Program Style, Design, Efficiency, Debugging, and Testing

SECOND EDITION

DENNIE VAN TASSEL

University of California
Santa Cruz, California

PRENTICE-HALL, INC.

Englewood Cliffs, New Jersey 07632

Library of Congress Cataloging in Publication Data

VAN TASSEL, DENNIE
   Program style, design, efficiency, debugging, and testing.

   Includes bibliographies and index.
   1. Electronic digital computers — Programming.
   2. Debugging in computer science.
   3. Computer programs — Testing. I. Title.
   QA76.6.V37 1978   001.6'42   78-9078
   ISBN 0-13-729947-8

For my wife,
   Cynthia

Printed in the United States of America

10 9 8 7 6

PRENTICE-HALL INTERNATIONAL, INC., *London*
PRENTICE-HALL OF AUSTRALIA PTY. LIMITED, *Sydney*
PRENTICE-HALL OF CANADA, LTD., *Toronto*
PRENTICE-HALL OF INDIA PRIVATE LIMITED, *New Delhi*
PRENTICE-HALL OF JAPAN, INC., *Tokyo*
PRENTICE-HALL OF SOUTHEAST ASIA PTE. LTD., *Singapore*
WHITEHALL BOOKS LIMITED, *Wellington, New Zealand*

Contents

Preface   *vii*

1   **PROGRAM STYLE**   *1*

Standards of Style   2
Comments   3
Blank Lines   9
Blank Spaces   10
Identification and Sequence Numbering   11
Selections of Variable Names   11
File Names   14
Standard Abbreviations   16
Splitting Words   17
Placement of Statements   18
Alphabetizing Lists   19
Parentheses   23
Indenting   24
Selection of Paragraph Names   29
Unreadable Programs   31
Conclusion   32
Programming Maxims   33
Exercises   34
References   40

2   **PROGRAM DESIGN**   *41*

The Simplicity Goal   41
Reading Programs   44
Problem Definition   44
Selection of Algorithm   46

Data Description   52
Selection of Programming Language   53
Generality   53
Libraries   56
Input/Output Formats   58
Operator Convenience   59
Modest Goals   59
Set Goals   60
Limiting Complexity   61
Structured Programming   62
Two Myths   87
Top-Down Coding   88
Chief Programmer Team   93
Development Support Library   98
Program Maintenance   100
Documentation   102
Rewriting   103
Programming Maxims   104
Exercises   105
References   111

3   **PROGRAM EFFICIENCY**   *113*

Nonconcern for Efficiency   115
Efficiency versus Reliability   115
Optimizing Compilers   116
Optimizing a Program   119
Execution Efficiency   123
Storage   125
Calculation of Constants   130
Initialization of Variables   130
Arithmetic Operations   131
Function Calls   140
Compiler Optimization   140
Avoidance of Loops   142
Loop Organization   142
Loop Optimization   143
Conditional Expressions   147
Logical Expressions   149
Subscripts   150
Input/Output   156
Explore New Commands   162
Warning Messages   163
Load Modules   163
Modules   163
Computer Lore   165
Conclusion   166
Programming Maxims   166
Exercises   167
References   174

Debugging versus Testing   177
Debugging Is the Next Hurdle   178
Errors in Problem Definition   179
Incorrect Algorithm   179
Errors in Analysis   180
General Errors   181
Physical Errors   182
Program Deck Marking   182
Simple Coding   183
Correctness   183
Syntax Errors   183
Types of Debugging   187
General Hints   190
Undefined Variables   191
Storage Map   192
Cross-Reference List   193
Typing Errors   193
Desk Checking   194
Attributes   195
Input/Output Errors   196
Psychology of Program Bugs   197
Numerical Pathology   197
Locating Errors   199
Defensive Programming   206
Assertions   209
Error Checklist   209
Program Dimensions   209
Debugging Aids   211
On-Line Debugging   215
Modules for Checking Programs   216
Automatic Checks   216
Getting It Right First   217
bebugging   218
Time Needed for Debugging   219
Preventing Bugs   219
Conclusion   221
Programming Maxims   221
Exercises   221
References   236

Beginning Programmers   239
Robustness   239
General Hints   240
How Much Testing   241
Exhaustive Testing   242
Specification Versus Program Testing   243

Early Testing   244
Design Testing   245
Testing Methods   248
Test Data   250
Sample Tests   260
Testing Mathematical Software   262
Modules   263
Program Library   265
File Testing   265
System Testing   265
Testing Aids   267
Use Your Program to Check Results   269
Validation   270
Adequate Time for Testing   271
How Well Has A Program Been Tested?   273
Retesting   273
A Test Group   274
Conclusion   276
Programming Maxims   276
Exercises   277
References   284

6 101 PROGRAMMING PROBLEMS   285

Number Problems   285
Game Problems   288
Graphic Problems   290
Cryptography Problems   291
Character String Problems   293
Statistics Problems   294
Compiler Problems   295
Sorting Problems   296
Mathematics Problems   296
Array Problems   298
Interest Problems   299
Business Problems   299
Change Problems   308
Calender Problems   308

APPENDIX: Team Projects   311

References   312

INDEX   313

Preface

This book was written for those who already know how to program, but who wish to increase their programming proficiency. Most of the information collected here could be classified as the "Lore of Programming." The contents cover five subjects that are seldom discussed in beginning programming books: the style or readability of programs, program design, efficiency or optimization of programs, debugging, and testing. These subjects are usually left for the programmer to learn by experience. Although experience is a good teacher, it is also rather slow and haphazard, leaving much to chance. Most of us have enough to learn by experience without leaving these important programming subjects for that slow process, too.

Since this is a revision some of you have seen the book before, so I will outline the major differences.

The Program Style chapter has been enlarged and parts redone. The Program Design chapter has been completely redone with all new material; the emphasis is now on top-down design and structured programming. The Program Efficiency chapter has stood the test of time and has changed little. The Program Debugging chapter has changed some, with added emphasis on getting the program right the first time. The Program Testing chapter has changed quite a bit, with more emphasis on top-down testing and a discussion of the newer, more sophisticated techniques of program testing.

Each chapter has a set of Programming Maxims that emphasize some of the main points in the chapter. These have been summarized at the end of each chapter. References have been pruned, and new references added. The 101 Programming Problems have been edited, combined, and added to, so although the count is still 101, there are many more problems because some problems suggest several programs. The 101 Programming Problems comprise a fairly complete set of programming problems and should provide something for every taste and background. The Exercises at the end of each chapter have changed greatly. They have been revised, reorganized, and several added.

It was a pleasure to revise this book because I like the book very much (author's don't always like their own books), and I had collected a great deal of new material. The book has been widely used and reviewed, so I have received numerous suggestions on how to make this edition even better.

I found out that the first edition has been used by a wide variety of audiences, ranging from professional programmers reading the book on their own, to undergraduate and graduate programming classes. Because of this I have divided the exercises at the end of the chapters into four categories: these being Review of Text, Problems, Programs, and Projects.

The Review of Text exercises are for you to read through to see how well you understood the chapter. You should be able to answer the questions in your head with no pencil and paper necessary.

The Problem exercises require more thought, and they will usually require pencil and paper to work out and write the answers. Many of the problems add greatly to the learning process, so it is suggested you try some of them and at least read them.

The Programs are small computer programs selected to emphasize the specific topics discussed in the chapter. These programs do not require much time and can be used for weekly assignments.

The Projects are either programs or projects that take much more effort and time. Many of the projects are open ended; that is, one could do a small version or a very complete version as time and motivation permit. Also, Projects often require the potential solver to read other articles and books to help solve the problem.

The Appendix, at the back of the book, contains a more detailed discussion of how the projects can be used as team projects with several people working on the project.

I wish to thank the many people who have helped me with this revised edition, especially the two reviewers: Richard Austing of the University of Maryland, and Brian Kerninghan of Bell Laboratories.

DENNIE VAN TASSEL

The purpose of programming is not the program,
but the result of the computation.

Alas, there are no prizes for coding;
the results are what count.

1

Program Style

One day, perhaps, computers will be able to write programs for other computers, or we will be able to write programs in English. But until then, we must deal with the dynamics of producing programs that other people can read. Not many would contest the simple idea that a programmer should at least be able to read his or her own program. Here is where programming style enters the scene.

Programming style is concerned with the readability of programs. If each programmer used a very individualistic style, the program might be incomprehensible to others. So style involves a selection of programming habits or techniques that appeal to experienced programmers because such habits produce programs that are correct, efficient, maintainable, and readable. The rules of good style are the result of consensus among experienced programmers. Once programmers become accustomed to a certain style, their own programs as well as other people's will be more easily understood. If all programmers used their own particular style, on the other hand, a garbled Tower of Babel would result.

A program's main purpose is to be read by humans rather than by machines. People must read and understand the program in order to correct, maintain, and modify it. If we were concerned only with the machine, programs would be written so that machines could read them easier than people could. Moreover, programs are documents for future reference, educational media for instruction on coded algorithms, and tools for further development of better programs. Consequently, program languages should be conducive to producing readable statements. Too often the element of readability is overlooked in the haste to obtain a workable program.

> *Programs are to be read by humans.*

It is doubtful that anyone would argue that readability is unimportant. The original programmers must always be able to read their own programs. Thus guidelines of programming style will also help them. Conventional language uses punctuation, paragraphing, ordering, and spacing to improve readability. Programmers can use similar aids to avoid abstruse programs.

Abstruse programs are usually difficult to modify, particularly if the original programmer does not do the modification. An unfortunate result is that it is generally easier to rewrite an entire program than modify someone else's. Program specifications are, in general, in a constant state of flux. Often we not only do not know what we want, but also, after getting results, we want the program changed. The tendency is to begin a program with modest ambitions and expand it continuously. If program-style guidelines are followed, some of the abstruseness in programs will disappear.

When a programmer is able to pick up someone else's program and see that it is organized and easy to read, the normal reluctance and confusion of updating or modification start to disappear. A readable program creates the impression that the original coder knew what he or she was doing. The program itself should convey as much of its logic and structure as possible.

If the programs are coded for an organization, the adoption of an agreed-on style will help make the programs the property of the organization instead of the private property of a single programmer.

STANDARDS OF STYLE

One argument against standards of programming style goes as follows: programming style is a matter of personal opinion and preference and thus should not be restricted. This argument simply says that chaos is better than order.

The rule for standards is

If there is more than one way to do something and the choice is rather arbitrary, pick one way and always do it that way.

The advantages of this philosophy are

By eliminating arbitrary parameters, communication can be more precise. By doing the same thing in the same way each time, communication is less susceptible to misunderstanding.

The disadvantages of standards are

1. They might restrict future growth and progress.
2. They might be too restrictive for universal usage.
3. They might be too cumbersome for universal use.

In the last two cases, the standards are generally ignored. The standards of style given here are merely a product of common sense and common usage by experienced programmers and are not meant to be restrictive.

A good set of standards can encourage future growth and progress by shifting people's attention to a new set of problems. For instance, it is no longer necessary to think about choosing how to write loops.

There seems to be little pressure for industry-wide style standards, but consistent standards within one installation are common. So a common practice is for each installation to establish style guidelines. Many of the suggestions in this book can be used to develop an installation standard. Once learned, the guidelines involve little extra effort.

COMMENTS

The desirability of comments would seem to be self-evident, and yet they aren't always included in programs. Comments are omitted to save time or keypunching, or "they will be put in later." Such excuses are rather lame because in a surprisingly short time even the original programmers will find that they have forgotten many of the details of the program. A program with explanatory comments is much easier to debug because there is more information to work with. When looking at someone else's program, a colleague is often forced to spend many hours tracing the program logic or simply re-writing the undocumented program when a change is necessary. In this case, all the original time "saved" is used up many times over.

An uncommented program is probably the worst error that a programmer can make and the sign of an amateur (even with 10 years experience); moreover, it is a good reason to fire a programmer. This statement may seem unusually harsh, but it is probable that many program managers would agree with it. Comments are like trail markers in an unknown forest. Only a fool would omit leaving such markers and thus let the trail become difficult to follow during debugging and testing.

When should comments be written? Generally a good rule is to write comments while writing the program. You are most familiar with the details at that time. Comments inserted later are seldom as satisfactory; also, remembering what should be commented will be difficult. A general rule is: the more comments the better. Very few production programs are overcommented.

> *Provide more comments than you think you will need.*

Good comments are not easy to do. Since their purpose is to convey an understanding of the program, they should be as well thought out and designed as the program code. Many comments can be acquired from the original top-down design elaboration (see Chapter 2). The design specifications must describe the program, and often some of the specifications can be used for comments. Comments are just as useful during the design and debugging stages as afterward. Consequently, it is foolish to wait until the program is finished to insert them. Doing so is similar to looking at a road map once a trip is finished. If you are having trouble using comments to describe what you are doing, it is probably because you don't *know* what you are doing.

There are three types of comments: prologue, directory, and explanatory.

Prologue Comments

Every program, subroutine, or procedure should have some statements at the beginning to explain what it does. The minimum expectations are

1. A description of what the program does.
2. Usage: How to call it or use it.
3. A list and explanation of the important variables or arrays.
4. Instructions on input/output. List any files.
5. A list of subroutines used.
6. The name of any special scientific methods used, together with a reference in which more information can be found.
7. Some indication of how long it takes.
8. Amount of core needed.
9. Special operating requirements.
10. Author.
11. Date written.

All this information must be supplied for documentation, and the best place to put it is right in the program so that it can easily be found. The program should be its own documentation. Figure 1.1 shows sample prologue documentation.

Use prologue comments.

Directory Comments

If the program is very long, it is worthwhile to provide a directory or table of contents in comment form at the beginning of the program. The table of contents should give the name, location, and function for each module. Hopefully, each module will be already labeled either by module name or comments to indicate its function.

Use directory comments in long programs.

Explanatory Comments

Explanatory comments are inserted in the program to explain any code that is not obvious simply by reading the code. Comments should appear before important loops or conditional statements, indicating what is being done. Properly done comments provide a narrative account of the flow of data and logic in the program. Pro-

```
C                                                                           TALL  10
C*********************************************************************************TALL  20
C                                                                           TALL  30
C          SUBROUTINE TALLY                                                 TALL  40
C                                                                           TALL  50
C          PURPOSE                                                          TALL  60
C             CALCULATE TOTAL, MEAN, STANDARD DEVIATION, MINIMUM, MAXIMUM   TALL  70
C             FOR EACH VARIABLE IN A SET (OR A SUBSET) OF OBSERVATIONS.     TALL  80
C                                                                           TALL  90
C          USAGE                                                            TALL 100
C             CALL TALLY(A,S,TOTAL,AVER,SD,VMIN,VMAX,NO,NV,IER)             TALL 110
C                                                                           TALL 120
C          DESCRIPTION OF PARAMETERS                                        TALL 130
C             A     - OBSERVATION MATRIX, NO BY NV.                         TALL 140
C             S     - INPUT VECTOR INDICATING SUBSET OF A. ONLY THOSE       TALL 150
C                     OBSERVATIONS WITH A NON-ZERO S(J) ARE CONSIDERED.     TALL 160
C                     VECTOR LENGTH IS NO.                                  TALL 170
C             TOTAL - OUTPUT VECTOR OF TOTALS OF EACH VARIABLE. VECTOR      TALL 180
C                     LENGTH IS NV.                                         TALL 190
C             AVER  - OUTPUT VECTOR OF AVERAGES OF EACH VARIABLE. VECTOR    TALL 200
C                     LENGTH IS NV.                                         TALL 210
C             SD    - OUTPUT VECTOR OF STANDARD DEVIATIONS OF EACH          TALL 220
C                     VARIABLE. VECTOR LENGTH IS NV.                        TALL 230
C             VMIN  - OUTPUT VECTOR OF MINIMA OF EACH VARIABLE. VECTOR      TALL 240
C                     LENGTH IS NV.                                         TALL 250
C             VMAX  - OUTPUT VECTOR OF MAXIMA OF EACH VARIABLE. VECTOR      TALL 260
C                     LENGTH IS NV.                                         TALL 270
C             NO    - NUMBER OF OBSERVATIONS.                               TALL 280
C             NV    - NUMBER OF VARIABLES FOR EACH OBSERVATION.             TALL 290
C             IER   - ZERO, IF NO ERROR.                                    TALL 300
C                   - 1, IF S IS NULL.  VMIN=-1.E75, VMAX=SD=AVER=1.E75.    TALL 310
C                   - 2, IF S HAS ONLY ONE NON-ZERO ELEMENT. VMIN=VMAX.     TALL 320
C                     SD=0.0                                                TALL 330
C                                                                           TALL 340
C          REMARKS                                                          TALL 350
C             NONE                                                          TALL 360
C                                                                           TALL 370
C          SUBROUTINES AND FUNCTION SUBPROGRAMS REQUIRED                    TALL 380
C             NONE                                                          TALL 390
C                                                                           TALL 400
C          METHOD                                                           TALL 410
C             ALL OBSERVATIONS CORRESPONDING TO A NON-ZERO ELEMENT IN S     TALL 420
C             VECTOR ARE ANALYZED FOR EACH VARIABLE IN MATRIX A.            TALL 430
C             TOTALS ARE ACCUMULATED AND MINIMUM AND MAXIMUM VALUES ARE     TALL 440
C             FOUND. FOLLOWING THIS, MEANS AND STANDARD DEVIATIONS ARE      TALL 450
C             CALCULATED.  THE DIVISOR FOR STANDARD DEVIATION IS ONE LESS   TALL 460
C             THAN THE NUMBER OF OBSERVATIONS USED.                         TALL 470
C                                                                           TALL 480
C                                                                           TALL 490
C          REFERENCE                                                        TALL 500
C             STATISTICS  BY MURRAY R. SPIEGEL                              TALL 510
C             SCHAUM PUBLISHING COMPANY                                     TALL 520
C                                                                           TALL 530
C          TIME-REQUIRED                                                    TALL 540
C             FOR 10 VARIABLES 20 SECONDS.                                  TALL 550
C             FOR 20 VARIABLES 45 SECONDS.                                  TALL 560
C             FOR 65 VARIABLES 95 SECONDS.                                  TALL 570
C                                                                           TALL 580
C                                                                           TALL 590
C          SIZE                                                             TALL 600
C             120 CARDS.                                                    TALL 610
C             OBJECT CODE   1960.                                           TALL 620
C                                                                           TALL 630
C                                                                           TALL 640
C          PROGRAMMER                                                       TALL 650
C             ABE SURECODER.                                                TALL 660
C                                                                           TALL 670
C          DATE-WRITTEN                                                     TALL 680
C             JULY 1978.                                                    TALL 690
C                                                                           TALL 700
C*********************************************************************************TALL 710
C                                                                           TALL 720
```

Figure 1.1 Subroutine TALLY

vide comments whenever you do something that may not be entirely obvious to another person. This documentation will then be carried along as part of the program itself. It can help a new programmer understand your program or help you understand earlier sections of the program while new parts are being written. A good rule might be a minimum of one comment every ten lines of code for high-level languages.

One problem with the foregoing rule is it may do just that — produce a comment every ten lines instead of where needed. It is meant to be an average instead of a comment on line 1, a comment on line 11, a comment on line 21, ... Another way to phrase the rule is to use a comment for each logically distinct subdivision of the program.

High-level languages are designed to be as readable and self-documenting as possible, but frequently the logic used by the programmer is not apparent to someone else reading the program. In such cases (and such cases are far more prevalent than programmers realize), comments are invaluable. In reading a program to a new programmer, you should have a comment in each place where you would have to stop to explain the coding to the other person.

The type of comment used is important. An English translation for each line of code is not necessary. You should assume that the reader is familiar with the language of the program. Therefore comments should explain the purpose of a group of program statements, not describe the operation of the statements. For example,

```
/* CHECK IF LESS THAN ZERO */
```

The above is not a good comment, since the person reading the program would know the programming language and be able to ascertain that a negative check was to take place. But the reader would not know *why*. And it is the *why* that comments are supposed to tell him or her. The code can tell us what is being done; the comments should tell us why it is being done. Instead of the useless comment above, this one should be used.

```
/*PERFORM NEGATIVE ACCOUNT PROCESSING IF TOTAL COSTS
     ARE LESS THAN ZERO.      */
```

This comment tells why a negative check is to be used. Comments should not explain programming language syntax but should indicate the purpose or tell what is happening in the logic of the program. Make the comment say something useful.

> *Comments should provide something extra —*
> *not just paraphrase the code.*

A test of commenting is that a programmer should be able to read only the comments and understand what the program is doing without referring to any other documentation. One reason that we do not comment enough is that we overestimate our ability. We believe that we will easily remember what a section of code does. Moreover, we do not expect many bugs, and so comments seem unnecessary. Past experience should point out the fallacy of such beliefs.

Placement of Comments

When using an assembly language, add a comment on most lines. Comments that are interspersed in the coding are easier to read when preceded and followed by a blank line. An additional method of setting off comments is to make a box of special characters. The box can then be used in several ways.

1. To create a box in which the comments appear.
2. To group a set of commands. This step is done by placing a comment line filled with special characters before and after the group of commands.
3. To set up a boundary that indicates that one comment applies to several lines of code.

In Fig. 1.1 a comment line of asterisks is used above and below the comments to form a box for the comments.

When including comments in the same line as the code, use a set column to start each comment. For instance, start comments at column 40 with columns 1–39 reserved for code. If a comment is on a line by itself, it is a good idea to indent comments beyond the beginning of code lines for easy recognition.

Structured programs (Chapter 2) usually require fewer comments than unstructured programs, since coding is more straightforward and branches are avoided. Thus there is less to explain by comments. In the past, comments were often used to explain messy coding. The remedy for messy coding is not to use comments but to recode so that messiness is eliminated. Structured programs also display logic by paragraphing: so comments should be placed on the right side of the program in order to avoid interfering with the paragraphing of the program. Some people justify comments on the right side. Generally, however, it is sufficient to place comments far enough over to the right so that indenting is not interfered with.

Indent comments the same amount as the code they refer to.

Correct Comments

The comments must be correct. In other words, they must be correct when originally inserted and modified when the program is modified. Incorrect comments are obviously worse than no comments, since the incorrect comments lead us astray.

Incorrect comments are worse than no comments at all.

BLANK LINES

Blank space is an often-overlooked method of improving the appearance of a program. Blank lines can be used for vertical spacing. Just as they are used in English to separate paragraphs, you can use blank lines to separate elements of your program. A single blank line can be used to separate each similar group of statements, and several blank lines should be used to separate any major section of the program. The use of blank lines will make any search for the major routines within a program much easier.

A blank line should follow any unconditional transfer of control to indicate a break in program flow. Blank lines before and after comments make the comments more prominent. Blank lines can be created by blank cards in a source deck or blank comment lines.

Some COBOL, PL/I, FORTRAN, and assembly language compilers have special commands that control carriage spacing on source statements. COBOL users can use EJECT, SKIP1, SKIP2, and SKIP3. PL/I users can specify a control column using job control language that will control spacing in the source listing. The WATFIV version of FORTRAN has the $EJECT and $SPACE options available for vertical spacing.

Skipping to a new page is similar to beginning a new chapter in a book. Both indicate a larger change than just a blank line (new paragraph). Blank space separates the program into meaningful units.

BLANK SPACES

In programming languages blank spaces are quite often optional. Yet it makes no more sense to leave out all the blank spaces in programs than it would to leave out all the blank spaces in written texts. Icouldalwayswritelikethisandyoucanreaditbutittakestoomucheffort.

Blanks should be left in all places that will improve the readability of the program.

It is possible to write statements like

```
DO10I=1,23,2
```

But the following one is much easier to read.

```
DO 10 I = 1, 23, 2
```

Liberal usage of blanks will add significantly to the readability of programs. Include blank spaces between items in data lists and before and after arithmetic operators (+, -, =). Sometimes blanks are desirable before and after the two operations (*, /). Blank spaces can be used to indicate operator precedence. Thus

```
1 + A*B
```

instead of the misleading

```
1+A * B
```

Use blank spaces to improve readability.

IDENTIFICATION AND SEQUENCE NUMBERING

Most programming languages allow for the identification and sequence numbering of lines of the source program in columns 73–80. Identification is normally punched in columns 73–76, and then columns 77–80 can be used for sequence numbering. Sequence numbering should be in increments of 10 in order to allow the insertion of new lines. COBOL programs should be sequenced in columns 1–6; then columns 73–80 can be used for identification.

Another advantage of sequence numbering in columns 73–80 is that you can also indicate program modifications there by putting NEW or FIX in these columns to indicate what was changed or added to the program. Obviously it is often useful to know what has been changed recently.

Sequence numbering helps prevent errors caused by programs being out of order. A careless operator could easily drop a program deck and "attempt" to put the deck back in order. Thus the programmers will usually have no indication that their program deck has been shuffled if it is not numbered sequentially. Of course, if your program is not on cards, sequence numbering is not as important.

Sequenced source programs are helpful when debugging because the sequence number can be used to locate a card or line in a large program quickly. Therefore the programmer should sequence number the source programs when first coding them. Sequence numbering and identification make a program look neater and more complete and thus, psychologically, seem more readable.

In order to encourage sequential numbering of source programs, every computer installation should provide a program to reproduce and sequence source decks. Then an interpreting keypunch can be used to interpret the new source deck. See program assignments at end of this chapter. Figure 1.1 shows a program that has identification and sequence numbering.

SELECTION OF VARIABLE NAMES

Variable names should be selected to best identify the symbolic quantities they represent. If there are no restrictions on name size, use names as long as necessary and not longer than necessary. For example,

$$X = Y + Z$$

has little mnemonic value and the variable names are poorly selected. The following is much better.

$$PRICE = COST + PROFIT$$

Proper selection of variable names is the most important principle in program readability. It is also the easiest and least expensive technique, since it usually takes just a little thought by the programmer and costs no more in machine time.

Variable names chosen may conflict with the default data-type assignments made by the language. You should, however, simply use appropriate kinds of declarations to override the default assignments. In fact, it is a good idea to declare all variables to ensure that they are the correct data type.

There are some *don'ts* to remember when selecting variable names and labels. Avoid visually similar names. Also, avoid unnatural spellings (phone and fone) and confusing characters (AX10 and AXIO). If you must use numbers in variable names, use the numbers only at the end of the name. Names should have a psychological distance. Names that sound alike, look alike, or are spelled alike are not psychologically distinct. Those that have too much meaning can be bad, too. An example is

$$FOUR = 12/5$$

Here the variable FOUR has two different meanings, the value 4 and the value stored in FOUR.

Selection of suggestive names should also be used when naming programs, paragraphs, procedures, functions, and subroutines. The program labels should match labels that you used in flowcharts or analysis so that you can relate them to the earlier procedural forms. This procedure should seem obvious, but it is often not done. Variable names that are prevalent in the subject area of the application should be selected.

> *Use good mnemonic names.*

It is easy to select good variable names in COBOL and PL/I, since both allow long names and have a separator character. FOR-TRAN is severely limited by short lengths for variable names (anywhere from 5 to 8 characters in different versions) and the absence of a separator character. ALGOL allows long variable names. "Cute" names that have no bearing on the task involved become completely unintelligible later when the program has grown "cold" or when a new programmer must modify the program. Unwise choice of variable names and labels can render an otherwise clear program nearly incomprehensible.

Here is one way to select a good symbolic variable name. When choosing variable names, try stating what the variable is to stand for in an English sentence and then pick the most important word.

Some programming languages have no reserved words. Consequently, the programmer is able to use any word as a variable name, even those normally used as commands. For instance,

FORTRAN

```
      DO 5 I6 = 1.34
14 FORMAT(I6) = I
   5 END = K*I
```

PL/I

```
IF IF = THEN THEN THEN = ELSE;
      ELSE ELSE = IF;
```

What do the preceding statements do? There are no typesetting errors. All are legal statements and unambiguous to the compiler, but notice how difficult they are to interpret because of predetermined meanings for the variable names. Avoid using words that could confuse the reader.

Different types (i.e., integer, real, complex, character) are often a problem for the programmer. However, the problem is not overwhelming, since such faults are usually easy to overcome, especially if the programmers adopt some naming convention in their mnemonics to identify types that are conceptually different to them. For example, in a program that uses a few complex variables all complex variable names could start with C or CMP. This prefix would remind you that the variable is a complex variable. A similar technique can be used to help identify files.

Begin integer variables with one of the following letters: *I, J, K, L, M, N*. The use of these letters to represent integer variables is so common and accepted that it is useful to follow the practice.

If the programming language allows a separator in the variable names (e.g., the dash in COBOL and the underbar in PL/I), then the separator should be used to separate the words. For instance,

COSTPLUS	should be	COST-PLUS
RECOIL	should be	REC-OIL
CRAFTER	should be	CR-AFTER
IDENTRY	should be	ID-ENTRY

The separator makes the names more readable and less susceptible to other interpretations.

Some programmers design whole programs in order that so-called cute phrases can be inserted.

```
ADD GIN TO VERMOUTH GIVING MARTINI.

ADD HOT-PEPPER TO CHILI GIVING HEART-BURN.
```

Although possibly fun at the time, it is not much fun when trying to modify the program, because the names used give no indications of what is happening. Good variable names will lessen the need for comments.

Programs can be nicely written

```
IF CONTENTS(PITCHER) < QUART THEN
    FILL(PITCHER)
ELSE
    POUR(PITCHER)
```

or they can be poorly written:

```
    IF       XCONT (PTCH
)   <        QT    THEN  XFILL     (
    PTCH
)   ELSE                   XPOUR   (
        PTCH)
```

FILE NAMES

When working with files in such languages as COBOL and PL/I, it is a good idea to select a prefix or suffix to identify each file. Then you can use this prefix or suffix on every subordinate item in the file description. In this example MASTER is used as the prefix.

```
FILE SECTION.
FD  MASTER-FILE,
     .
     .
     .
01  MASTER-RECORD.
    03 MASTER-NAME      PICTURE X(20).
    03 MASTER-ADDRESS   PICTURE X(40).
    03 MASTER-NUMBER    PICTURE 9(08).
     .
     .
     .
WORKING-STORAGE SECTION.
01  MASTER-WORK-AREA.
    05 MASTER-COUNT     PICTURE 9(04).
```

If each file has a unique prefix, it is much easier to read the program. The prefix will help locate the field in the program listing and indicate which fields and work areas are together logically. Another useful convention is that file names should contain the word FILE and record names should contain the word RECORD.

Use a prefix or suffix on file names.

This technique allows for prefixes on identical names, such as a date field. For instance,

```
MASTER-DATE
TRANSACTION-DATE
REPORT-DATE
```

Even though three different date fields are used, each one is easy to identify because of the prefix. If you do not use the prefix method, you are forced to use different abbreviations, such as DATE, DTE, DAT, which do not adequately label the fields.

When selecting record names, use record-oriented instead of job-oriented names. The following names are job oriented.

```
01  OUTPUT-FILE.
    05 OUTPUT-NAME
    05 OUTPUT-ADDRESS
```

These names would be usable only once — that is, when the file is an output file. On the next job the record might be an input file and the preceding labels would not make sense.

A more careful selection of names will allow the same record names to be used in several interconnected programs. For instance,

```
01  MASTER-FILE.
    05 MASTER-NAME
    05 MASTER-ADDRESS
```

The foregoing record name can be used for the record in every program that might use the record.

The use of the same names for identical files in different programs means that programmers can immediately identify the file. Program managers might find it advantageous to set up a standard file label when one file is used in many programs.

STANDARD ABBREVIATIONS

Each programming manager may find it advantageous to develop a list of standard abbreviations. Doing so will be helpful when the program is read by others besides the original programmer. Otherwise the following abbreviations

```
MSTR
MAST
MST
```

will all be used to abbreviate MASTER. Simply stated, the use of standard abbreviations helps programmers understand old programs that must be modified. Using standard abbreviations and standard variable names is especially advantageous when many programmers are working on a large system.

For those who like to abbreviate in order to save keypunching or who must abbreviate because of variable name-length restrictions, a set of rules is available for abbreviating that will help maintain readability. These rules were developed by Michael Jackson in an excellent article in the April 1967 issue of *Datamation*. His rules for abbreviating are as follows.

1. Abbreviate every significant word in the name, up to a maximum of three words.
2. Initial letters must always be present.
3. Consonants are more important than vowels.
4. The beginning of a word is more important than the end.
5. Abbreviate to between 6 and 15 letters in all.

These rules are especially helpful to FORTRAN programmers because FORTRAN programmers are forced to abbreviate. Keeping in mind the preceding rules, here is an algorithm for abbreviating.

The abbreviation within a word is formed by deleting vowels successively from the right-hand end of the word until either all vowels have been deleted (except the initial letter of the word if that is a vowel) or the word is reduced to the required size. If all vowels have been deleted and the word is still too large, the procedure is repeated, deleting consonants until the required length is obtained.

Names	Abbreviations
COST PLUS	CST PLS
ACCOUNTS RECEIVABLE	ACCNTS RECVBL
RECORD	RCRD
TRANSACTION	TRNSCTN

SPLITTING WORDS

Some programming languages allow the splitting of names or literals between two lines. It is never necessary to split a word and seldom necessary to split a literal. If a word cannot fit on the current line, begin the word on the next line. Although it may be permissible to split a word, the use of this option by the programmer tends to make the program more difficult to read and maintain.

If you are splitting a statement over two lines, split after an operator. For example,

Careless form

```
A = B - C
    - (D + 2)
```

Better form

```
A = B - C -
    (D + 2)
```

The second example leaves a minus sign dangling on the first line which will immediately indicate to a reader that the statement is to be continued on the next line. In addition, if the second line should get lost in the first example, a syntax error would not appear, but you would always get a syntax error in the second example if the second line was lost.

PLACEMENT OF STATEMENTS

Some programming languages allow several statements on one line — for instance,

PL/I

```
X = A**3; IF (A < B) THEN CALL FINISH; B = COS(C);
```

COBOL

```
FD  CARD-IN, RECORDING MODE IS F, LABEL RECORDS ARE
    OMITTED, RECORD CONTAINS 80 CHARACTERS, DATA RECORD IS CARD-SALES.
```

Using multiple statements on one line is usually a bad practice for two obvious reasons. First, it makes the program difficult to read; and secondly, it prevents the use of other reading aids, such as paragraphing.

A better approach is to place only one statement on each line.

PL/I

```
X = A**3;
IF (A < B) THEN CALL FINISH;
B = COS(C);
```

COBOL

```
FD  CARD-IN
    RECORDING MODE IS F,
    LABEL RECORDS ARE OMITTED,
    RECORD CONTAINS 80 CHARACTERS,
    DATA RECORD IS CARD-SALES.
```

This approach not only makes the program more readable but also facilitates the removal or modification of one statement without disturbing the other statements.

For example:

ALGOL W

```
A=14.2; FOR I:=1 UNTIL 10 DO BEGIN X(I):=0;K:=I*K;Y(I):=K;END;
```

Here is the same example with each statement on a new line.

ALGOL W

```
A := 14.2;
FOR I := 1 UNTIL 10 DO
   BEGIN
      X(I) := 0;
      K := I*K;
      Y(I) := K;
   END;
```

Perhaps you noticed that the two preceding program segments are not the same. Can you find the error? If you do find the error, notice how many statements you must retype in the first example in order to correct it. (*Hint:* It is in the first statement.)

Another reason to place one statement at most on each line is that syntax error messages always indicate the line number. So, if only one statement is on each line, it is easier to locate the syntax error.

One statement per line is enough.

This suggestion also applies to headers, such as paragraph headers or labels. By placing each paragraph header on a separate line, it is not necessary to disturb the line containing the paragraph name for any later rewriting or rearranging of the contents of that paragraph.

ALPHABETIZING LISTS

Programming languages contain many variable name lists, and the order of the lists is left up to the programmer. Two examples are lists of variable names whose precision or mode is being declared and subroutine parameter lists.

The reason for alphabetizing the list is to make it easy to find a name in the list. Here, for instance, are two lists.

FORTRAN

```
INTEGER BETA, Z, KEP, COST, PRICE, DOBT
REAL I, AMOUNT, SIZE, K, BETS
```

If you wanted to find out if BETS is integer or real you would need to scan both lists completely. If the lists are extremely long, as is normal in large programs, you may find this process both time consuming and difficult. If the variable lists are alphabetized, however, the task becomes relatively simple.

```
INTEGER  BETA, COST, DOBT, KEP, PRICE, Z
REAL  AMOUNT, BETS, I, K, SIZE
```

It is not necessary to alphabetize all variables of one type in one declarative. Frequently, it is useful to keep variables with similar uses together.

```
INTEGER     BUFF1, BUFF2, CHAR, TERMTR

INTEGER     COST, PRICE, TAX
```

The table that follows shows some of the commands that can use alphabetized lists.

FORTRAN	PL/I	COBOL	ALGOL W
INTEGER	DECLARE	File names	INTEGER
REAL	Parameter lists	Working storage variables	REAL
COMMON			LONG REAL
DIMENSION		Parameter lists	STRING
COMPLEX			LOGICAL
DOUBLE PRECISION			COMPLEX
Parameter lists			BITS
			Parameter lists

Alphabetizing can also be used in argument lists. For example,

CALL SUB1 (A, B, CTAX, X, Z)

Since the calling statement arguments must be matched with the subroutine or procedure parameter list, it isn't always possible to alphabetize the lists completely. Also, some people prefer to order argument lists by function, such as output first and input last.

Another place in which alphabetizing can be used is in the sequence of subroutines or procedures. Putting your subroutines in alphabetic order, whenever possible, will help you locate them faster. In FORTRAN subroutines are separate programs, and so alphabetizing is quite simple. In PL/I the procedures can easily be arranged alphabetically.

Alphabetize lists.

FORTRAN

If the statement numbers are in no particular sequence in large FORTRAN programs, it is quite difficult to find a statement number. And since statement numbers are completely arbitrary, it is possible to renumber all the statement numbers once the program is debugged so that they are in sequence. A program can be provided to do so. The resequencing program should be able to start at any desired number and increment by any desired increment. See Projects at the end of this chapter.

FORTRAN and BASIC use numbers for labels. In these languages, if the program or subroutine contains two separate logical blocks of code, it is advisable to reserve the first digit or two of the statement numbers for block identification and to use the remaining digits to label the statements within the block. For instance, if there are three distinct blocks, then the first block could use the 1000s, the second block the 2000s, and the third block the 3000s.

COBOL

Alphabetizing is not as easy in COBOL because the order of the paragraphs may affect the logic of the program. In order to maintain complete freedom of name choice, select regular mnemonic paragraph names but add a sequence number. For example, if the paragraph names are

TEST-LOOP
RUN-ERROR
REPORT-OUT

then these paragraph names can be changed to indicate the relative location of that paragraph within the program by

TEST-LOOP-600
RUN-ERROR-610
REPORT-OUT-620

The numbers used should allow for the insertion of new paragraphs.

In procedure-oriented languages like PL/I, procedures are often nested within other procedures. In this case, alphabetizing the order of procedures is limited by the order of the nesting. One suggestion for helping to locate nested procedures is to use outer procedures as a prefix or suffix on the nested procedures. To illustrate,

PL/I

```
SCAN:   PROCEDURE
             .
             .
             .
        SCAN_CHECK:   PROCEDURE
             .
             .
             .
            SCAN_CHECK_TRACE:   PROCEDURE
             .
             .
             .
            END SCAN_CHECK_TRACE;
            SCAN_CHECK_TRAP:   PROCEDURE
             .
             .
             .
```

```
        END SCAN_CHECK_TRAP;
        END SCAN_CHECK;
        SCAN_DEBIT:   PROCEDURE
             •
             •
             •
        END SCAN;
```

Since SCAN is the outer procedure, the programmer uses it as a prefix on the inner procedures.

Another technique that indicates the order, but that provides less information is to number the labels. That is, the procedure is SCAN, and the labels in the procedure are SCAN010, SCAN020, and SCAN030. Whenever lexicographic labeling is used, be sure to leave gaps in the label numbering for inserting later changes so that the ordering scheme can be kept.

Alphabetizing is one prerequisite for good readability. The second is neatness. That is, lists should be organized in columns. For example, note how difficult it is to read

```
OCOMMON ALPHA,BETA,CHI,DELTA,EPSIL,ETA,GAMMA,IOTA,
1KAPPA,LAMBDA,MU,NU,OMEGA,OMICR,PHI,PI,PSI,RHO,
2SIGMA,TAU
```

compared to

```
OCOMMON  ALPHA,  BETA,   CHI,    DELTA,   EPSIL,  ETA,
1        GAMMA,  IOTA,   KAPPA,  LAMBDA,  MU,     NU,
2        OMEGA,  OMICR,  PHI,    PI,      PSI,    RHO,
3        SIGMA,  TAU
```

Not many readers will disagree that the second example is clearer than the first. In order to space columnwise, the programmer must allow enough room for the maximum number of characters used in variable names. Similar spacing should be used in all data lists, including input/output lists.

PARENTHESES

When properly used, parentheses greatly improve the readability of programs. Since mathematical and logical operations are governed by order of operation, programmers can quite often get by with few parentheses, but this situation makes reading and correcting a program much more difficult. The following examples illustrate this.

With few parentheses	*With extra parentheses*
`A*B*C/(D*E*F)`	`(A*B*C)/(D*E*F)`
`A*B/C*D/E*F`	`(A*B*D*F)/(C*E)`
`A**B**C`	`A**(B**C)`
`A/B/C/D`	`((A/B)/C)/D`
`A**B*C`	`(A**B)*C`
`X.GT.Y.OR.Q`	`(X.GT.Y) .OR. Q`
`A+B.LT.C`	`(A+B) .LT. C`

The basic rule is: when in doubt, overparenthesize — not only to improve readability, but to prevent errors. Programmers often underparenthesize in logical expressions with the result that the program is incorrect.

Parentheses are cheaper than errors.

INDENTING

Indenting (also called paragraphing) refers to the process of indenting commands to indicate that they belong together. Although this step does not affect the logic of the program, it greatly improves the readability. It is comparable to English writing practice, where a paragraph is a group of related sentences. Good indenting displays the logical structure of the program. As simple a matter as the proper indenting of program text on a page can have a profound effect on the reader's ability to comprehend the program. Your program should be pleasing to the eye.

Indenting Example

No indenting:

```
IF (I<=1) THEN FACTORIAL := 1 ELSE BEGIN FACTORIAL := 1; F
J := 2 UNTIL I DO FACTORIAL := FACTORIAL * J END;
```

With indenting:

```
IF (I<=1) THEN
    FACTORIAL := 1
ELSE
    BEGIN
        FACTORIAL := 1;
        FOR J := 2 UNTIL I DO
            FACTORIAL := FACTORIAL * J
    END;
```

The first rule of indenting concerns groups of statements bracketed by one of the following pairs.

FORTRAN

```
DO ... CONTINUE
```

ALGOL

```
BEGIN ... END;
```

PL/I

```
DO; ... END;
BEGIN; ... END;
PROCEDURE; ... END;
```

Loops are one common place where indenting can be used. Examples of loops that make use of the process are shown below.

FORTRAN

```
    DO 10 I = 1, 16
        C = 0.0
        DO 8 K = 1, 12
            C = C + B(K)
            D(K) = SQRT(K*1.0)
  8     CONTINUE
        A(I) = C
 10 CONTINUE
```

PL/I

```
DO I = 1 TO 16;
   C = 0.0;
   DO K = 1 TO 12;
      C = C + B(K);
      D(K) = SQRT(K);
   END;
   A(I) = C;
END;
```

ALGOL W

```
FOR I := 0 UNTIL 4 DO
   BEGIN
      X(I) := 0.0;
      B(I) := C(I);
   END;
```

In order to make absolutely clear to a reader of the program which two symbols form a pair, start both symbols in the same column. Statements enclosed by the pair are generally indented three spaces. These examples of nested loops show how paragraphing can help illustrate where loops start and end.

Loops are not the only place that indenting can be used; paragraphing is used to illustrate grouping of commands.

PL/I

```
IF (A<B) THEN
   DO;
      C = A;
      A = B;
      B = C;
   END;
```

FORTRAN

```
   IF (A .LT. B) GO TO 16
      C = A
      A = B
      B = C
16 VAL = TAN(X)
```

The general rule is to put the IF statement on a line by itself, indenting all statements conditioned by it.

These examples illustrate which commands are grouped together by an IF statement. Similar grouping is possible with IF...THEN...ELSE commands.

PL/I

```
IF (A < B) THEN
   DO;
      A = -A;
      B = A*B;
   END;
ELSE
   DO;
      A = A*B;
      B = -B;
   END;
```

Consistent indentation of three spaces is commonly used. This space is sufficient to indicate indentation and allows for several levels of indentation.

Use indentation to show the program structure.

Input/output statements can also be indented.

COBOL

```
READ file-name
   AT END
      statement.
WRITE record-name
   BEFORE ADVANCING identifier LINES
      AT END-OF-PAGE
         statement.
```

PL/I

```
GET FILE (SYSIN)
   (PRICE, SALES_NUMBER);
PUT FILE (SYSPRINT) EDIT
   (TASK, NEW_RATE)
   (SKIP(2), COL(4), A, F(7) );
```

Complex IF statements that involve compound conditionals are easily read if indented properly. One technique is to line up the IF, AND, OR, THEN, and ELSE.

COBOL

```
IF     (PARTS-NUMBER-PREFIX IN
        MASTER-HISTORY-FILE IS LESS THAN
        CURRENT-NUMBER-PREFIX,
OR      CURRENT-DATE IS EQUAL TO ZERO),
AND     CURRENT-COST IN DETAIL-INVOICE-FILE
        IS GREATER THAN 10.00
THEN
        (True commands)
ELSE
        (False commands).
```

In languages where variables are declared, the attributes should be lined up in straight columns to make reading easier.

COBOL

```
05 TOTAL-RECORD-COUNT   PICTURE 9(03)   VALUE ZERO.
05 FILLER               PICTURE X(04)   VALUE SPACES.
05 TOTAL-PAGE-COUNT     PICTURE 9(04).
05 FILLER               PICTURE X(23)   VALUE 'TOTAL COUNT OF RECORDS'.
```

PL/I

```
DECLARE  COST       FIXED(5)          INITIAL (0),
         TAXES      FIXED(5,2),
         HEADINGS   CHARACTER(22)     INITIAL('TOTAL COUNT OF INSERTS');
```

In files, indentation should be used to indicate which items are subordinate items.

COBOL

```
01 NEW-PARTS-AREA.
    05  NEW-SEQUENCE-NUMBER     PICTURE 9(03).
    05  NEW-PAY-NUMBER.
        10  NEW-DEPT-CODE       PICTURE 9(02).
        10  NEW-EMPLOYEE-CODE   PICTURE 9(03).
    05  NEW-CHARGE-DEPT         PICTURE X(05).
```

The preceding indentation illustrates the data structure.

A similar structure can be used with arithmetic statements. This structure is the lining up of all equal signs.

```
A    = B + C
SIGN = BASE*COUNT
COST = PAY + BONUS
```

This step improves the neatness of the program and makes arithmetic statements more readable. Similarly, statements that exceed one line should have their turn lines indented so that they align at the right of the equal sign.

```
SIG = B*B + C/DES - COS(A) +
          PLAT/TEST
```

This statement will fit in with the columnar placement better than the following one.

```
SIG = B*B + C/DES - COS(A) +
PLAT/TEST
```

ALGOL W and PL/I allow procedures within procedures. In order to understand the structure of the program, it is important that the nested procedures be carefully indicated. One method to indicate the nesting is by indenting nested procedures. Figures 1.2, 1.3, and 1.4 are examples of this indenting.

SELECTION OF PARAGRAPH NAMES

Just as dividing a long essay into paragraphs makes reading easier, the dividing of a long program into paragraphs, sections, or subroutines improves readability by breaking it up into logical units. This procedure is also similar to dividing a book into chapters to avoid monotony and organize the materials.

The names chosen for the sections should describe the intent of, or the processing activities involved in, the section. The use of sections also provides a convenient place for inserting comments. Place the comments at the beginning of each section, explaining the use of that section.

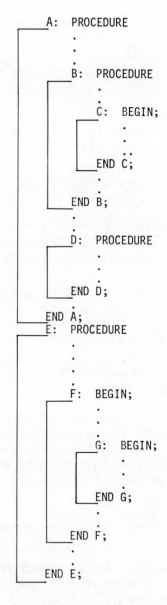

PL/I Indentation

Figure 1.2 PL/I indentation

```
BEGIN
REAL X,Y;
READ (X);
Y :=X;
IF X=0 THEN WRITE (0)
ELSE IF X<0 THEN WRITE("ERROR, INPUT OUT OF RANGE")
ELSE BEGIN
WHILE ABS((X-Y*Y)/X) >.000001 DO
Y:=.5*(Y+X/Y);
WRITE (Y)
END
END.
```

Figure 1.3 Sample Program: no comments or indenting.
What does the program do? Look on the next page.

UNREADABLE PROGRAMS

In engineering drawing a supervisor usually signs the drawings when he or she agrees that they look nice and conform to company or professional standards. In programming we do not see the second signature, often not even the first. Clarity and style are ignored; everyone wants to know if the program works, and, if not, when it will. It would seem worthwhile to have nontrivial programs bear the signature of two people who certify that the program is reasonable in style and format. This small requirement by a programming manager would result in better designed programs at almost no cost. It would also make the original programmers much more conscious of style and clarity because of the knowledge that a second signature was necessary. And they would know that someone else would be reading the program. If a supervisor cannot read the code and understand what is happening, how will maintenance people fare when it is time for the inevitable changes and program maintenance?

Beginning-level programmers believe that they are writing programs for machines. Experienced programmers know that they are writing programs for humans. A long line of people will be reading most programs. First, the original programmer will read it and reread it, frequently while writing, testing, and debugging the program. Next, all those who must do maintenance on the program will read the program many times. We learn to write language by reading. Perhaps the reason we do not learn to program by reading programs is because so many of them are painful to read.

Programs that no one understands exist because the original programmer moved on and others modified the original program without really understanding it. Such programs are black boxes that accept an input and provide an output with no one knowing how it works. As a result, these programs are accepted until the inevitable

```
BEGIN

COMMENT THIS PROGRAM READS IN A SINGLE REAL NUMBER OFF AN INPUT CARD
        AND PRINTS THE SQUARE ROOT OF THAT NUMBER ON THE OUTPUT PAGE
        IT USES NEWTON'S ITERATION METHOD TO CALCULATE THE SQUARE ROOT OF
        THE INPUT NUMBER UNTIL AND ACCURACY OF 10**(-6) IS OBTAINED -
        THE BASIC IDEA OF THIS ITERATIVE METHOD IS THAT IF X IS AN
        APPROXIMATION OF THE SQUAREROOT OF Y THEN (X+Y/X)/2 IS
        AN EVEN BETTER APPROXIMATION OF THE SQUAREROOT OF Y - THUS
        WE SHALL KEEP USING THIS ITERATIVE APPROXIMATION UNTIL
        WE OBTAIN THE DESIRED ACCURACY, NAMELY UNTIL THE RATIO OF
        THE DIFFERENCE OF X SQUARED AND Y WITH Y IS LESS THAN 10**(-6)

VARIABLE DEFINITION:
        INPUT - THE NUMBER READ OFF THE INPUT CARD - IE THE NUMBER
            WE'RE TO FIND THE SQUAREROOT OF
        APPROXIMATION - THE CURRENT APPROXIMATION OF THE SQUAREROOT
            OF INPUT;

REAL INPUT,APPROXIMATION;
COMMENT INITIALIZATION - GRANTED INPUT IS NOT A VERY GOOD ESTIMATE
        OF THE SQUAREROOT OF INPUT, BUT IT'S GOOD ENOUGH FOR OUR
        PURPOSES;

READ(INPUT);
APPROXIMATION:=INPUT;
COMMENT NEWTON'S METHOD WILL ONLY WORK IF WE ARE GIVEN A POSITIVE
        NUMBER, SO WE MUST FIRST CHECK TO MAKE SURE WE ARE DEALING
        A POSITIVE NUMBER;
IF INPUT=0 THEN
        WRITE(0)
ELSE IF INPUT<0 THEN
        WRITE("ERROR, INPUT OUT OF RANGE")
ELSE
    BEGIN
    WHILE ABS((INPUT-APPROXIMATION*APPROXIMATION)/INPUT)>.000001 DO
        APPROXIMATION:=.5*(APPROXIMATION+INPUT/APPROXIMATION);
    WRITE(APPROXIMATION)
    END
END.
```

Figure 1.4 Same program with comments, indenting, and good variable names.

changes occur, and then the program is discarded and rewritten because it is no longer understandable.

CONCLUSION

I hope I have shown that the small extra effort needed to make a program readable is minimal in comparison to the cost of revising, locating error, or rewriting an abstruse program. The rate of software production is about ten fully checked-out instructions a day. At this cost, a little effort at readability can be quite profitable.

One mark of a good programmer is the ability to write readable programs. Anything else, in the long run, will be more costly both in programmer's time and computer time.

Two reasons are often given for badly written programs.

1. It is to be a "fast and dirty" program for limited use.
2. It is a crash project that is already late.

But because programs have a tendency to stay around longer than planned and to grow in use far beyond the original plan, it seems worthwhile to write a good program the first time. Also, careful coding will save time in testing and revisions.

A great deal is said about the need for good documentation. If programs are readable, they become an important element in documentation. Another reason for demanding readable programs is that the code in the program is the only part of the documentation that is guaranteed to be accurate and up to date. The idea behind readable source languages is that the documentation of the program is the program itself.

PROGRAMMING MAXIMS

Programs are to be read by humans.

Provide more comments than you think you need.

Use prologue comments.

Use directory comments in long programs.

Comments should provide something extra — not just paraphrase the code.

Indent comments the same amount as the code they refer to.

Incorrect comments are worse than no comments at all.

Use blank spaces to improve readability.

Use good mnemonic names.

Use a prefix or suffix on file names.

One statement per line is enough.

Alphabetize lists.

Parentheses are cheaper than errors.

Use indentation to show program structure.

Use indentation to show data structure.

Chapter Review

1. Define the following terms.
   (a) Prologue comments
   (b) Directory comments
   (c) Explanatory comments
   (d) Indenting

2. Why should programs be readable?

3. How often should comments be inserted?

4. Name some obvious places to put comments.

5. Each program needs some general comments. What items should be included in these introductory comments?

6. How should variable names be chosen?

7. What rules can be used to produce readable abbreviations for variable names?

8. What considerations should be used in naming files?

9. What are the advantages of using standard abbreviations?

10. Where should blank lines be used?

11. Why is ample use of spaces desirable?

12. Why should an identification name be punched in program cards?

13. Why shouldn't you sequence number a program by units?

14. Why shouldn't multiple statements be placed on the same line?

15. In your programming language, where could alphabetized lists be used?

16. Find some examples in a program where parentheses will improve readability.

17. Modify one of your programs so that indenting is used. Does it improve readability?

18. Can you think of any other generalized techniques to make programs more readable?

19. Is there a statement in your programming language to cause an eject in the source listing?

20. What does the following program do? Criticize the program from a style point of view and then rewrite it.

```
45  READ(5,32)X,Y
    IF(X.GT.40)GOTO10
32  FORMAT(2F8.2)
    GOTO21
10  R=Y*40+Y*1.5*(X-40)
 1  WRITE(6,32)R
    GOTO45
21  R=Y*X
    GOTO1
    END
```

21. What does the code below do?

FORTRAN

```
     DO 5 I = 1, N
       DO 5 J = 1, N
5          XMAT(I,J) = (I/J) * (J/I)
```

After you figure out what this piece of code does, recode it in a clearer manner. Hint for non-FORTRAN programmers: I, J are integer variables that always result in integer results by truncation if necessary. Find three examples of tricky or cryptic coding and present them to the class for recoding.

22. If your programming language has no reserved words (i.e., FORTRAN, PL/I), write a small program, using variable names that are usually used for commands. See if someone else can figure out what the program does.

23. Try reading some programs. Some sources are program libraries, friends, and wastepaper baskets. Give such programs a grade (A to F) on style and readability. Were you able to learn anything by reading them?

24. Is computer programming an art or a science? Some people believe that it will always be an art; others believe that it is a science. After all, it is called computer science! Write a paper discussing the pros and cons of this question. To begin, decide on the difference between art and science. A good place to

start researching this topic is in Donald E. Knuth, "Computer Programming as an Art," *Communications of the ACM*, December 1974.

Programs*

25. Pick a problem out of Chapter VI.
    (a) Write the program in the worst possible style.
    (b) Write the same problem in the best possible style.
    (c) Try to use no GO TOs.

26. Write a program to read *N*; then read *N* numbers. Sort the numbers in ascending order and print the sorted numbers.

27. For *I*, *J*, *K*, and *L* positive integers less than 20, what integers satisfy the following relationship?

$$I^3 + J^3 + K^3 = L^3$$

28. Write a program to read the age of 100 individuals. Count the number of individuals in each block of 10 years. That is,

$$
\begin{aligned}
&\text{years} \quad 0\text{--}9 \\
&\text{years} \quad 10\text{--}19 \\
&\text{years} \quad 20\text{--}29 \\
&\qquad \text{etc.}
\end{aligned}
$$

Print the results of your counts in some readable fashion.

29. Write a program for these number problems.
    (a) Use the digits 1 through 9 in different combinations and the operators plus and minus to obtain the total 100. You shouldn't need a computer to find some of them.
    (b) Do part (a), but restrict the solutions so the digits appear in ascending or descending order. Here are two examples.

$$123 + 4 - 5 + 67 - 89 = 100$$
$$9 - 8 + 76 - 5 + 4 + 3 + 21 = 100$$

    (c) Do the same as part (b), but use hexadecimal digits (123456789ABCDEF) to obtain the hexadecimal 100.

30. Write a program that reads a source program and punches a new source program with sequence numbers in columns 73–80. The

---

*The programs work best if several people can do the same problem. Then compare the results and rank the programs according to style.

program should be able to start at any desired number and increment by any desired value.

31. Write a program that reads a integer number greater than zero in decimal representation and gives as output the decimal and English representation of the number. If the input was 7 204 52 0, the output would be

```
  7   SEVEN
204   TWO HUNDRED FOUR
 52   FIFTY TWO
```

The last number is to be a zero, and no number is to be larger than a billion.

Projects

32. Develop a set of guidelines for indenting (paragraphing) in your programming language. Then circulate the guidelines and see how many people agree or disagree. Modify them as needed until a consensus develops, then send me a copy.

33. Write a program that will accept an unparagraphed source program as input and return a paragraphed program. See Exercise 32. This is not an easy project, but it is possible. Start by indenting loops.

34. FORTRAN or BASIC. Write a program that accepts a source program and resequences statement numbers. The program should accept any starting value and any increment. A nice added feature is the option that allows you to indicate which number to start with at several places in the program. Thus you would be able to start the program at 10 and then later on you could indicate another area that is to start at 1000.

35. COBOL or PL/I. Write a program that will read a source program and provide a new source program where all the paragraphs and procedures have a numerical suffix.

36. A lazy (and smarter) way to do the preceding exercise is to locate an already written program to resequence the statement numbers. Then check it out, document it, and make it generally available to users.

37. Find a friend who will read your programs (Does anyone have such a friend?) and, in return, you will read theirs. Each of you can then make suggestions and notes on each other's programs.

Develop a set of guidelines for criticizing each other's programs so that the notes are helpful but not ego-shattering. One traditional suggestion is that the reader must always find something positive. Look up ego-less programming in Weinberg's book, which appears in the References in Chapter 2.

38. In any programming language, it is possible to develop a list of *do's* and *don'ts* for good style. Develop a list for your programming language, using this chapter as a starting point. Pass your list around and see if you can obtain a consensus. Then send me a copy of your list.

39. A program can be written to enforce the style guidelines. (See above project.) That is, a source program is read by the "Enforcer," and any violations of style are flagged. Write an Enforcer program.

40. Write a program that reads an X array and an Y array. Then scale and plot the data on either a line printer or terminal output. If you have a plotter, use the plotter for output.

41. Write a program to read a source program and output some or all of the following.
    (a) How many and percentages for each type of statement: Comments, `GO TO`, `IF`, `DO`, etc.
    (b) How long are variable names? How many one-character names, two-character names, three-character names, . . . ?
    Can you use the preceding information to develop some scale of good and bad programs? For a similar study, look up Donald E. Knuth, "An Empirical Study of FORTRAN Programs," *Software—Practice and Experience*, April–June 1971.

42. Write a program that generates nonempty sequences of zeros, ones, and twos without nonempty, elementwise, equal, adjoining subsequences, and generates these sequences in alphabetic order until a sequence of length 100 has been generated. Here are some sequences.

```
0
00       *
01
010
0100     *
0101     *
0102
01020
010200   *
010201
```

The sequences followed by the asterisk are no good. If you have trouble or would like to see a nice solution, the problem is discussed in Dahl, Dijkstra, and Hoare, *Structured Programming* (New York: Academic Press, 1972, pp. 63–67).

43. *Palindromes.* A palindrome is something that reads the same way backward and forward. The unit in a palindrome can vary. Sometimes it is a letter (WOW or MOM) or a number (4884 or 121) or words: STRAP ON NO PARTS.
    (a) Find some integers N which when squared are palindromes.

    $$26 = 676$$

    (b) Find some palindrome integers N which when squared are palindromes.

    $$22 = 484$$

    (c) Generalize the above for powers larger than 2.
    (d) Write a program that is also a palindrome.
    (e) *Conjecture.* Begin with any positive integer. If it is not a palindrome, reverse its digits and add the two numbers. If the sum is not a palindrome, treat it as the original number and continue. Stop the process when a palindrome is reached. Here is an example for 78.

$$
\begin{array}{r}
78 \\
+\ 87 \\
\hline
165 \\
+\ 561 \\
\hline
726 \\
+\ 627 \\
\hline
1353 \\
+\ 3531 \\
\hline
4884 \\
\end{array}
$$

    Check this conjecture out for the first 100 integers. *Side note:* 196 is the first number where it isn't known if it works. For reference, see Howard W. Bergerson, *Palindromes and Anagrams*, New York, Dover Publications, 1973 and Martin Gardner, "Mathematical Games," *Scientific American*, August 1970.

44. Write a program that will do one of the following conversions.
    (a) FORTRAN to BASIC
    (b) BASIC to FORTRAN
    (c) ALGOL to FORTRAN
    (d) FORTRAN to ALGOL
    You may wisely decide to implement only part of the conversion.

45. Write a program that is also poetry.

46. Write a program that is iambic pentameter.

REFERENCES

Conrow, Kenneth, "NEATER: A PL/I Source Statement Formatter," Program 360D–03.6.018. *SHARE Program Library*, Triangle Universities Computation Center, P.O. Box 12076, Research Triangle Park, N.C. 27709.

Conrow, Kenneth, and Ronald G. Smith, "NEATER2: A PL/I Source Statement Reformatter," *Communications of the ACM*, November 1970.

Jackson, Michael, "Mnemonics," *Datamation*, April 1967.

Kernighan, Brian W., and P. J. Plauger, *The Elements of Programming Style*. New York: McGraw-Hill, 1974.

Ledgard, Henry F., *Programming Proverbs*. Rochelle Park, N.J.: Hayden Book Company, 1975.

Scowens, R. S., and B. A. Wichmann, "The Definition of Comments in Programming Languages," *Software — Practice and Experience*, April–June 1974.

Large monolithic programs are like a plate of spaghetti:
pull it here and something moves on the other side.

A good rule is to expect the worst at all times
and program accordingly.

I don't program half as
good as I know how already.

2

Program Design

Program design affects program style, reliability, efficiency, debugging, testing, and maintainability. As a result, it is an important part of any program development. It is also an area, however, in which recommendations for one project or one programmer do not always work for a different project or programmer.

One obvious suggestion for better program design is: design before coding. In the rush to get "something" started, the tendency is to start coding before the design stage is completed or sometimes before it is even started.

Small programs do not, of course, prove as difficult as large programs. Small programs can easily be coded and comprehended by one person. But how can we intellectually organize programs that are so large that they cannot be comprehended by one person? Much work is being done on this problem, but for the present we are all amateurs when it comes to building *large* programs. Here are a few thoughts on program design.

THE SIMPLICITY GOAL

Simplicity in program design is the first step in writing a readable program. Coding should be simple. This is often called the *KISS principle* (Keep It Simple, Stupid). Sophisticated coding is not desirable because complex logic or tricky coding can become very expensive when debugging or modifying needs to be done. Unusual coding (i.e., taking advantage of obscure machine-dependent capabilities) often impedes program checkout and certainly hinders future maintenance by programmers unfamiliar with the program.

> *KISS: Keep It Simple, Stupid.*

Someone has suggested that if you have a clever programmer, one who can do things in obscure ways, fire that person. There is something to be said for that advice, because if you can write a program that is so clever, so complicated, and so obscure that only you can understand it, the program is worthless. The program must be tested and maintained by you and others, and those clever and obscure qualities will make it that much more difficult.

Complex programs are sometimes written in an attempt to convince everyone that the programmer is indispensable. Although it may be a valid goal from the programmer's point of view, it is not from management's standpoint. Management's goal should be maximum clarity. Complex programs merely cause headaches and are an indication of bad programming. Complex or tricky programs are difficult even for the original programmer to debug or modify and often prove an embarrassment when he or she is unable to get the program working correctly.

The structure of the program should make apparent sense. For example, if a test that has several outcomes is performed, it is most reasonable to list the code for each outcome in a sensible order, as by increasing magnitude of the test parameter. This method is most reasonable because a reader would expect it that way.

Another area in which simplicity is important is in individual statements. During syntax checking the compiler could produce a message as follows.

SYNTAX ERROR AT LINE 37.

If line 37 is something like the following:

$$A = B/*C$$

then the error is easy to locate. But if the statement is quite long or if there are several statements on line 37, the error can be difficult to discover.

Another use of simple statements is in trying to locate an execution error after a line number is given. For instance,

FIXED OVERFLOW AT LINE 56.

If the statement at line 56 is short, the error is easier to pinpoint. But we should not go to the other extreme. To illustrate,

ROOT1 = (-B + SQRT(B*B - 4*A*C)) / (2*A)

That is easier to understand than

```
BB = B*B
A1 = A*C
A2 = 4*A1
B1 = BB - A2
B2 = SQRT(B1)
BOTTOM = 2*A
TOP = -B + B2
ROOT1 = TOP/BOTTOM
```

which is not only inefficient but also prone to errors. Moreover, it is more difficult to understand.

The problem is: How do you decide what is a simple statement and what is a complex statement? The answer will vary, depending on the users and their familiarity with the programming language and the problem being programmed. One obvious guideline is that, in programming a numerical expression, the statement should not exceed one line.

Psychologists suggest that seven items are a good length to restrict statements. This is the same length as are local telephone numbers, and it seems to be a good limit. Each programmer can adjust the limit up or down, according to individual needs. In addition, each programmer must decide what an item is in a statement. As a programmer becomes more familiar with the language, it is usually natural to use longer statements.

Another way to improve simplicity in programs is to use consistency in coding techniques. Doing so will help to reduce confusion. For example, all program switch variables should be used in the same manner. That is, a value zero (0) is used to mean *off*, whereas a value unity (1) means *on*. Similarly, it may be desirable to use the same table lookup method for all tables in one program. On input, use the same field width for all real data and use the same field width for all integer data. This practice will eliminate many input errors. It is also best to avoid mixing real and integer data on the input data record when possible.

READING PROGRAMS

The program should be read by someone besides the programmer. If the programmers *know* that others are going to read the program, their entire attitude toward coding changes. Code becomes commented, paragraphed, clear, and concise.

One method used at some installations to ensure simplicity in program design and coding is the *program buddy system.* In this system each program is to be understood by at least two programmers. The first programmer does the coding, but a second programmer is expected to understand and review the program. This procedure has two positive benefits. First, it ensures that understandable programs will be produced. Secondly, if the first programmer should leave for some reason or be unable to finish the program, another will still be familiar with the project.

A similar setup is the program standards evaluation. Here a set of installation programming standards is established. Then each program is compared to these standards to ensure that the standards are met before the program is put in the program library. Generally all programmers take turns doing the evaluating.

PROBLEM DEFINITION

There is nothing more devastating in a development activity than an incomplete and/or incorrect specification of software requirements. If customers cannot define their needs or if the programmer (by programmer is meant whoever is writing the design specifications) cannot understand what the customer wants, serious trouble can be expected in the software development. It has been said that the perfect program is one that would deliver exactly the output desired when given a vague description of the user's needs. Seldom does a vague description result in the desired output.

One way to help clarify the description of user needs is to carry on a continual series of reviews for developing a mutual understanding of both the requirements (as stated) and the actual customer intent (if different). These reviews will prove successful if they uncover problems that might not surface until much later. It is important to recognize the importance of the completeness and consistency of the preliminary design. Realism at the beginning of the design stage is preferred over changes when the system reaches "puberty" (i.e., the stage before maturity when the facts of life become apparent).

Well-Defined Problems

Both well-defined and ill-defined problems exist. Ill-defined problems do not have a clear-cut programming design and solution. Unhappily, most programming problems start out ill-defined ("Write a payroll program"). But if you can turn the problem into a well-defined one *before* writing it, you will save yourself much work. If the problem is ill-defined to start (with gaps in the design), you will begin programming and then discover this fact while programming or after giving the "completed" program to the user. Afterward the program must be modified to match the correct design. Much program modification and maintenance occur because no one bothered to get the problem design straight originally.

Programming problems are usually originated by someone besides the programmer. There are two reasons why the programmer may start without a clear understanding of the problem. First, the originator of the problem may not have a clear understanding of the problem; secondly, the programmer may not understand what the originator wants due to lack of communication. When the programmer and the problem originator are not the same person, the programmer must work with his or her understanding of the problem.

A written description of the problem should be prepared by the problem originator. This step is necessary even if the programmer is the problem originator. Such a description forces the problem originator to think about the problem and, hopefully, to define a clear goal. Next, a conference between the problem originator and the programmer should take place. If the problem is complex, it may be best to have a conference even before the originator attempts to write up the problem. In this way, the problem originator may develop a greater appreciation of the capabilities and limitation of computers (or the programmer or both). Such discussion often helps the problem originator clarify his or her own thinking.

The programmer should then rewrite the problem specification, using a computer orientation. What is needed is a concise but thorough description of the problem, which may range from a few sentences for a small problem to a large book for a large system. It will become the basis for much documentation.

Next, the programmer and problem originator should go over the written specifications together to ensure understanding on both sides. This process may need to be repeated several times before both believe that they understand the specifications. It is important that the problem originator understand that he or she is going to get exactly what is specified. Later changes or additions are not only expensive but also delay completion of the project. Any haste at the problem definition stage will cause difficulty later on.

> *Get it right at the design stage.*

At some point it is best to freeze the specification. After this, no changes or additions may be added to the specifications. Any revisions are saved until a later time. Even if changes are accepted after programming has begun, some additional cost and time should be added to the schedule. Furthermore, the added cost and schedule charge should be quite heavy for all changes. This is one way to control changes and allow extra time for programming. Many projects have slipped schedules because of changing specifications. It is important to charge a fee for all changes. Users who are allowed to make a small output heading change free of charge will not understand why they cannot make a small change in the master input file without causing delay and added cost. Consequently, it is preferable to accustom the user to paying heavily for all changes. Doing so might result in more carefully drawn design specifications in the future.

SELECTION OF ALGORITHM

The most important step in having an efficient and correct program occurs before the program is written. It is the selection of the best algorithm for the program. This statement assumes that correct language has been chosen and that a problem specification has been completed. Thus a good algorithm is a necessary but not a sufficient condition for a good program. If the user can state the problem in a clear algorithmic form, the design process will be easier. Here is a simple example.

$$Y = Ax^3 + Bx^2 + Cx + D$$

The most straightforward approach to finding the value of this equation would be

$$Y = A*X**3 + B*X**2 + C*X + D$$

But repeated multiplication is more efficient than exponentiation for small integer powers, and so the equation could be changed to

$$Y + A*X*X*X + B*X*X + C*X + D$$

This form requires six multiplications and three additions. Many people might believe that this equation could not be improved, since we have already improved it once. Yet even this simple problem can be greatly improved. For example (polynomial factoring — Horner's method),

$$Y = Ax^3 + Bx^2 + Cx + D$$

$$= x(Ax^2 + Bx + C) + D \qquad \text{Factor an } x.$$

$$= x(x(Ax + B) + C) + D \qquad \text{Factor an } x.$$

Now our equation would be

$$Y = X * (X * (A * X + B) + C) + D$$

which requires three multiplications and three additions. We have decreased the number of arithmetic operations. We have also increased the accuracy. This is called the *nested* form of the polynomial.

This example of improving an algorithm should help illustrate the rule that an hour of planning is usually worth five hours of programming. Too often all planning is skipped, and the first algorithm that comes to mind is programmed. Another example worth discussing is the problem of determining if a number N is a prime. A prime number is a number that is divisible only by 1 and itself. For example, 3, 5, 7, 11, 13, and 17 are primes. The numbers 4, 9, 21, and 35 are not primes. Figure 2.1 is one algorithm to find if N ($N > 1$) is prime.

This algorithm divides 2, 3, 4, . . . , $n - 1$ into n until a number divides n exactly or until n is reached. This is not the most efficient way to determine if N is prime; however, it is an all too common first approach to the problem.

A little analysis would reveal that it is not necessary to check to see if all even numbers less than N are divisors. You need only check

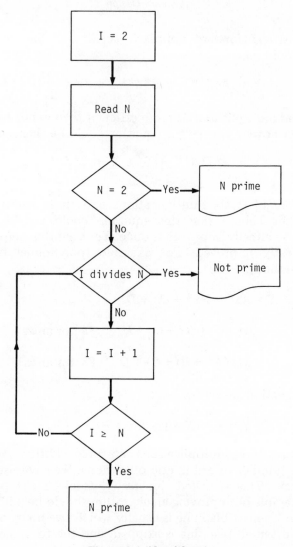

Figure 2.1 Algorithm 1

the number 2, because 2 will be a divisor if any other even number is a divisor. Then all that is needed is a test for divisibility by the odd integers 3, 5, 7, and so on. This simple modification will reduce the calculations by about half. Armed with this new knowledge, we can proceed to draw a new flowchart as in Fig. 2.2.

This algorithm divides 2 and then the odd integers into *n* until a number divides *n* exactly or until *n* is reached. Most programmers, relieved at reducing their calculations by half, would start programming immediately. But since I am trying to stress the importance of

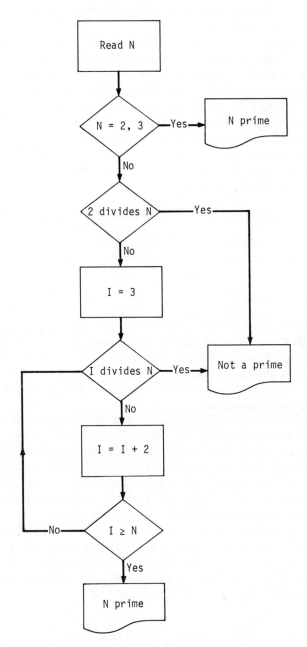

Figure 2.2 Algorithm 2

carefully selecting an algorithm before starting to program, a little more analysis will be used.

The next step is to notice that all we must do is to test divisors that are less than or equal to the square root of N. (If there is a divisor larger than the square root of N, there must be a divisor less than the square root of N.) If this point is not immediately evident, try a few examples. So Fig. 2.3 is our new flowchart.

This algorithm divides 2 and then the odd integers less than or equal to the square root of n until a number divides n exactly or until the square root of n is reached.

Let us examine the number of divisors that we must check in each case in the three groups.

N	Algorithm 1 All Is	Algorithm 2 2 and Odd Is $< N$	Algorithm 3 2 and Odd Is $< \sqrt{N}$
10	8	5	2
100	98	50	5
1000	998	500	16

By comparing the second and fourth columns in the last row we can see that about 60 times as many numbers must be checked in method 1 as in method 3. From an efficiency point of view, selection of the correct algorithm is the most important step in this example and in many other programs.

Now we have an efficient method to determine if a particular number is a prime number. But what was the original problem? Was it to determine if a particular number is prime, or was it to generate prime numbers? If it was the first, then we probably have a good algorithm. If our goal was to generate prime numbers (i.e., generate all primes less than 1000), then we picked the wrong method completely. We could have used the Sieve of Eratosthenes.

This raises the question: How does one select a good algorithm? The first rule is: don't immediately start programming the first algorithm that comes to mind; at least consider several. Then choose the best one. If you consider only one algorithm for solving a problem, it is doubtful that you will select the best.

Select the problem algorithm most carefully.

There are many sources of computer algorithms. Donald Knuth's *The Art of Computer Programming*, Vols. 1–3, (Reading, MA:

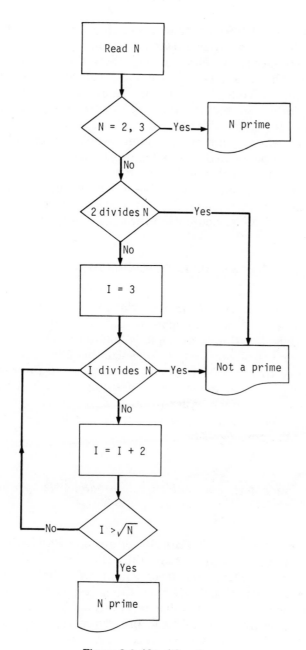

Figure 2.3 Algorithm 3

Addison-Wesley, 1969) contain a wealth of basic computer algorithms. This is an obvious first place to look, and all professional programmers should be familiar with these three useful books. See also Alfred Aho et al., *The Design and Analysis of Computer Algorithms* (Addison-Wesley, 1974), which covers many computer algorithms. Another source is *Collected Algorithms from the CACM* (Association for Computing Machinery). Next, consult the literature in the field where your programming problems come from. Algorithms can also be located in existing programs that can be from your installation or from programs in interchange groups. If an algorithm from the literature can be used, the design and implementation will be easier and more reliable. A good algorithm is a necessary condition but not a sufficient condition for a good program.

DATA DESCRIPTION

Another factor similar in importance to algorithm selection is data description. A well-thought-out data description can eliminate pages of coding. A simple example is failure to use an array when an array is the most obvious way to organize the data. Another example is the ability to use references and pointers. If you needed to trace relationships between parents and offspring through several generations, it would be much easier to do it with pointers and references. We want to choose a representation that is fairly natural for the problem under consideration.

> *Choose a data representation that matches the problem.*

Malcolm C. Harrison's *Data Structures and Programming* (Scott, Foresmen and Company, 1973), Ellis Horowitz and Sartaj Sahni's *Fundamentals of Data Structures* (Computer Science Press, 1976), and Donald E. Knuth's *The Art of Computer Programming*, Vol. 1, are three good places to familiarize yourself with the different types of data structures. FORTRAN programmers interested in nonnumerical applications should look at A. Colin Day's *FORTRAN Techniques* (Cambridge University Press, 1972). Almost any data structure can be simulated in any language, and these techniques are adequately discussed in the preceding references, but you should not overlook the option of using a programming language that has the desired data structure.

SELECTION OF PROGRAMMING LANGUAGE

Often the programming language is already established by installation standards or programmer background. There are good reasons for installation standards. If too many different languages are used for production programs, program maintenance becomes much more difficult. At the same time, however, the temptation to use a programming language simply because it is familiar should be resisted.

If the programmer is able to select the programming language, the highest-level language suitable for the task is usually the best choice. Higher-level languages have statements that do the work of two or three statements of lower-level languages. Therefore fewer potential errors per unit of code are generated. Use of a library of prewritten, pretested, error-free subroutines and functions has the same effect.

If the programming language does not fit the task, problems in programming, efficiency, and debugging result. It is amazing how many programs are still written in assembly language. Moreover, many people try to do business applications in FORTRAN and numerical applications in COBOL. A great deal of trouble can be avoided by using a proper programming language. The use of a particular programming language will influence the thinking process involved in the design.

GENERALITY

Generality refers to the concept of program independence from a particular set of data. If a program is highly dependent on the data, then it is not general.

A very simple example of nongenerality is the following piece of code.

FORTRAN

```
READ (5,12)  (A(I), I=1, 25)
SUM = 0.0
DO   20   I = 1, 25
    SUM = SUM + A(I)
20 CONTINUE
```

This code reads in a vector A and sums the elements. But everything depends on the vector having 25 elements. If the program must be modified to handle a different number of elements, we must search through the program, changing each 25 to the new value. This approach is error prone, since it requires us to find *each* place where 25 is used for the vector **A**.

A much better approach is

```
N = 25
READ (5, 12) (A(I), I = 1, N)
SUM = 0.0
DO   20   I = 1, N
     SUM = SUM + A(I)
20 CONTINUE
```

By changing the value of **N**, we can handle any size vector from 1 to **N** (as long as **N** does not get too large).

A good general program will also handle the degenerate cases (i.e., zero or 1) and print an error message when **N** is too large. Not only is the program then general, but it also avoids errors.

Use variables for parameters, not constants.

A program can be made general by using variables instead of constants for parameters. If constants are used, then, when the parameters change, someone is forced to change every statement in the source program where the obsolete constants appear. This process is wasteful of programmer time and, of course, prone to errors. The use of constants instead of variables has no effect on program efficiency, and so there is no reason to use constants. Whenever practical, we wish to be able to respond to a change in the environment simply by changing a parameter of the program rather than by searching through the program to find which parts are affected by the change.

It is easy to miss a statement in which a desired constant appears and then have an incorrect program. It has been suggested that a good text editor could be used to automatically change every place a certain constant appears. Although creative, the idea is foolish, since the same constant could be used in the program for another purpose and so should not be changed. This situation illustrates another possibility of error when making constant changes. Not only can you miss changing a constant but you can also easily change one that should not be changed. Much program maintenance occurs because the original programmer used constants instead of variables for parameters.

Some obvious places where variables can be used instead of constants are in the cases below.

1. Size of tables, arrays, and lists
2. Tax rates, discount rates, scientific constants, and percentages
3. Input/output device designators.

Other steps can also be taken, such as leaving space in tables and keeping all change-prone parameters in one place. Then these parameters can be initialized in one place and heavily commented. In a simple program this procedure can occur at the beginning of the program. In a program having many subroutines it is sometimes useful to have one subroutine initialize all parameters. Otherwise a change in a parameter may require a change in several subroutines, with the resulting possibility of error.

In addition, parameters can be useful during testing. For instance, if a parameter is used for table size or number of work areas, it can be reduced during testing in order to cause a table or workspace to overflow easily. Then you can ensure that the error routines work properly for these error conditions.

Experienced programmers know that bringing generality into programs will save work later and make the program more robust. Always look for minor amendments or additions that will make a routine useful elsewhere. In this way, generalized subroutines can be contributed to a program library for use in other programs. Once a programmer or department starts this policy, a library of useful, tested subroutines is gradually built up. This situation eliminates much dull and repetitious coding.

> *Design generality into the program.*

Another reason for writing general programs is that programs tend to require modifications. Generality can often anticipate many future changes in the program specifications. Also, a careful examination for feasible generalizations may help clarify the design of the program. The search for generality can usually help anticipate future modifications and adaptations.

In order to improve program design, decrease debugging and testing, and thereby reduce the amount of work needed in programming, use program libraries that are already available. Plagiarism in programming is no crime. In fact, it is the intelligent way to do your programming.

The first type of library consists of the functions and subroutines available with the programming language. Included are all the standard functions, such as square root, sine, cosine, and absolute value. Become familiar with supplied functions and subroutines by examining those in the programming language manual. Built-in functions supplied with the language are certainly better programmed and tested than any we could write ourselves. So it would be wasteful to program a routine that was already available with the language.

> *Don't reprogram the square root function.*

The next source of functions and subroutines is your local installation. Most installations have some available — the only hitch is to determine what is available and how to use them.

Why use library programs? One reason is to increase reliability and reduce complexity. Programming is no longer so new that major improvements can be achieved by junior programmers doing the same thing over one more time. This fact is already accepted for such utilities as sort, or merge, or functions like square root or cosine.

Yet frequently it does not extend to building up a library of reusable parts for programs. When each module is uniquely programmed for a complex structure, the user must bear the full cost of design and testing of the special module. When standard pretested modules are used, however, the cost of design and testing can be spread among a larger group of users. And so greater care can be taken at the original design and testing. Reliability can be much improved by the use of already existing routines.

One program had the following set of code.

```
        IF A < B THEN GOTO 10
        GOTO 20
10      IF A < C THEN GOTO 30
        GOTO 25
```

```
 30      SMALL = A
         GOTO 100
 20      IF B < C THEN GOTO 50
 25      SMALL = C
         GOTO 100
 50      SMALL = B
100      ....
```

If you study this code, you might figure out what it is trying to do. Besides the fact that it is nearly unreadable, this is a very common operation usually provided by a built-in function. That is, find the smallest element of a group of elements, and the above could be programmed by

$$SMALL = MIN(A, B, C)$$

Although familiar with MAX and MIN functions, when was the last time that you scanned the list of available library functions in your programming language? All of us have spent hours or days writing a routine only to discover later that a library function (or utility program) was already available to do the same thing.

When designing a new electronic gadget, engineers do not design each transistor and capacitor from scratch. Instead they select off-the-shelf power supplies, transistors, and capacitors. Too often programmers *do* start from scratch.

Another source of library programs consists of books on programming and computer use. Quite a few books contain programs that are useful for library programs. Some effort should be made to become familiar with your own subject matter.

Generally each computer manufacturer has a user's group that distributes programs at a nominal cost. This source should not be overlooked. People in the chemistry field have collected together chemistry programs by refining the process a little. Information on this group is available from Quantum Chemistry Program Exchange, Indiana University, Bloomington, Ind. 47401. Good statistics programs are available from several groups (BMD statistics program available from University of California at Los Angeles, and the SPSS available from the National Opinion Research Center at the University of Chicago). Other disciplines should imitate these groups.

The final source of library programs is yourself. By programming in modules and keeping the principle of generality in mind, you will slowly build up a source of useful subprograms.

INPUT/OUTPUT FORMATS

Input and output data formats are part of the design phase. Input formats should be designed for maximum user convenience and avoidance of errors. Order of variables and data formats that are natural to the user will help prevent errors and make usage easier.

Consistency in input format is frequently helpful in avoiding input errors. That is, a format of (I7, I8, I9, I8) is much less desirable than a consistent (4I10) format. In the first format it is difficult for a user to remember the input formats, but it is easy to remember that all formats are ten-column fields.

Output specifications vary greatly. Sometimes exact instructions are provided for output so that everything will fit on special forms. Often, however, the programmer lacks such firm guidelines. Many output lists appear that have pages of numbers with no identification whatever. Usually even the programmer cannot tell what the numbers represent without referring to the code.

The output should be capable of being understood without reference to any other sources. Good output provides

1. Identification of the output report
2. Description or function of the report
3. Date
4. Pages numbered.

In addition, every item printed should be labeled. Data output in tabular form can have columns or rows labeled.

Data should be grouped together by function or logical groups with blank lines or page ejects for separators. I have often seen people take computer output and retype it for inclusion in reports. Not only is this step wasteful in time but it is also a source of errors. Instead the output reports should be designed so that they could be reproduced and published without any editing being required.

Good formatting of output is not always popular with programmers facing unrealistic completion dates, but there are several reasons for doing it. First, nicely formated, appropriately labeled output is an aid to the programmer when debugging and testing. Unlabeled output requires constant reference to source code to see what is printed. And the appearance of output is often the sole yardstick by which the programmer's skill is judged. Users who receive attractive-looking reports will assume that the programmer is a skilled craftsperson.

OPERATOR CONVENIENCE

An important feature that is commonly overlooked in the design situation is the computer operator. Someone must run the job, locate the input/output tapes, mount disks, and change paper forms. Although it may be impossible to shape the job for operator convenience, it is often possible to provide a little help. In certain jobs the operator is requested to put in 2-part paper, 4-part paper, and then 2-part paper again. A little change in design of the output stream would have changed the order of output so as to eliminate a form's change. Another simple aid is to use labeled tapes so the operating system can verify that the correct tape is mounted.

One way to gain insight into the operator situation is simply to ask the operator how your new XYZ system is running and if there are any operating problems. Experienced programmers know that a good relationship with computer operators is desirable. Some installations require their programmers to operate the computer occasionally. I believe that all programmers should be required to work in the machine room at least once a year for several days. It is always a learning process.

MODEST GOALS

We are often too ambitious when designing a program in that we attempt to handle all possible exceptions. This attempt leads to extremely large and complicated programs. Instead we should design programs that will handle almost all cases; then we should set up code that will *identify* the remainder and put them aside for manual processing. Frequently, a great deal of code is used for extremely rare events. The operating system for the IBM 360 has code to handle leap years as part of its permanently resident date routine. (Frederick P. Brooks, Jr., *The Mythical Man-Month*, p. 56 — "must" reading for anyone interested in software). This is an event that occurs every four years, and Brooks felt that it could have been left to the operator. Many software projects that might have been successful but that failed can be traced to overambitious design. OS/360 is one obvious project that was too ambitious for its time. Programming, as in other areas of life, could benefit by a more modest evaluation of what we can do successfully. A program that behaves correctly with 99% of the data and rejects the other 1% is more desirable than a program that accepts all data but appears to behave randomly part of the time. And a modest working program is more useful than an unfinished grand program.

SET GOALS

Sometime early in the design stage goals should be set. Examples include

1. High reliability level
2. Certain completion by a specific date
3. Minimal development time or minimal cost
4. Simplicity and ease of maintenance
5. Efficiency — storage or speed
6. Ability to accept changes as progressing
7. Generality or ease of use.

Each programming project usually has some goals, but frequently they are not written down. Sometimes the programmers are not aware of the goals, or two programmers may perceive different goals even when working on the same project. One programmer may be trying to minimize storage usage at any expense, whereas another may be trying to minimize development cost at any expense.

> *Set realistic project goals early and explicitly.*

To illustrate, suppose that a program must be finished by January, that it is to be used only once, and that if it is not done by January, it is of no use. Here the goals are not efficiency and maintainability. In contrast, a weekly update program will be used for a long time. Efficiency and maintainability are important, but if the program were to be a week late, it would not be too serious. Establishing and writing down goals ensure that everyone is working for the same one. Once established, goals should be ordered by importance and given weights in case tradeoffs are necessary.

Once a software system is operational, new goals may become necessary. A system may be too slow or too large, or new requirements may be posed for the system. The fitting of an existing software to new goals is called *retrofitting*. Retrofitting will continue to occur as new functions are added or old functions are dropped.

COMPLEXITY

All of us are familiar with two dimensions in programs: storage and time. Yet there is another dimension that must be controlled — complexity. The more complex the program, the more difficult it is to control, test, debug, and maintain. By limiting complexity, we can obtain a much more manageable product. Today such methods of limiting program complexity exist.

Computer programs are some of the most complex structures ever assembled. Moreover, because of repeated execution with new sets of data, programs are the most thoroughly exercised of complex structures. Many complex structures that contain errors are saved because the error factor is never tested. For example, only during an earthquake is an earthquake-proof building adequately tested.

At various times in history the human race has built some very complex structures and successfully accomplished operations of impressive complexity with few important errors. A successful structure or operation is one in which errors of design and implementation can be handled during use. What are some of the techniques for controlling complexity? How do they work? How can they be applied to programming?

There are two approaches to quality assurance: either the product is exhaustively tested or quality is built in. Exhaustive testing is impossible in most computer programs, and so we must control complexity in order to limit the number of possible errors.

The technique that is normally used to control complexity is to divide the process or structure into small, manageable parts and combine them to accomplish the specified function. It is the basis used by mass production methods as well as by all organizations, governmental and industrial. Yet increasing the size of a program increases complexity disproportionately. As size doubles, complexity can easily quadruple. So a software project that is twice as large as a previously successful project cannot be done merely with twice as much effort or people. This often-overlooked fact has produced many disastrous software projects.

Controlling complexity is a desirable feature in programming. We do so by specifying the function of each module in an independent way. Each module must produce its specified outputs from specified inputs. To the extent that this independence is realized, it is possible to cascade and combine software modules into a larger structured system.

Modules and top-down design (explained later in the chapter) allow us to control complexity by having levels of understanding.

The details of lower levels can be ignored if the information is not needed. For example, if people are reading a main routine and see a call that produces report headings, they can skip the report-heading routine if they are not interested and keep following the main logic. If the report headings are coded in-line, they would be forced to read the code.

Modules are powerful weapons to control complexity. First, modules separate sets of variables from other sets of variables. Thus modules reduce the impact of many possible program errors by isolating the error to a particular module. For example, the larger a module is, the greater the possibility of using the same variable for two different purposes. Also, the larger the module, the more difficult it is to determine what will happen if a small change is made in one part of the module. Finally, modules reduce the number of possible paths through a program, which is an important element for controlling complexity.

The next step in controlling overall complexity is to control the complexity within each module: this process is commonly called *structured programming*.

STRUCTURED PROGRAMMING

One method that leads to better programs is structured programming. Its goal is to organize and discipline the program design and coding process in order to prevent most logic errors and to detect the ones that remain. Structured programming concentrates on one of the most error-prone factors of programming, the logic. Structured programming has three important characteristics.

1. Top-down design
2. Modular programming
3. Structured coding.

These three characteristics are discussed below.

Traditionally programmers have programmed in a personal manner, each using his or her own rule of program structure. Although the program might start with some clear structure, as the program progresses and the need for changes or corrections becomes apparent, a large number of GO TO statements and labels are used to get it all together. Thus we often have a clear structure at the beginning, but during subsequent unit and integration testing, as well as later maintenance, the original logic becomes completely obscured.

Unstructured	Structured
IF p GOTO label q	① IF p THEN
IF w GOTO label m	A function
L function	B function
GOTO label k	② IF q THEN
label m M function	③ IF t THEN
GOTO label k	G function
label q IF q GOTO label t	④ DOWHILE u
A function	H function
B function	④ ENDDO
C function	I function
label r IF NOT r GOTO label s	③ (ELSE)
D function	③ ENDIF
GOTO label r	② ELSE
label s IF s GOTO label f	C function
E function	③ DOWHILE r
label v IF NOT v GOTO label k	D function
J function	③ ENDDO
label k K function	③ IF s THEN
END function	F function
label f F function	③ ELSE
GOTO label v	E function
label t IF t GOTO label a	③ ENDIF
A function	② ENDIF
B function	② IF v THEN
GOTO label w	J function
label a A function	② (ELSE)
B function	② ENDIF
G function	① ELSE
label u IF NOT u GOTO label w	② IF w THEN
H function	M function
GOTO label u	② ELSE
label w IF NOT t GOTO label y	L function
I function	② ENDIF
label y IF NOT v GOTO label k	① ENDIF
J function	K function
GOTO label k	END function

Figure 2.4 Examples of structured and unstructured coding

Figure 2.4 illustrates the normal unstructured code on the left and structured code on the right. The most obvious difference is that the left side uses GO TOs and labels. Read the program on the left from the beginning to the end, following the logic of the program. Then notice the dearth of branches on the right program and read it.

Top-Down Design

Top-down program design is similar to top-down report writing. Reports are structured hierarchically and written from the top of the hierarchy — that is, starting with a brief synopsis. The design

normally begins with an investigation of the goals of the project and
a determination of the major tasks involved in accomplishing these
goals. If the project is large, the initial division of the project should
be done by a person who is highly competent and experienced.

A first approach is to write what you want to do in English first.
This step is often quite revealing. Frequently, you find that you cannot write the problem in English. If so, don't expect to be able to
program it either. And it is much easier to rewrite a program in
English at design specification time than to rewrite it in a programming language when it is supposed to be complete. So it is important
to get it right during the design stage instead of later during the
programming or checkout stage.

Write it in English first.

This technique involves first specifying a program in the broadest
outline and then gradually refining the structure to fill in the details.
The design consists of a sequence of refinement steps. And at each
step we want to identify the major functions to be accomplished.
In each step a given task is broken up into a number of subtasks until
the subtasks are simple enough to be coded into a module with high
reliability. This is the traditional and essential top-down approach
used in building complex structures in other disciplines, such as
engineering, mass production, and report writing. The system design
can then be validated by simulations or walkthroughs. Each module
can have one sentence describing the action that is to take place. As
soon as a module takes more than a line or a short paragraph to
explain, redesign it.

Next, the data should be described, indicating the essential
structure and the major processes to which the data will be sub-
jected. This description should include carefully selected samples
to illustrate the functions and their most important variations.
These examples will be useful later as test cases. Each module should
have the test data described when the module is described. Since
program testing is inevitable, it is good practice to identify testing
needs (weak or critical points) early in program design. Logical
testing of various abstractions of the program should reduce actual
testing needs of the final program. In order to do this "hand testing",
specifications must be precise enough to be testable.

> *Design test data early.*

A major advantage of this method of working is that it guarantees that the documentation is produced. The documentation always begins during the design specification phase, but often this initial work is lost or misplaced by the time that final documentation is started at the end of the project. Ideally, much of the documentation should be completed even before coding begins. It should also lead to better programs. The programmer is forced to think about the structure, the data, and the testing of his program more carefully than usual in order to describe it on paper.

The use of structured programming suggests that program correctness is more likely to occur simply because of the way that the program is developed. By performing the complete system design from the top-most levels, we are more certain that the software will meet its goals and that any errors missed when implementing will become apparent as early as possible. It is important to design first before any coding takes place. Writing any code produces a psychological barrier to later design improvements. We should be willing to do several design iterations before coding occurs. Most programmers acquire the habit of starting to code too early on small projects where design is less critical. Most programs are not designed; they are created on a coding form.

> *Design before coding.*

Now that top-down design has been explained, stop and try to do a top-down design for getting a man dressed. Start with the broadest outline and then continually refine the instructions until you have a complete set of instructions.

Let us try it. A gross first step might be to state the goal:

Get dressed.

Then a first level refinement might be:
Dress bottom half.
Dress top half.

We might break the bottom half into two steps.
  Put on undershorts and trousers.
  Put on shoes and socks.

Next, we can break the top half into two steps:
  Put on undershirt.
  Put on shirt.

Now we can do a final top-down design:
  Put on undershorts.
  Put on trousers.
  Put on shoes.
  Put on socks.
  Put on undershirt.
  Put on shirt.

Thus we have a fairly detailed design specification. The next step is to hand simulate it and check for errors. There is an error! If you cannot find the error by hand simulation, try to use the design specification to get dressed tomorrow morning.

Most current software development methods allow design specification errors that have been committed early in the development cycles to remain undetected until testing and implementation. The cost of finding and correcting an error in the system increases, however, as the program nears completion. Errors found during design specification are relatively inexpensive to correct (redo the design) compared to errors found during final system testing (reprogram the job). Also, errors found later involve more people and necessitate communication among groups (i.e., the programmers, those doing the documentation, and the users).

Get it right at the beginning.

In most cases, incorrect implementation is the result of incomplete or inconsistent design specifications. Boehm's article (see References) indicates that up to two-thirds of software errors are introduced during design specifications. Consequently, here is where our major effort to reduce errors should occur, since it is the area of largest payoff in designing reliable software. Good programming cannot save a bad design.

An ill-designed program is so common that a new word has entered the vocabulary to describe it. A *kludge* is a system described as "an ill-sorted collection of poorly matched parts, forming a distressing whole." The term originated from an article entitled "How to Design a Kludge" by Jackson W. Granholm in the February 1962 issue of *Datamation*. Five other articles followed in later issues, and four of these appear in a book edited by Jack Moshman, *Faith, Hope and Parity* (Thompson Book Company, 1966). The term has now come to mean any ill-designed program, documentation, or even a whole computer center.

Modular Programming

In order for structured programming to succeed, the program must be planned in a modular fashion. Modular programming is the process of dividing your program into logical parts called modules and the successive programming of each part. Once a large monolithic problem is divided into smaller, logical, more workable units, it is easier to understand and read the program. This is a normal technique to control complexity — divide and conquer. If the top-down design of the entire problem has been prepared, the task has already been partitioned into subtasks for possible modules.

Two goals apply when using modular programming.

1. We must be able to convince ourselves that the program module is correct, independent of the context in which it will be used.
2. We want to be able to put modules together to form larger programs without any prior knowledge of the inner working of a module.

Scientific routines or utilities are examples of successful modules. We use the square root function in any context and expect it to have no side effects on other parts of our program. We would like our own modules to interact with the same independence.

SIZE OF MODULES

No one can say exactly what is a good size for a module, but one commonly used limit is about 60 lines of code. This number is selected because it is about the length of code that can be conveniently understood. That is, it is easy to keep in mind and comprehend. And it all will fit on one page or can be conveniently read at a computer terminal. Obviously there are exceptions, but the 60-line limit is a good guideline that works rather well. The main guideline is that the module be easy to keep in mind and comprehend.

Some people use larger modules and others use guidelines in addition to lines of code. We want a module that accomplishes one easy-to-comprehend task. Some programming shops allow modules to be up to 100, 200, or even 300 lines of code. Obviously an upper limit of 300 would be rarely needed and questionable. Several successful large programming projects (see articles by Baker) have kept the 60-line maximum and found it quite workable. If unable to program a subtask in 60 lines, there is a good chance that you are programming more than one subtask, in which case you should be using more than one module. Although we may be unable to set an exact maximum size for a module, there is general agreement that small modules are better than large ones.

> *Short modules are nice modules.*

Some installations put the module limit in memory size, 4096 bytes or 1024 words. But doing so seems less natural than using the more obvious line limit. It is apparent where 60 lines end, but it is not as apparent where 4096 bytes ends.

INDEPENDENCE

It is important to strive for independence between modules or subroutines. To achieve modular independence, the module should be independent of (a) the source of the input, (b) the destination of its output, and (c) the past history of the module's use. Otherwise the module is dependent on combinations of other modules and complexity increases greatly. Obviously there is some dependence (i.e., the parameter and calling sequence), but by breaking the main program up into functional units called modules, some independence is possible.

Each module should have a different purpose that is somewhat independent of the other modules. We would like a unit that is logically self-contained, one in which input and output are well defined. There is a good reason for trying to achieve subroutine independence: a change in one subroutine will be less likely to affect the rest of the program. A change in one module or part of the program that causes problems in another part of the program is called the *ripple effect*. The ripple effect can be reduced by minimizing connections between modules, which minimizes the paths along which changes or errors can propagate into other parts of the system. An easy way to reduce the ripple effect is to avoid use of global variables (i.e., COMMON storage) and to use small modules. We minimize the relationships between modules by maximizing the relationship among elements in the same module (called the *module strength*) while minimizing the interrelations between modules (called *module coupling*). Thus we want closely related elements to fall into a single module and unrelated elements to fall into a separate module. A high degree of independence using structured programming and minimally interacting modules has the advantage of limiting the effects of software bugs to the module in error.

One goal in using modules is to reduce complexity. Complexity with modules can arise from three sources: functional complexity, distributed complexity, and connection complexity. *Functional complexity* occurs when the module is made to do too many things. In this case, so many tests are needed to distinguish which of the functions is to be done that the logic is completely obscured. *Distributed complexity* is a condition in which a common function is not identified so that it is distributed among several modules, thereby losing a chance of reducing the complexity of the overall program. *Connection complexity* occurs when modules interact on common data in unexpected ways.

Imposing a size restriction on subprograms does not guarantee the production of modular programs. Some programmers have heard of modularity and write the program in one piece and then divide the program into four or six equal parts so that they can say they write modular programs. Needless to say, this is not the correct approach. We wish to use the natural divisions of the problem for modules — the natural divisions obtained in the top-down design phase.

Any program of appreciable complexity consists of a number of distinct steps. Thus the design begins with an investigation of the general goals of the project. And this process leads to a determination of the main tasks involved in accomplishing these goals. These major task definitions are usually the first phase of program design and, hopefully, will lead to a good indication of modular division.

In order to judge the independence of modules, we wish to determine the following. If one feature of a program changes, how will this fact affect the rest of the program? If we can replace a module by a new module that accepts the same input and produces the same output and the program remains unaffected, then the modules are independent. If there are items that are prone to change (i.e., tax deductions in a payroll program), we want to isolate them in one module to facilitate later changes. A little advance planning in regard to future changes can pay large dividends during later maintenance.

DEFINING THE MODULE

Good modules should be similar to mathematical functions. In mathematics there is a square root function. We call this

$$SQRT (X)$$

The square root function will only operate on nonnegative numbers. So the domain of the function is the nonnegative numbers. A *domain* is a set of permissible input values. The function is undefined for values outside the domain. For each valid argument of X, a value will be returned by the function. The set of possible output values is called the *range*.

We would like our modules to be defined this way. And just as the computer square root function checks the argument to ensure that only values within the domain are used, your module should do the same. When the square root function receives an argument outside the domain, an error message is usually provided. This is called a *side effect*. Sometimes the side effect also includes an error code that can be processed. Thus a module should have the following features.

1. An algorithm for solving the problem
2. A domain of permissible input values
3. A range of possible output values
4. A set of side effects

If these items are carefully defined for each module, the result will be cleaner modules and hence better programs. Often the domain of input is not checked and the side effects are not defined.

One additional observation on side effects should be mentioned. The side effect should seldom terminate the program execution. Instead the error is identified, and it is up to the calling module to decide what to do. So we do not want the square root function to terminate the execution of the program when receiving a value outside its domain (i.e., a negative value). We want some predictable value to be returned (often zero) and a warning of the error. Then the calling module must decide whether to terminate or proceed executing. This method ensures program generality, since the error is identified and the calling program can do whatever is necessary.

It is because of side effects that program maintenance is so difficult. A definition for side effect is the following. If a module Mx cannot be replaced by a module Mz, where Mx and Mz may have the same input and same output, it is because Mx has side effects. An example of a module with side effects is

```
IF (MAP (1) .LT. 0) STOP
      .
      .
      .
FUNCTION MAP (N)
   COMMON I, K, L
      .
      .
      .
   I = 0
   K = K + 1
   L = K * L
   MAP = MAP - K
   RETURN
END
```

The innocent-looking IF statement has a number of side effects that you can only detect by prowling all the way through the FUNCTION and elsewhere. The preceding example also illustrates why the use of global variables or COMMON is often discouraged. That is, side effects can too easily be hidden by the use of global variables.

METHOD OF CODING

Code segments should be formed as follows. Each segment should have one entry at the top and one exit at the bottom. If other segments are called for within a segment, they are also entered at the top and exited at the bottom, back into the calling segment.

The mainline routine should make all decisions governing the flow of data to proper processing routines. Variables common to all modules should be defined as part of the mainline routine in COMMON. Variables not needed by all modules, however, should be restricted only to those modules needing them.

Next, within each segment there should be a minimum of paths.

Smaller modules mean a smaller number of paths to test out. A very simple structure is preferable. Each routine should accomplish only one logical task. Each routine should perform all its own house-keeping to ensure noninterference with other segments. In this way, a processing routine will have tight logical control of its segment. No decision outside the segment should determine the processing within a segment; and, similarly, no decision within a segment should determine the processing outside the segment. The clarity of the program as a whole depends heavily on the clarity of the structure of each individual module.

Thus each routine is a closed routine. Control is transferred to the processing routine from the mainline routine; and when the routine has performed its function, it sends control back to the main-line routine. A processing routine can call another routine, but returns are always made to the calling routine.

CHESSBOARD PROBLEM

Problem: Print a chessboard. Fig. 2.5 is a sample chessboard. This problem can be used to demonstrate the ideas of top-down design and modularity. First, try it yourself. There are probably many good solutions, and your solution may even be better than mine. But the only way you will know if you understand some of the techniques covered in this chapter is to try an example yourself. Do a top-down design of this chessboard problem, breaking the problem into modules. Then look at my solution. If still interested, code the problem and run it.

A first step in the top-down design is to describe what we want to do. The problem is to print a chessboard similar to the chess-board figure. Our program could be

CALL PRINT-CHESSBOARD

Since we do not have a command that will do so, we must subdivide our problem a little more. A next step might be

CALL TOP-MARGIN

CALL MIDDLE

CALL BOTTOM-MARGIN

Next, let's expand MIDDLE. MIDDLE actually seems to have two tasks, since there are two types of rows. So let's try this.

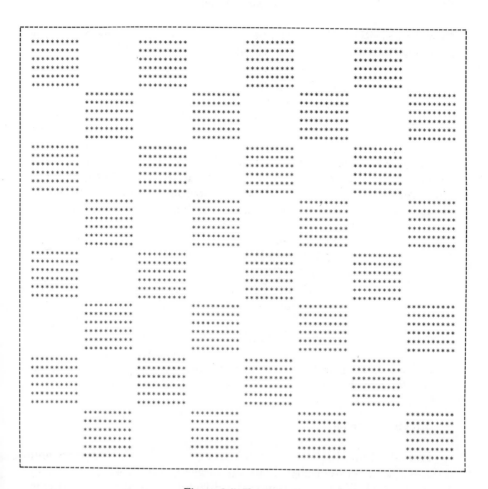

Figure 2.5 Chessboard

```
CALL FIRST-ROW-TYPE

CALL SECOND-ROW-TYPE
```

Here FIRST-ROW-TYPE is a module that gets us a complete first row. The same is true for SECOND-ROW-TYPE. And if we do this four times, we get the eight middle rows of the chessboard.

```
DO 4 TIMES
    CALL FIRST-ROW-TYPE
    CALL SECOND-ROW-TYPE
DOEND
```

Now FIRST-ROW-TYPE can be expanded. What we want to do is print a certain type of row six times.

```
FIRST-ROW-TYPE
    DO 6 TIMES
        PRINT FIRST-ROW
    DOEND
```

Similarly with the second row. We have a rather good top-down design of the whole problem and the modules are laid out. Perhaps you already noticed that the top and bottom margin are the same. So here is one version of the program written in some metalanguage.

```
CHESSBOARD
    CALL MARGIN
    DO 4 TIMES
        CALL FIRST-ROW-TYPE
        CALL SECOND-ROW-TYPE
    DOEND
    CALL MARGIN
```

Notice we have not bothered about how the procedures will be coded. We want to avoid these details as long as possible.

Structured Coding

Humans tend to be sequential processors. We like to read and process things sequentially. Thus the larger the number of breaks in sequence (GO TOs), the greater the difficulty we have in following the logic of the program. A person trying to read a program after going by several conditional transfers will be completely confused because of the multiplicity of possible paths.

Structured coding is a method of writing programs with a high degree of structure; this provides us with programs that are more easily understood for testing, maintenance, and modification. Arbitrarily large and complex programs can be written by using a small set of basic programming structures.

This principle is used in hardware design, where we know that any logic circuit can be formed out of elementary AND, OR, and NOT gates. It is based on a theorem in Boolean algebra. Since it is established on solid theoretical grounds, it need not be reproven for each new case. It is the task of the professional engineer to be able to design logic circuits out of these basic components. If an engineer cannot do so, then his or her competence as an engineer is in question.

STRUCTURED CODING THEORY

Structured coding is based on some simple logic structures out of which any proper program can be formed. It is based on the mathematical proven Structure Theorem (see Projects at the end of the chapter), which states that any *proper program* (a program with one entry and one exit and no infinite loops or unreachable code) can be written by using only the following logic structures.

1. *Sequence* of two or more operations
   (MOVE, ADD, ...)
2. *Selection* of one or two operations
   (IF THEN ELSE)
3. *Iteration* (or loop control) of an operation while a condition is true.
   (DO WHILE)

Figure 2.6 illustrates these basic logic structures. When proper programs are combined by using the three basic control logic structures (sequence, selection, and iteration), the result is also a proper program. Note that each structure has only one entry and one exit. A program of any size or complexity can be developed by the appropriate iteration and nesting of these basic structures within each other. When only these three structures are used in a program, no unconditional branches or statement labels are needed. Each structure always proceeds from the beginning to the end without arbitrary branching. Structured programs of this type greatly reduce the complexity of a program.

Sequence is a formalization of the idea that program statements are executed in the order that they appear in the program unless something is done to change the sequence. The fact that sequence is a control logic structure is sometimes overlooked. *Selection* is the choice of two actions based on some conditional. It is called the IF THEN ELSE. *Iteration* is used to execute a group of code repeatedly while a condition is true. The iteration control structure is activated by the DO WHILE or the iterative DO.

An important point is that, wherever a function box appears, any of the three basic structures can be substituted and we still have a proper program. So in looking at Fig. 2.7, we see three functions in sequence. If we wished to change function B by placing a selection

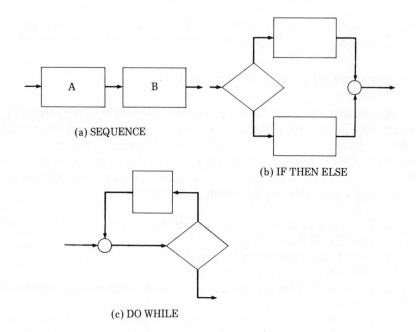

(a) SEQUENCE

(b) IF THEN ELSE

(c) DO WHILE

Figure 2.6 Structured logic

logic structure, we would end up with a diagram like Fig. 2.8. The ability to substitute control logic structures for functions and still have a proper program is called *nesting* of structures.

Although it is theoretically possible to write all well-formed programs using nothing more than the three basic logic structures shown here, we will find that programming is easier if we expand our repertoire a little. Extensions to the three basic logic structures are permitted as long as they retain the one-entry, one-exit property. The DO UNTIL and CASE statements are usually added. Figure 2.9 illustrates these two logic structures.

DO UNTIL provides a form of looping similar to the DO WHILE. There are two differences between the DO WHILE and DO UNTIL.

1. The DO WHILE terminates when the condition is false; the DO UNTIL terminates when the condition is true.

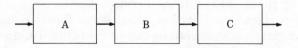

Figure 2.7 Sequence structure

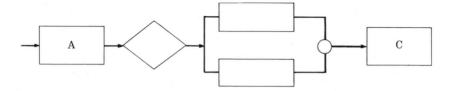

Figure 2.8 Nested structure

2. In the DO UNTIL the condition is checked after the statements are executed, so that the statements are always executed at least once.

The CASE structure is a multibranch, multijoin figure used to select one of a set of functions for execution, depending on the value of an integer expression. In the major programming languages, the CASE statement is available only in ALGOL.

Several concepts already covered are necessary to support this structure. First, logic structures should be indicated by indenting so that the logic relations in the code correspond to the physical position in the listing (paragraphing). Next, the code should be segmented into groups of code (modules) that are easily comprehended. Finally, code should be standardized so that it can be read from top to bottom without having to jump around because of branches.

Programs written this way reduce complexity, since they can be read from top to bottom typographically. The jumping around so typical of GO TO programs doesn't exist. Actually, when the basic logic structures are used correctly, there is little need for GO TO statements, and so it is easy to avoid them. Another characteristic

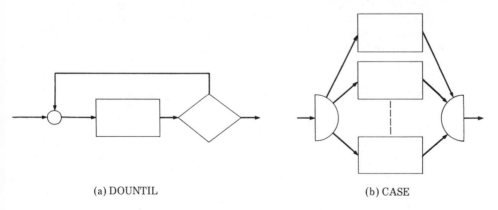

(a) DOUNTIL   (b) CASE

Figure 2.9 DO UNTIL and CASE

is that structured programs require a more detailed design before coding. Otherwise maintaining the required structure is impossible, and we must resort to branches to take care of overlooked exceptions.

In order to obtain a simple structure for each segment of the program GO TO statements should be avoided. Each segment should consist of straight-line sequencing with IF THEN ELSE, DO loops, CASE statements, or decision tables. Older languages, such as FOR-TRAN or COBOL, do not have enough language constructs; consequently, it is difficult to avoid the use of all GO TO statements.

Because several programming languages are difficult to use without some GO TOs and because it is impractical to take GO TOs away from someone who has been using them for 20 years, here are two guidelines that will help to limit their use.

1. Do not use GO TOs to execute some code when a CALL or a PERFORM can be used instead.
2. GO TOs should only branch forward. To branch backward implies a loop. Then the appropriate loop construct should be used.

Normally you should be able to avoid GO TO statements except in very special circumstances, such as the simulation of a control logic structure in a programming language that lacks it.

The quality of a program is often inversely proportional to the number of GO TO statements included in it. GO TO statements make large programs very difficult to read. In a GO TO-ridden program the reader must read a few lines of code, jump to a point several lines or pages down, read a few more lines of code, jump to another page, and so on. To complicate matters, many of the branches are either conditional branches or multibranches so that we are often unsure as to the correct branch to follow. After such skipping around, the reader has forgotten what he or she was trying to do. The goal of structured programming is to let the reader read the program from top to bottom, following the logic of the program.

USING STRUCTURED CODING CONSTRUCTS

PL/I and ALGOL have most of the preceding recommended programming commands, and, as a result, it is easy to write structured programs in these languages. In addition, both have a block structure so that a block of code can be conditionally executed. Because no major programming language has all the recommended programming commands, we will show how these commands can be simulated in any language.

PL/I has sequence, the IF THEN ELSE, the iterative DO, and the DO WHILE as part of the language, Also, PL/I has a grouping feature so that blocks of code can be conditionally executed and procedures or subprograms can be activated by using a CALL or %INCLUDE statement. The DO UNTIL is not part of the conventional PL/I instruction set, but it can easily be simulated as follows.

```
/*   DO UNTIL  */

MORE_TO_DO = '1'B;
DO WHILE (MORE_TO_DO);
    .
    .

    IF (condition)
    THEN
        MORE_TO_DO = '0'B;
END;
```

MORE_TO_DO would have to be declared as BIT(1). The preceding DO UNTIL will always be executed at least once because the tested condition is only changed at the bottom of the DO WHILE.

Also, the CASE statement is not part of the conventional PL/I. Here is how to simulate a CASE statement in PL/I.

```
/* CASE */
CASE_INDEX = expression;
IF (CASE_INDEX < 1 | CASE_INDEX > case_max)
    THEN CASE_INDEX = n;
GOTO CASE (CASE_INDEX);


CASE1:
    DO;
        .
        .

        GOTO END_CASE;
    END;
```

```
        CASE2:
            DO;
               .
               .
               .
             GOTO END_CASE;
            END;

        CASE3:
            .
            .
            .
        CASEn:
            DO;
             .
             .   This case takes care of the error case selection.
             .
             GOTO END_CASE;
            END;
        END_CASE:  ;
```

This simulation of the CASE statement requires the following declaration as well.

```
    DECLARE
        CASE (1:n)
                LABEL
                INITIAL (CASE1, CASE2, CASE3, ..., CASEn);
```

This example will handle any number of cases. It is important to check the CASE_INDEX to ensure that it does not exceed its used range. The CASE statement is especially useful when we wish to select from a large number of alternates. For instance, suppose that it is necessary to select one of 50 routines based on a two-digit code. It is certainly possible to write 50 IF statements, but common sense tells us that the preceding CASE statement would do it much better. Null cases can be used by having only the GO TO statement in the case. Also, the same function can be selected by several different values simply by including more than one label in front of one case.

    If there is a small number of cases or if there is no convenient numerical code, nested IF statements can be used to simulate the CASE structure.

```
IF (CODE = 'A')
THEN
    CALL CASE_A_PROC;
ELSE
    IF (CODE = 'C')
    THEN
        CALL CASE_C_PROC;
    ELSE
    IF (CODE = '3')
    THEN
        CALL CASE_3_PROC;
    ELSE
        CALL CODE_ERROR_PROC;
```

The code can be made more efficient by ordering the most likely selected code first.

ALGOL

Most versions of ALGOL have all or most of the recommended structured programming structures. A CASE statement is usually included. If there is no DO UNTIL, it can be simulated in the same way that it is in PL/I.

COBOL

Structured coding is not difficult in COBOL. COBOL has the sequence structure, the IF THEN ELSE structure, and the CALL statement for subprograms. It also has the PERFORM verb, which can be used like an iterative DO to execute paragraphs of code repeatedly. COBOL allows statements to be grouped by not ending any except the last with a period. This is a limited blocking structure, since it does not allow nested blocks and requires that no statements in the group terminate with a period.

When IF THEN ELSE is used to execute single statements conditionally, there are no problems. The IF THEN ELSE can be used to execute groups of statements as long as no period terminator is used on the statements within the the groups.

```
IF (condition)
THEN
    statement-group-1
ELSE
    statement-group-2.
```

The problem arises when we want an IF THEN (without an ELSE) in statement-group-1. What is needed is the following.

```
IF (condition p)
THEN
    IF (condition r)
    THEN
        statement-group-1
ELSE
    statement-group-2.
```

The problem occurs because the ELSE will be paired with the wrong THEN. COBOL pairs the ELSE with the most recent THEN. In the preceding example we wanted the ELSE paired with the first THEN as paragraphed. A period before the ELSE would cause a syntax error. This problem is solved by adding an ELSE and NEXT SENTENCE clause.

```
IF (condition p)
THEN IF (condition r)
    THEN
        statement-group-1
    ELSE
        NEXT SENTENCE
ELSE
    Statement-group-2.
```

When using nested IF statements, the foregoing ELSE NEXT SENTENCE is the best way to avoid the mismatched THEN and ELSE problem.

The PERFORM with the COBOL UNTIL works like the conventional DO WHILE because the condition is tested prior to the execution of the paragraph. It looks as follows.

```
PERFORM paragraph
    UNTIL (condition).
```

In simulating the DO UNTIL, we wish the paragraph always to be executed at least once. We can do so as follows.

```
PERFORM paragraph.
PERFORM paragraph
    UNTIL (condition).
```

The CASE statement can be achieved by using the COBOL GO TO... DEPENDING statement. The statement is

> GO TO case-1, case-2, ..., case-n
> DEPENDING ON IDENTIFIER.

Each named paragraph must end with a GO TO statement that branches to a common collection node. Only one paragraph will be branched to by the preceding GO TO, and it automatically handles a value of *n* outside the planned range. The main part of the CASE statement is similar to the one explained in the PL/I section.

FORTRAN

It is less easy to write structured programs in FORTRAN since it has no grouping structure of IF THEN ELSE. There are several ways to solve this problem. FORTRAN has an IF THEN statement, and so that part is easy to handle. If single statements are to be executed after a THEN and ELSE, it may be best to use two IF statements in the sequence.

> IF (condition) statement-1
> IF (.NOT. condition) statement-2

The first IF statement handles the THEN part and the second IF statement the ELSE part. FORTRAN has no block feature; when a block of statements that depends on the IF statement is to be executed in FORTRAN, we can do the following.

```
C      IF THEN ELSE.
          IF (condition) GOTO 50
          .
       done if false
          .
       GOTO 75
50        . . .
       done if true
          .
75     CONTINUE
C      END IF THEN ELSE.
```

If the ELSE part is not needed, it reduces to

```
C       IF THEN.
        IF (NOT condition) GOTO 75
        .

        then part
        .
75      CONTINUE
C       END IF THEN.
```

which is not quite as good as having an IF THEN ELSE with blocks, but it works all right. Also, it conforms to the rules of GO TO (i.e., GO TOs, when used, should only branch down and not up). FORTRAN has a good subroutine feature that can often be used to execute blocks of code conditionally.

The DO WHILE can be implemented several ways in FORTRAN. First, we have the iterative DO loop, which is often sufficient. The easy way to simulate the DO WHILE is to use a standard FORTRAN DO loop with a very large terminator parameter.

```
C       DO WHILE.
        DO 100 K = 1, 100000
        IF (condition) GOTO 150
        .

        .

        .
100     CONTINUE
150     CONTINUE
C       END DO WHILE.
```

The DO UNTIL simply has the test at the bottom with the condition reversed.

```
C       DO UNTIL.
        DO 100 K = 1, 100000
        .

        .

        .
        IF (NOT condition) GOTO 150
100     CONTINUE
150     CONTINUE
C       END DO UNTIL.
```

The CASE construct is the last one needed. It is implemented in FORTRAN with the computed GO TO as follows.

```
C       CASE STATEMENT.
        IF (KASE .LT. 1 . OR.KASE .GT. 4) KASE = 5
        GOTO (10, 20, 30, 40, 50), KASE
C       CASE 1.
   10   CONTINUE
          .
          .
          .
        GOTO 200
C       CASE 2.
   20   CONTINUE
          .
          .
          .
        GOTO 200
C       CASE 3
          .
          .
          .
C       CASE n+1, ERROR CASE.
   50     CONTINUE
          .
          .
          .
  200     CONTINUE
C       END CASE.
```

This method can be expanded to handle any number of cases. The preceding segment will conditionally execute one of the paragraphs. The GO TOs used always branch downward. It is important to check the computed GO TO to ensure that it does not go outside the possible range.

Summary of Structured Programming

One side benefit of structured programming is that the program can be reviewed by using a structured walkthrough. A *structured walkthrough* is a review session in which the originator of the program design or code explains it to colleagues. This review process should detect errors very early in the programming process, when they are least expensive to fix. Structured walkthroughs are covered in detail in Chapter 5.

From the point of view of readability, many advantages result when programmers use structured programming. A large program is first broken into logical units similar to the way that a book is broken into chapters and the chapters into sections. Each logical segment is restricted to one page of code with a simple structure, and so the reader can easily comprehend what each segment does. There is one entry at the top and one exit at the bottom of the code. Finally, GO TO commands are omitted so that the code can be read straight through without jumping around. Figure 2.10 is an example of a program that uses too many GO TO commands.

```
GOTO: PROCEDURE OPTIONS (MAIN);

        /*  A PROGRAM THAT USES TOO MANY GO TO'S.
                 WHAT DOES THE PROGRAM PRINT?  */

        K = 0;
        GO TO L4;
L2:     PUT LIST ('D'); GO TO L3;
L7:     PUT LIST ('E');  GO TO L5;
L4:     PUT LIST ('H');  GO TO L7;
L3:     PUT LIST ('O');  GO TO L1;
L5:     PUT LIST ('L');  K = K + 1;
        IF K < 2 THEN GO TO L5;
        GO TO L3;
L1:
        /*   DOES YOUR PROGRAM USE GO TO'S LIKE THIS?   */

    /*  WARNING: THE PROGRAMMER GENERAL HAS DETERMINED
             THAT THE USE OF GOTO STATEMENTS IS DANGEROUS
             TO THE GENERAL HEALTH OF YOUR PROGRAM.       */

END GOTO;
```

Figure 2.10 Too many GO TOs

Minimize use of GO TOs.

In COBOL and FORTRAN it is difficult to avoid GO TO statements completely. In addition, programmers with a long history of programming in these languages are accustomed to "thinking" in terms of GO TOs. Thus it may be difficult to avoid their use. Perhaps in COBOL and FORTRAN it is best to pretend that only a few GO TO statements are available and that they should be used sparingly. A small program may need one GO TO statement and a larger program two or three. Simply by keeping the concept of avoidance in mind, it is possible to think of a redesign of a program that will avoid most GO TO statements.

TWO MYTHS

A myth exists that if the programming manager or teacher issues a ukase banning all GO TO statements, well-designed programs will result. I do not agree. I have seen people go through contortions simply to avoid using a single GO TO. Instead a more reasonable approach is try to obtain a GO TO-less program — with "less" meaning fewer. On some problems in some languages all GO TOs can be avoided; on other problems in other languages it is extremely difficult to avoid all GO TO statements.

Structured coding often leads to the purist syndrome in which the goal is to write perfectly structured code in every situation. It should be realized that structured coding is not an end in itself; the goal is a good program. Structured coding is a means of achieving better, more reliable, more maintainable programs. In even the best of company a GO TO is occasionally needed (e.g., exist from a group of inner loops on an error condition). But to prevent the exception from becoming the rule, documentation and management approval are desirable for each violation of structured coding standards.

The use of the four-letter GO TO can be appropriate even in the best structured program. (For further details, see Donald E. Knuth, "Structured Programming with GO TO Statements", *ACM Computing Surveys*, December 1974.) It is not merely the absence of GO TO statements that is desired but the presence of structure. Good structure automatically results in fewer GO TOs.

The increased interest in structured programming has produced the view that correct, reliable programs will follow. Although possibly true, it is naive to expect perfect programs. Even though the field of engineering has a much firmer basis than programming, we still hear of a bridge or a dam failing upon completion. Mathematicians have long had a rigorous approach, and yet the history of mathematics is littered with errors. An interesting paper entitled "Fidelity in Mathematical Discourse: Is One and One Really Two?" by P. J. Davis (*American Mathematical Monthly*, March 1972) discusses the frequency of errors in mathematical papers. Several hundred errors have been discovered in the National Bureau of Standards' *Handbook of Mathematical Functions*. An editor of *Mathematical Reviews* estimated that 50% of all mathematical papers are flawed. And there is a 130-page book that lists errors made by first-rate mathematicians. In sum, programs should be designed to catch malfunctions. A program design that checks for reasonableness and errors will be the most reliable.

Although structured programming is popular and GO TOs unpopular, it must be concluded that there are no set rules according to which clear, understandable, and provable programs can be constructed. Guidelines exist, but the individual programmer's style, clarity, and creativity (or lack of it) will contribute significantly to the final program.

TOP-DOWN CODING

Coding should proceed from the top down. That is, the mainline program is coded first. This skeleton coding is best done if it is machine and language independent. The notation should mirror the problem instead of the target machine or programming language. Rather than aiming at finished code, the first steps should be concerned with exploring sizes of critical modules and with the complexity and adequacy of modules. As each level is coded, it should be hand simulated to see if it is correct and will work in principle. It is important to "test" out the higher levels of the design completely before designing the lower levels. The importance of being complete (and certain) at each higher level is often overlooked in the top-down approach.

As the skeleton coding is repeated and checked at each lower level from the top, the form of the actual program will be laid out. And as each level is written, it is important to ensure that it will do the job because any errors at this level will be disastrous. The top-down coding is used to ensure that the design will work from the beginning.

The skeleton coding technique helps avoid the problem of large rewriting effort. For example, most large programs are modified extensively as they are coded and certain problems, restrictions, and desired changes become apparent. Because of this last-minute redesigning, coding, and testing, quality is usually lacking in the final program. By doing skeleton coding first, some of the problems may be discovered before a great deal of effort has been put into the programming. This skeleton coding should be done in pseudo code.

Pseudo Code

Pseudo code is an English-type code that allows the program logic to be expressed in a highly readable manner. It often replaces flowcharts and is similar to programming languages. The idea is to allow us to state the logic of the program clearly, ignoring machine constraints. Pseudo code cannot be compiled and executed. You can develop your own pseudo code or use my suggestions.

1. Use only structured constructs.
   (a) Sequence
   (b) IF THEN ELSE
   (c) DO WHILE
   (d) DO UNTIL
   (e) CASE
   (f) CALL
2. Use ENDDO to indicate the end of DOs. Use ENDIF to indicate the end of IFs.
3. Use indentation to indicate block structure.

If the same pseudo conventions are used by everyone in one installation, then everyone will be able to read the pseudo code. Pseudo code should be part of the documentation and can be used in place of or in addition to flowcharts.

Here is a problem to write in pseudo code.

Problem: Write a program to print out change for a dollar when given purchase prices of less than a dollar. You wish to give back the minimum number of coins.

Try the problem yourself before looking at my solution. In order to encourage you to try your own solution, I will postpone mine for a few pages and give you another example. After you find your solution, go through the solution, checking to see if it will actually work. Here is another problem.

Problem: Read a series of numbers 1, 2, or 3 and count the number of each. Print the results when reading a 9.

Here is my pseudo code solution.

```
Read a number.
DO WHILE (not 9)
   IF 1 THEN
      add 1 to 1-count
   ELSE IF 2 THEN
         add 1 to 2-count
      ELSE IF 3 THEN
            add 1 to 3-count
         ENDIF
   ENDIF
   Read next number.
ENDDO
Print results.
```

Notice how only structured constructs are used and how the paragraphing indicates the structure. Try doing the same problem using a DO UNTIL, a CASE statement, or arrays. The pseudo code must later be translated into a programming language so that it can be executed. Pseudo code is used to get the program logic correct in the beginning, before the actual coding begins.

Two advantages of pseudo code are

1. The program logic can be written out unencumbered by programming language or machine restraints.
2. The logic of the program is written down so that others (including nonprogrammers) can read it.

Thus it allows you to write the program in a pure, structured form before having to face all the intricacies of the machine or programming language.

Write it in pseudo code before coding.

Here is a similar but harder problem to try.

Problem: Read some text, setting up a table of all words found and how many times each word appears. When there is no more text, print a table indicating each word found and the number of occurrences.

Actual Coding

The actual coding should also proceed from the top down with the Job Control Language (JCL) being coded first, followed by the mainline routine. Figure 2.12 depicts the essence of the top-down approach. It can usually be done by one person, which helps ensure the integrity of the basic design. Since the program is modularized, the mainline will be short and will call modules or subroutines. These modules can be simulated by putting in stubs. A *stub* is a very small set of code, which is used as a substitute until the actual code can be completed. A program stub can be of two types: a dummy module or a substitution module. A *dummy module* is one that performs no processing but merely returns control to the calling module. A *substitution module* is one that does simple processing until the more

```
DO WHILE (amount > 0)
   IF amount >= 50
   THEN
       subtract 50 from amount
       Print 50
   ENDIF
   IF amount >= 25
   THEN
       subtract 25 from amount
       Print 25
   ENDIF
   IF amount >= 10
   THEN
       subtract 10 from amount
       Print 10
   ELSE
       IF amount >= 5
       THEN
           subtract 5 from amount
           Print 5
       ELSE
           Print amount
           set amount to zero
       ENDIF
   ENDIF
ENDIF
```

Figure 2.11 Change problem

complicated module can be coded. It is needed when the calling module cannot proceed until the substitution module provides something. An example would be a situation where a complicated input routine was needed. The substitution module might supply some simple data. These program stubs may read dummy files where necessary to keep the program under test executing. The use of calls to dummy subroutines permits compilation and debugging at a much earlier stage of programming.

The stub is used so that testing of the other segments of the program can be started. A program stub must permit any code that references it to continue executing. It is best that the stub meet any interface requirements so that later interface changes are not needed. Often the stubs will have only one or two statements. Sometimes they will simply print out a statement: "GOT TO XY ROUTINE", indicating to the tester that they have, in fact, been executed, thus testing the logic of the next higher-level unit. Otherwise it may be necessary to return some values so that the upper levels of the program can be checked out. After the mainline is coded and checked out, the next level down is coded and checked in the same fashion. The lower-level units are continually added in the same manner. A program unit is coded only after the unit that invokes it has been

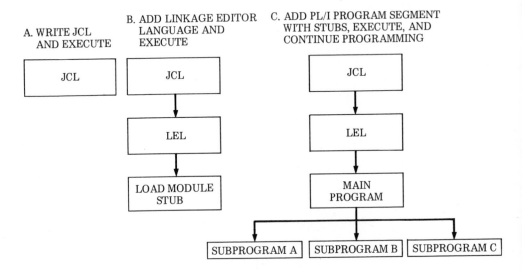

Figure 2.12 Top-down development

coded and tested. This process results in the highest-level units, usually the more critical, being tested the most frequently.

As the project proceeds from top to bottom, additional, less skilled people can be used to program the lower-level modules. It is important that highly skilled, experienced programmers do the initial top-down skeleton and actual coding. Besides making use of the professionals' expertise, the procedure also gives less experienced programmers something to work for — that is, the chance to direct their own projects someday. All coding should be read and checked by at least two people.

What top-down development actually implies in everyday production programming is that the system is built in such a way as to eliminate or minimize writing any code whose testing depends on code not yet written or data not yet available. It requires careful planning in a large project, since some programs must be partially completed before others can be begun. This continual integration of code is tested as it is produced, thereby reducing the test cycle that usually occurs at the end of the project.

Top-down coding does not imply that implementation must proceed rigidly down the tree level by level. Some branches will intentionally be completed before others. Branches that are prone to change may be completed earlier in order to obtain some reaction from the eventual user.

Top-down expansion of a problem is always difficult. Textbook examples make it look easy by rolling out a set of smooth top-down expansions. In reality, even for these simple problems I floundered for quite a while, trying to get a nice solution. And I have the major advantages of a well-defined problem and a very good algorithm. In real life, often neither one is available. So be prepared for a rough time when you do your top-down expansion. It is not easy and requires hard work. Yet after algorithm selection, a good design is the second major element in a successful program. A bad algorithm or a bad design cannot be saved by clever coding. There is always the urge to start coding, but it should be resisted until the design is done. Coding is a minimal part of the problem. Most major decisions must be made before coding begins. Once coding does begin, it is difficult to change direction. So it is important to get started on the correct path at the beginning. Frequently, there is more than one good way to solve a problem.

The situation is similar to driving across the country in a car. If we start driving before consulting our map, the initial direction that we start in can determine the rest of the trip. So it is important to plan where and how we are going first.

CHIEF PROGRAMMER TEAM

Does it all work? Today many programming projects use the techniques covered in this chapter. Some report a high degree of success in turning out large, error-free programs. Also, many individuals who have adopted structured programming techniques report a quantitative jump in their programming productivity. Two of the early successes combined all the techniques of structured programming and added what is called a "Chief Programmer Team" (CPT).

The Chief Programmer Team organization was first reported by J. D. Aron in *Software Engineering Techniques* (edited by Buxton and Randell). It was then called the "Super-Programmer Project." A combination of structured programming and a new organization of programming talent succeeded in programming a 50,000-instruction program in one-fifth the normal time with almost no errors. After this success, the CPT organization was further refined in *The New York Times* project.

The second project was to build an information bank for *The*

New York Times. The task took 22 months and included about 83,000 lines of code. About 11 people-years of effort was involved. The file processing system passed a week of acceptance testing without errors and ran for 20 months until the first error was detected. In the first 13 months only one program error resulted in system failure. The system control programmers achieved about 10,000 lines of source code and one error per people-year. In both projects Harlan Mills was the chief programmer. For a more detailed study of this project, see References at the end of the chapter.

This situation is in contrast to OS/360, which was over a year late and still has over 1000 errors in at all times, even after going through 21 releases. When IBM 360 OS was in so much trouble and other large projects were in similar trouble, some of these groups started analyzing and studying what programmers actually did. A startling fact discovered by more than one source was that on these large programming projects the average rate of debugged instructions coded per person-day was five to ten instructions. Obviously it did not take a person a whole day to code five instructions. So what was being done the rest of the day? (Interested readers are referred to Brooks' *The Mythical Man-Month.*) Basically, on large projects most time is spent communicating, rewriting code, testing, and debugging. The problem is to get the program right the first time, since debugging is obviously too expensive.

The nucleus of a chief programmer team consists of a chief programmer, a backup programmer, and a programming librarian. The chief programmer decides when and how many additional programmers may be needed. If many programmers are involved, a project officer may be added to take care of administrative, financial, legal, and personnel matters so that the chief programmer can concentrate on technical management. It is important that the chief programmer's main goal be the technical development of the program.

Team Member Responsibilities

The chief programmer's principal job is to design and code the program, and all team members report directly to the chief programmer. The chief programmer designs and codes central critical segments of the program system and assigns other segments to team members. As these segments are completed and added to the system, the chief programmer reviews the segments to ensure that they do what they are supposed to do and that they adhere to the standards of clarity and structured programming. The chief programmer makes all final decisions and is responsible for the success of the project.

The backup programmer is equal in skill to the chief programmer and helps with the design of the program. The backup programmer involvement at every level is necessary because he or she must be able to assume leadership of the project if necessary. Some of the backup programmer's other duties may be to develop the strategy and tactics to be used to program the project. This process also allows the two people to discuss the major structure and design of the problem. While the chief programmer codes the central critical segments, the backup programmer can provide the test data, thus offering a different view of testing. The chief and the backup programmer review each other's code and also review code produced by other members of the team. The other programmers, in turn, read and understand the code written by the chief programmer that defines the program stubs with which they must interface. As a result, at least two programmers fully understand every line of the developing program.

The programming librarian keeps all records of the project in the Development Support Libraries (described in the next section). Records that show the current status of the program and testing are kept. As new or modified modules are added to the system, the programming librarian will replace new listings in the notebook and indicate the new current status. The programming librarian is responsible for keeping all records, running programs with test data, and replacing old stubs or segments with new segments. Although one benefit is that less clerical work is needed on the part of the other programmers, the programming librarian is not considered merely a clerk but an equal member of the team.

The librarian position is a difficult one to define. Generally the skills needed are not those of a programmer. Instead someone is needed who can interact with a computer system, initializing computer runs and updating data files. Also, the librarian should be able to handle such secretarial duties as typing documentation. So often someone with secretarial skills is selected and then trained in the necessary computer skills. The librarian's purpose is to take over a great deal of clerical work normally done by programmers, thereby providing a more concentrated use of the latter. This simple aid has raised the productivity of programmers greatly.

Additional Members

Depending on the size and character of the system under development, additional team members are included in the CPT as the development cycle progresses. Since the chief programmer is the principal designer of the program, his or her duties will begin early in the development cycle. Soon afterward the next two major people — the backup programmer and the librarian — will join the team. Extra members will be added if the project is large or if specialized application, hardware, or software knowledge is needed. As a rule, the team should not exceed seven people.

Large programs are very complicated structures. By introducing the CPT into programming, skilled senior people again have a position in which they are needed the most. The use of senior people in detailed program coding illustrates another set of circumstances in today's operating system environment. The job control language, data management access methods, utility facilities, and high-level source languages are so powerful that there is a need as well as an opportunity to use senior-level people at this detailed but critical coding level. Software available today is so complex and extensive as to require a good deal of study and experience to utilize. Only senior people can provide this necessary level of skill.

The team approach offers many advantages. First, less skilled people are given a chance to work on large projects in junior positions and see the whole project evolve. This association with skilled people — the three main team members — allows junior members to gain both professional and technical skills. All work produced is reviewed for integrity by senior members. Also, since junior members will be reading the mainline code, this is also reviewed. Thus programming is moved from private art to public practice where all see both the progress and the errors being made by others. Junior members are involved in an environment in which they can hope to advance as other new projects are needed.

Gerald Weinberg in his *Psychology of Computer Programming* suggests that egoless programming will contribute to better programs. Egoless programming means that all programs are public property and are reviewed by other team members. The CPT forces a high degree of public scrutiny. The librarian is responsible for picking up all computer output, good or bad, and filing it in notebooks of the development support library (see later section), where it becomes part of the public record. In contrast, in non-CPT programming the bad runs go into the wastebasket. This establishment of all program data and computer runs as public assets instead of private property of individual programmers contributes to the egoless programming principle.

Some Reflections on the CPT

It is important that the Chief Programmer (CP) be given the time, responsibility, and authority to perform the technical direction of the project. Typically, the CP is responsible for three types of activities:

1. Technical management — the supervision of the technical aspects of the project,
2. Personnel management — the supervision of the people reporting to him or her, and
3. Contract management — responsibility for relations with the customer.

The first responsibility is the most important for the success of the project. If the number of people involved becomes larger than seven, personnel matters will dominate the CP's time. This situation is avoided either by keeping the number smaller or by bringing in an individual to handle all extraneous personnel matters. Or if the number of people must be larger than seven, then it may be best to split into two teams. Similarly, if the customer interface responsibilities become too time consuming, a program manager should be employed to handle nontechnical matters with the customer.

The backup programmer title sometimes connotes the idea of second best. It may be true but hard to avoid, since a leader must be designated. If the backup programmer is as skilled as the CP, then perhaps the roles can be interchanged in the next project. The backup programmer should be a peer to the chief programmer, since she or he may be called on to take over the project. It is important that the CP have an open relationship with the backup programmer so that problems can be discussed in an atmosphere of mutual trust. So it is important that the chief programmer have the right to refuse a backup programmer; otherwise the entire project can be disastrous.

Possible Problems

It is not yet clear how well the CPT organization will transfer to very large projects. CPTs seem to work well in medianly large projects in which one individual can still comprehend the whole project. But when we consider something like the IBM 360 Operating System, which cost $50 million dollars and took 5000 people-years, it is clear that one chief programmer cannot grasp the entire project. Levels of CPTs can be used, but their effectiveness may decline as the number of CPTs increases and as they must communicate with each other. Chief programmer teams have worked successfully on projects that were about two orders of magnitude less than the IBM 360 OS. A technique that works well on one size project is not guaranteed to work on a project that is a hundred times larger. It is a hard lesson for software people to learn. But it is true in most other fields, too. On the other hand, past organization methods for large programming projects have done so poorly that it is doubtful that CPTs could lead to worse results.

The second point that is unclear is how well CPTs will work in more prosaic surroundings than the two often-cited successful examples. These two examples are atypical for several reasons. First, the chief programmer was an extremely skilled individual. Harlan Mills has a Ph.D in mathematics, is an IBM Fellow, and is quite skilled in computers. Differences of 25 to 1 in programmer performance have been shown, and so the skill of the individual programmer can easily be the most important factor in a project's success or failure. Secondly, the CPT was backed by the unlimited resources of IBM. Other CPTs will not have such advantages. Thirdly, the CPT organization may not appeal to some individuals, projects, or organizations. The chief programmer should be skilled in team management, able to provide technical representation to the customer, and good at management of his or her own time. He or she should also be able to keep the project going and should contribute to and criticize the efforts of other team members in a skillful manner. Individuals possessing these skills may be difficult to obtain. Early results were impressive, however, and the CPT organization is going to appeal to some people and some organizations.

DEVELOPMENT SUPPORT LIBRARY

The Development Support Libary (DSL) is used to store and maintain all the machine- and external-readable structured code being tested and integrated into the system. This system is maintained by the librarian and is used to keep all documents so that they are visible to all project members. The main goals are

1. Keep current project status organized and visible at all times. Anyone interested in the project can thus find out the status of the project or study the project without depending on someone else to interpret it.
2. Allow the librarian to do most of the clerical work of library maintenance, thereby freeing the rest of the project workers from clerical tasks. Doing so enhances program productivity.

All machine-readable data involving the system should be stored on the computer in a library. Included would be source code, Job Control Language, and test data. The librarian must ensure that a backup copy is made and maintained. This internal machine-readable library ensures that there is only one current set of each type of data or that different versions of on-going systems can be segregated.

The external-readable library mirrors the internal machine library. There should be a current status binder for each type of data kept in the internal machine-readable library. Thus there would be a binder of source code, job control language, and test data. There would also be binders of test runs, which are used to keep the project status visible to all concerned with the project. Superseded output is kept in an historical file to assist in disaster recovery and be available for looking at earlier results. And because the chief programmer is directly involved in the project and the status of the work is highly visible and understandable, management can react to problems sooner and more effectively than when CPTs are not used.

Changes to any of the data are done by a programmer making additions or corrections to the external-readable library in the binders or by writing programs or data on coding sheets. The librarian then makes these changes to the internal library and has the job run. Thus the librarian significantly reduces the clerical effort and wasted time of the programmers. Figure 2.13 illustrates the parts of a DSL.

The prime criterion determining if the DSL is properly used is whether the project as a whole is entirely dependent on the DSL for its operation. Programmers should use the source code in the DSL as a basic means of communication and should rely on it to answer questions on interfaces. Managers can use the code in the DSL to determine the progress of the work. Users can use the code in the DSL to determine progress and possibly use the system on an experimental basis without depending on others. If all the programmers do not funnel all the runs through the librarian, then the integrity of the DSL declines and most of the benefits disappear. The real value of the DSL is that all data is there.

The main characteristics of the DSL are as follows.

1. The DSL must be able to maintain both internal and external machine documents as explained above.
2. The library is used throughout the project from the beginning design stage to the final testing and delivery of the system.
3. The external library binder of past runs will indicate both the history and current status of the project.
4. The code itself should be the prime reference for questions of data formats, program operation, algorithms, and so on.
5. Preferably the librarian will inititiate all runs and handle

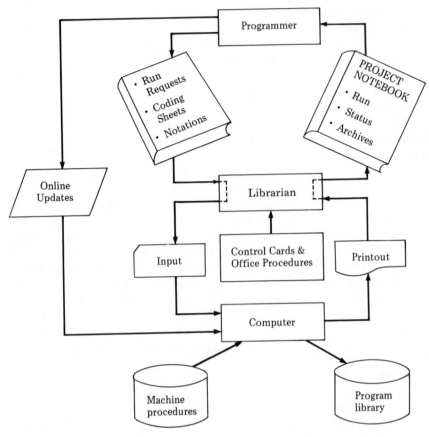

Figure 2.13 Operational procedure for development system library

the filing of runs to maintain the integrity and visibility of the project.

The archival runs are useful for several reasons. People can trace the evolution of a routine or look at earlier versions. Earlier generations of object code or run results are less valuable than source code and test data. One side advantage of the DSL is that backup of all files can easily be made and kept off premise to ensure recovery in case of disaster.

PROGRAM MAINTENANCE

Programmers often forget how long some programs last. Programs exist that were written back in the early 1960s. Some of these programs were written for the IBM 1401 and are now run on present machines by 1401 emulation.

The October 1972 issue of *EDP Analyzer* is devoted to program maintenance. This issue is worthwhile reading for anyone interested in program maintenance. The authors found that DP organizations commonly spend 50% of their programming time on maintenance and that an average production program will be maintained by ten different people before being rewritten or discarded. The original cost of the program was usually only a small fraction of the programming cost.

Alvin Toffler's *Future Shock* describes the difficulties individuals and organizations experience when change occurs too rapidly. The same is often true in programming. Changes arrive before the program is even completed. Management may change, laws may change, or volume may change. In addition, the programming staff changes, and so the original programmer is no longer available. Even if no additions or improvements are needed in a production program, the system changes. Computers and peripherals are changed. Updates are added to the operating system, and the original program must often be modified to take advantage of the new environment.

Programs that can be easily transferred from one execution environment to another are called *portable*. Portability is important if you wish to sell software to many users or if you wish to be able to take your programs to a new environment. The most obvious method used to keep a program portable is to use ANSI COBOL or ANSI FORTRAN. A similar concept is adaptability. *Adaptability* is the ease with which a program can be altered to fit different user images and system constraints. The major distinction between the two concepts is that portability is concerned with changes in the environment, whereas adaptability deals with changes in the structure of the algorithm. The concepts are discussed in detail in a good article by Poole and Waite in *Advanced Course in Software Engineering*, edited by M. Beckman et al. (New York: Springer-Verlag, 1973).

Thus if software is to be used over a period of time, it must be designed so that it can be continually changed to keep pace with the new environment. On the IBM operating system (IBM 360 OS) approximately four times as much was spent on maintenance as on development. So maintainability, in this case as well as many others, was more important than original costs.

A fact that is familiar to most programmers but not usually verbalized is that a programmer has a relatively low chance of success when he or she modifies a production program. Boehm (see References) discovered that if the change involved less than 10 statements, the chance of success is 50% on the first attempt. But if the change involves as many as 50 statements, the chance of success drops to 20%. The difficulty with making changes or corrections during maintenance is that the fix may be right locally but wrong globally. A program that is difficult to modify is called *fragile.*

Since maintenance costs often exceed the original programming costs, programs must be designed for maintainability. Maintenance costs are generally a hidden cost. One method used by computer centers to make them more visible is to add a maintenance cost on every production program. That is, if a program requires 3 people-years to finish, then program maintenance must be budgeted at one person or one-half person per year during its useful life. This procedure helps make it apparent to management why more programmers are needed each time they add a new system.

Some installations have discovered that one way to reduce maintenance is to allow the maintenance programmers to rewrite some routines completely. It was found that only a few routines or programs accounted for most maintenance. If these troublesome routines can be identified and rewritten, the maintenance costs associated with them often decline.

Maintenance is often confused with a continuation of debugging. In the rush to meet a deadline or to avoid delay, a partially debugged program is released before being adequately debugged and tested. If pressure for program completion is intense, this pressure to get the job out, tested or not, is difficult to resist.

One way to impress on programmers the importance of designing maintainable programs is to make each programmer do maintenance for a specific period of time. No programmer should be allowed to escape this task. In fact, all new programmers should be assigned to program maintenance for the first six months to impress on them the value of commented and well-documented clear programs.

In order to plan for maintenance at the program design stage, a list of possible changes should be included. Then if this list is kept in mind, the program design can be adapted so that these changes will not be too disrupting.

Plan for program changes.

DOCUMENTATION

Documentation should not be a process that is begun once the program is finished. Instead it should be an on-going effort, starting at the problem definition. No matter how good the program is, it will only work if adequate instructions are included for its use. Even if the program is for personal use, written instructions are usually necessary to avoid forgetting how to use the program. And if the program is to be used by others, a set of well-organized, detailed, written instructions are needed.

> *Start documentation at the design stage.*

Programs are not physical objects that can be understood by touching and handling. Moreover, when a program is inside a computer, it cannot even be seen. On large programs it is useless to provide a program listing and expect it to be used for documentation. Either the program listing is too long to be read or too much effort is required even in short programs to figure out what the program does.

Badly documented programs must be dissected by a combination of doctor, detective, and archeologist. The detective pieces together the incomplete documentation, the doctor diagnoses the symptoms, and the archeologist examines the historical evidence in the form of old output. Since all these skills are needed to figure out underdocumented programs, it is not surprising that the program is usually discarded and rewritten.

REWRITING

Programmers should not be afraid to rewrite a program. Program writing is a creative task and, like other forms of composition, often requires more than one draft. When writing a program, it often becomes obvious that the first effort was done incorrectly. Thus rewriting will help produce a neat, efficient, and debuggable program.

> *Don't be afraid to start over.*

When working with large programs, it is often advisable to write a small program to simulate the main details of the large one. The large program may require extensive input/output and much time to program or test. The simulator can involve no input and simplified output. This small program should involve at least a couple orders of magnitudes less work than the real program. Even though only an approximation of the final solution, the simulator should provide invaluable help in examining the problem to be programmed. Algorithms and design can be checked out. The simulator can be pseudo code that is hand executed. Or the simulator can be written on an interactive system in something like BASIC or APL and then used to check out the design and algorithm.

One way to check for the need for rewriting is to adopt the buddy system. That is, each program must be understood by the original programmer and at least one other programmer. If the programming is being done by a team, at least two people are already familiar with the code. But in small one-person projects often no one else looks at the code. This buddy system offers programming management a bonus. If one of the programmers leaves, there is still another programmer available who understands the program.

PROGRAMMING MAXIMS

KISS: Keep It Simple, Stupid.

Get it right at the design stage.

Select the problem algorithm most carefully.

Choose a data representation that matches the problem.

Use variables, not constants for parameters.

Design generality into your program.

Don't reprogram the square root function.

Set realistic project goals early and explicitly.

Write it in English first.

Design test data early.

Design before coding.

Get it right at the beginning.

Short modules are nice modules.

Minimize use of GO TOs.

Write it in pseudo code before coding.

Plan for program change.

Start documentation at the design stage.

Don't be afraid to start over.

EXERCISES

Chapter Review

1. Define the following terms.
(a) KISS	(b) Generality
(c) Complexity	(d) Independence
(e) Kludge	(f) Proper program
(g) Top-down design	(h) Modularization
(i) Structured programming	(j) CPT
(k) Program stub	(l) Pseudo code
(m) DSL	(n) Portable
(o) Adaptability	(p) Fragile
(q) Side effect	(r) Retrofitting

2. What are the duties of the following people?
   (a) Chief programmer
   (b) Backup programmer
   (c) Program librarian

3. What features of your programming language make structured programming awkward? Easy?

4. Why is it more difficult to program large programs than small programs?

5. Give some examples of simplicity and nonsimplicity in coding programs.

6. How do you think your programming would change if you used the program buddy system?

7. Set up a list of good programming standards for your programming language.

8. What are some of the advantages of modular programming? What are some disadvantages?

9. Give some examples of generality and nongenerality in coding programs.

10. Define structured programming. List as many characteristics of structured programming as you can. Look at other sources for their definition of structured programming and see if you can come up with a good definition.

11. Find a book of computing algorithms or a book of programs that is in your field of interest.

12. Many people have spoken against using EQUIVALENCE in FORTRAN, REDEFINES in COBOL, or DEFINED in PL/I. These statements allow one storage location to have several names assigned to it. When do you think the use is justified? What type of errors could be made during later program modification because of use of these features? State some of the arguments for both sides.

13. Most programming languages allow the use of global variables. This is done through use of COMMON in FORTRAN, the LINKAGE SECTION in COBOL, and EXTERNAL in PL/I. What troubles can global variables cause? When should they be used and when not? State the arguments for both sides.

14. Find one command in your programming language that you feel is absolutely dangerous and a candidate for banishment. Why would you banish it? When is it used now and what could you substitute for it? State the arguments for both sides.

15. One often-overlooked fact in the rush to computerize is that many problems shouldn't be computerized, or, at best, only marginal benefits can be obtained by computerization. In the problems below, classify each as yes, no, or questionable in regard to the value of placing the problem on a computer.
    (a) Payroll for 250 people.
    (b) Payroll for 12 people.
    (c) Payroll for 3 people.
    (d) A program to parse English sentences.
    (e) Arithmetic progressions: sum the first 100 integers.
    (f) Geometric progressions: sum 2, 4, 8, 16, 32, . . . , 2**20
    (g) A program to find the next three times Friday is the 13th.
    (h) Take a checkerboard and remove opposite corners. Write a program to determine how to lay checkers on the checkerboard so that each checker covers exactly two squares and all squares are covered.
    (i) Write a program to determine the maximum number of knights that can be placed on a checkerboard so that no knight can capture any other knight.

(j) Develop a table of 1000 random numbers.
There is a good chapter on this subject, "What is a Computer Problem?," in *Computing: A Second Course* by Fred Gruenberger (San Francisco: Canfield Press, 1971).

Programs

16. An integer can be represented as a sum of its parts, called *partitions*. Thus 4 can be represented as

    4
    3 + 1
    2 + 1 + 1
    2 + 2
    1 + 1 + 1 + 1

    $P(n)$ is the number of partitions, $p(4) = 5$. Write a program to read n and print the partitions of n and $P(n)$.

17. Write a program that reads some text and prints the frequency of different words in the text.

18. Write a program that prints the song "The Twelve Days of Christmas."

19. Generate the first 1000 prime numbers by using the first algorithm in this chapter, Fig. 2.1. Then improve the program as suggested and notice the difference in execution time.

20. *Sieve of Eratosthenes.* Program the prime number problem by using the following method. Generate a list of positive integers from 1 to N. Start with 2 and delete all multiples of 2. The next number that has not been deleted is the next prime, which is 3. Starting with 3, delete all multiples of 3. The next nondeleted number is 5, which is the next prime. Delete all multiples of 5, and so on. The list of numbers remaining will be the prime integers.

21. Write a detailed synopsis for the following program and then use it to write the program. The program is to read in integers and select the second largest value. The last number is a zero. Next, generalize the problem. That is, select the Nth largest value where N is read in each time.

22. *Bank deposit.* Develop a synopsis for the following problem and program it. Interest is paid monthly at 6%. Deposits made by the 10th of the month receive interest for the whole month. In order to discourage people from making frequent withdrawals,

anyone making more than five withdrawals in one month with a minimum balance of less than $1000 is charged 50¢ a withdrawal for all withdrawals over five. Interest is paid monthly on minimum balance during the month.

23. Program the character string subroutines below.
    (a) Write a subroutine that accepts integer numbers that have been read as a character string and convert them to integer values. Do the same for real numbers. Numbers can be positive or negative signed.
    (b) Write a subroutine that accepts an integer number and returns a character string with commas separating groups of three digits.

$$1567842 \rightarrow 1,567,842$$

    Write a subroutine to reverse the process. Do all this for real numbers, too.
    (c) Write a subroutine that does check protection. That is, the subroutine accepts a real number and returns a character string with a dollar sign and three asterisks in front of the number.

Projects

24. *Traveling salesman.* Write a detailed synopsis for the following problem. The salesman has 16 cities in his territory. Since he buys his own gasoline, he always wishes to drive the shortest distance. Each Friday he is given a list of cities he must cover the next week. He can visit the cities in any order and does not always visit all cities.

25. *Labyrinth and Minotaur.* Write a detailed synopsis for the following problem. The synopsis should be clear enough so that someone could use it to write a program. Indicate all modules and their interfaces. Input is a 21 by 21 array of zeros (no path) and ones (path). You are to write a program that reads the above array and finds a path. Your Minotaur starts at the center of the array. If your Minotaur is on a square, he can move to any of the four contiguous squares, provided that they have a one in them. A zero is a blocked path. After you find a path out of the array, print the array, indicating X in the path. Show only the direct path. That is, do not print backtracking.

26. Write a program to print an exact copy of itself. No input statements are allowed.

27. Write a program to print a 100-character sequence of digits 0, 1, and 2 such that no two adjacent subsequences are identical. There is a solution to this problem in the book by Dahl listed in the References.

28. *Simmons factorial conjecture.* Only four factorials can be expressed as a product of three consecutive integers. Here are two.

$$4! = 2*3*4 = 24$$
$$5! = 4*5*6 = 120$$

Can you find two more? Can you find any more and prove the conjecture incorrect?

29. Write a program to find all the ways of cutting an $n \times n$ checkerboard into two equal parts (not counting rotations and reflections). If n is odd, the center position is left out. (*Hint:* Try a 4×4 first. Then add the restriction that the two pieces must be identical in shape. Using the restriction, there are 15 different ways on a 5×5.)

30. Find out how old some of the programs are at your installation. Can you determine how many people have worked on these programs? Do you have any programs still around that are emulated on present machines? What is done when these programs must be modified?

31. The December 1974 issue of *ACM Computing Surveys* is devoted to structured programming. Look it up and read it over.

32. Program complexity is difficult to judge. One method of measuring complexity is to sum the number of nonsequential paths through the program. Does this seem like a good measure? Judge some programs, using this rule. Complexity is discussed on page 41 of Aron's *The Program Development Process*. It is also discussed in a book on structured programming by Harlan D. Mills. Read them and see if you can develop some guidelines on measuring the complexity or clarity of computer programs.

33. Look up some of the famous articles on the GO TO controversy. One good place to start is with Donald E. Knuth, "Structured Programming with GOTO Statements," *ACM Computing Surveys*, December 1974.

34. Lay out the design in a rough fashion for a payroll program. Look at some actual payroll checks so that you can see what some of the deductions are. Then as a class or individually, list all the possible changes that could affect the payroll program. If others did the assignment, collect the changes together and then redesign the payroll program so that it can be easily adapted to new changes. This exercise can be tried on many other programs, too.

35. The Structure Theorem states that any proper program is equivalent to a program that contains as logic structures only
    (a) Sequence of two or more operations.
    (b) Conditional branch to one of two operations and return (IF THEN ELSE).
    (c) Repetition of an operation while a condition is true (DO WHILE).
    Work out some examples, using a short program segment to see if this works. How practical would it be to reduce all programs to the preceding form? For references, consult C. Bohm and G. Jacopini, "Flow Diagrams, Turing Machines, and Languages with Only Two Formation Rules," *Communications of the ACM*, May 1966 and Harlan D. Mills, "Mathematical Foundations for Structured Programming," *IBM Report No. FSC 72-6012*, 1972.

36. Produce a deck of cards or paper tape that, when loaded into your computer either backward or forward, will execute the same way. For a more complicated version, have the program punch a copy of itself.

37. Try to develop some rules for dividing programs into good modules. Two articles by D. L. Parnas in the May 1972 and December 1972 issue of *Communications of the ACM* may be of some help.

38. Every compiler provided by a computer manufacturer usually contains the standard language constructs (ANSI COBOL or ANSI FORTRAN) and some extensions. These extensions are provided as a marketing scheme to lock you into their computers and thus make your programs not portable. If you wish to thwart this marketing scheme and keep your programs portable, you must eschew the extensions, which is often difficult because the extensions offer nice features. For one of your compilers, determine what the extensions are and what the standard

constructs are. Next, develop a program that reads source code and prints the source program, flagging all nonstandard features of the language. This program is sometimes called the "Enforcer."

39. Write a paper on the future of programming (not computers). Areas to examine are: future use of COBOL, FORTRAN, PL/I, and BASIC; role of structured programming; programming proofs; automatic programming; and so on. Good background for this project is Edsger W. Dijkstra, "The Humble Programmer," *Communications of the ACM*, October 1972.

40. Write a paper on the history of programming. A good place to start researching this topic is Jean E. Sammet, *Programming Languages* (Prentice-Hall, 1969).

REFERENCES

Armstrong, Russell M., *Modular Programming in COBOL.* New York: John Wiley & Sons, 1973.

Aron, Joel D., *The Program Development Process.* Reading, Mass.: Addison-Wesley, 1974.

Baker, F. Terry, and Harlan D. Mills, "Chief Programmer Teams," *Datamation*, December 1973.

Baker, F. Terry, "Structured Programming in a Production Programming Environment," *IEEE Transactions on Software Engineering*, June 1975.

Beckmann, M., et al., *Advanced Course on Software Engineering.* New York: Springer-Verlag, 1973.

Boehm, Barry W., "Software and Its Impact: A Quantitative Assessment," *Datamation*, May 1973.

Buxton, J. N., and B. Randell, *Software Engineering Techniques.* NATO Science Committee 1969. Available from Scientific Affairs Division, NATO. Brussels 39, Belgium.

Dahl, O. J., Edsger W. Dijkstra, and C. A. R. Hoare, *Structured Programming.* New York: Academic Press, 1972.

Dijkstra, Edsger W., "GO TO Statement Considered Harmful," *Communications of the ACM*, March 1968.

Improved Program Technologies — An Overview. IBM Corporation, GC20-1850, 1974.

An Introduction to Structured Programming in COBOL. IBM Corporation, GC20-1776, 1975.

An Introduction to Structured Programming in PL/I. IBM Corporation, GC20-1777, 1975.

Maynard, Jeff, *Modular Programming.* Philadelphia, Pa.: Auerbach Publishers, 1972.

McGowan, Clement L., and John R. Kelly, *Top-Down Structured Programming Techniques.* New York: Petrocelli/Charter, 1975.

Naur, Peter, and Brian Randell, *Software Engineering,* NATO Science Committee, 1968. Available from Scientific Affairs Division, NATO. Brussels 39, Belgium.

"Special Issue: Programming," *ACM Computing Surveys.* December 1974.

Stevenson, Harry P. (Ed.), *Structured Programming in COBOL.* New York: Association of Computing Machinery, April 1975.

"That Maintenance Iceberg," *EDP Analyzer,* October 1972.

Wirth, Niklaus, "Program Development by Stepwise Refinement," *Communications of the ACM,* April 1971.

Wirth, Niklaus, *Systematic Programming: An Introduction.* Englewood Cliffs, N.J.: Prentice-Hall, 1973.

Yourdon, Edward, *Techniques of Program Structure and Design.* Englewood Cliffs, N.J.: Prentice-Hall, 1975.

Why do we never have time to do it right,
but always plenty of time to do it over?

High efficiency reduces operating costs and makes things
possible that are impossible if the programs are inefficient.

3

Program Efficiency

In programming the primary concern is never efficiency, it is reliability. An efficient program is irrelevant if it does not yield the correct answer. Here is Van Tassel's rule. If the program need not be correct, it can be made as efficient as desired. Programs are written to accomplish some task, not to run in some short period of time. If the task is not accomplished, all the time is wasted.

Another factor to be considered is that reliability is not an add-on feature, whereas efficiency is. An efficient but unreliable program can seldom be made reliable, but a reliable (albeit inefficient) program can be optimized and made more efficient. Thus speeding up is the second step in programming. The first step is to have a correct program. There is no need to speed up an incorrect program. Unreliable software is worthless, no matter how efficient.

If it doesn't work, it doesn't matter how efficient it is.

Generally the wisest approach is to design and write the program the best possible way without too much concern for efficiency. Then *if* the program is useful in its present form *and* if the program is costly to run, *and* if the program will be run many times, *and* if the priorities of the project and the firm so permit, *then and only then* should optimization be considered.

With this point in mind, the rest of the chapter is divided into two parts: methods to find what to optimize and line-by-line optimization techniques. A typical program spends most of its time executing a very small part of the code (often about 5%), called the *critical region*. Usually only this critical region of the code is hand optimized by a programmer. Tools like profilers are available to locate these critical areas of the code. Profilers are discussed in the testing chapter.

Undoubtedly the pursuit of efficiency leads to abuse. It has been observed that programmers waste enormous amounts of time thinking or worrying about the speed of noncritical parts of the program. Remember that today's computers are so fast that it makes little difference if some statements that are executed only a few times are efficient. Savings can be achieved only inside loops that are to be executed many times.

But an inefficient program is like discovering a tooth with a missing filling. You can never leave it alone. You have to probe it, work around it, push on it, think about it, not because it is necessary but simply because it is there.

There are programmers who consider a concern for writing efficient programs archaic. This point is true for small programs doing small tasks on fast machines with large memory. But for any important program there is a necessary performance. It should be established in the design phase. And it affects both time and space. That is, we may say that a program should process ten transactions a second and the whole program must not require more than 150K.

Or, for a compiler, we may require it to process xx instructions per minute. For commercial programs, space is often more critical than time. If you are selling a program that requires 200K, then you have excluded from your market all the machines that have less than 200K. If the program can be kept under 150K, you can double your possible market (and profits).

To do so, the software designer must set target sizes and throughput goals. There items must be broken up and assigned to each module. Brooks' Chapter 9, "Ten Pounds in a Five-pound Sack," in *The Mythical Man-Month* (see References in Chapter II) has some worthwhile advice on handling the problem in a large programming project. At one stage it was found that their OS/360 FORTRAN compiler was processing only five statements per minute; therefore some major revisions were necessary.

Establish efficiency goals at the design stage.

NONCONCERN FOR EFFICIENCY

There are three types of programs, and efficiency assumes different meanings with each one.

The first type of program is a highly used program. It includes operating systems, compilers, scientific subroutines, and airplane-reservation systems. Efficiency is a primary goal in these systems because of their high use and the need for a specific performance.

The second type is a production program that is used often on long runs. This type of program is written by a professional programmer. Although efficiency is important, program maintenance is usually more so.

The third type is one that is written by a nonprogrammer, a business person or scientist. This person's time is generally the most valuable commodity. Here efficiency only has value in that the program must fit in the available core and must execute in a reasonable time.

Consequently, when writing a program, the following question should be considered: How efficient does the program need to be? Obviously you should only modify programs that are going to run a considerable number of times. "Code bums" are people who eliminate 10 microseconds execution time from a seldom-used program while taking 2 hours of programmer time and many minutes of compile and test time. Obviously nothing is saved. In addition, as in any program change, you may be adding a program bug. But human nature being what it is, there will be a continual interest in program efficiency.

EFFICIENCY VERSUS READABILITY

Many of the techniques that make a program more efficient are not detrimental to program readability. These techniques should be used as a matter of course. But since I have attempted to make a thorough survey of efficient programming techniques for source programs, a few of the efficiency suggestions can be *quite* detrimental to providing a readable program.

Completing a readable program is, as noted, more important than completing an efficient program. The reason is that readable programs are easier to debug, modify, and maintain. And every major program must be revised, updated, or otherwise maintained by people other than the ones who originally wrote the program.

The extreme case is when the program *must* be made more efficient. Either the program will not fit in core or it is taking too long to execute. Or the program is to be put in a library, thereby resulting in heavy use. Then efficiency becomes very important, and readability should be sacrificed for greater efficiency.

Readability is usually more important than efficiency.

OPTIMIZING COMPILERS

Program efficiency is important at two stages of program development: at the compile stage and at the execution stage. If the compiler is too slow, a great amount of time will be used during compilation. If program execution is slow, much time will be used during execution. But compilers that produce efficient object code tend to be large and slow because of the work needed to optimize object code.

Thus there is a tendency toward using two compilers for each source language at the same installation. The first compiler is an extremely fast compiler, but it produces inefficient object code. This compiler is used during the debugging stage of program development. The second compiler is usually slower, but it produces efficient object code by optimizing the code. This compiler is used for producing object modules.

WATFIV is a very fast FORTRAN compiler that produces good debug messages but relatively slow object code. WATBOL is a very fast COBOL debugging compiler. Both compilers are available from the University of Waterloo, Waterloo, Ontario, Canada, N2L 3G1.

ALGOL W is a very fast ALGOL compiler that is available from Stanford University. Several PL/I compilers are available. PL/C is a very fast debugging compiler that is available from Cornell University. PL/I Optimizer is an optimizing compiler that is available from IBM. COBOL optimizers are discussed in Stanley M. Naftaly et al., *COBOL Support Packages* (New York: John Wiley & Sons, 1972).

However, many installations have only one compiler for each language. Even then correct selection of compiling options can reduce both compiling time and execution time. At the debug stage assembly listing and object decks are normally not used, and so they should not be supplied by default. Also, other options, such as dumps, maps, and cross-reference lists, are of no use if the programmer doesn't know how to use them or seldom uses them. A careful study of compiler options can result in either defaults or a recommended option list that can save considerable time. Two procedures can be established to call the same compiler: the first would be a *production* version that is fast and has few extra options; the second is a *debugging* version that provides most of the extras, such as a map and cross reference list.

Some of the compilers available at present allow the user to select the resource that he wishes to optimize. That is, the user can request either that execution storage be minimized or that execution time be minimized. The optimization of one resource is done at the expense of the other.

Unfortunately, not a great deal can be said about increasing the compiling speed. A few programming tricks can reduce compiling time, but they are either trivial or extremely compiler dependent. Techniques that work for one compiler do not affect a different compiler for the same machine.

Some compilers compile more efficiently if variable name lengths are evenly distributed. Other compilers compile more efficiently if statement labels are evenly distributed by the last character. Trivial techniques that will reduce compiling time for any compiler include eliminating unused labels and expressions. Labels prevent certain types of optimizations, and so unused labels also prevent execution optimization. On reruns all source program errors should be corrected, and the number of warning diagnostic messages should be minimized whenever possible.

Efficient programs run more cheaply — and cost is always important. If a program uses too much time or storage, the problem cannot be solved on a small machine.

The last few years have seen a phenomenal growth in the use of the minicomputers; therefore it is likely that the writing of efficient programs will continue to be important to the majority of computer users. Compilers for smaller machines do a poorer job of optimizing code than compilers for larger machines. Thus the place where optimization is needed the most is the place where it is available the least. If a larger optimizing compiler is available for larger versions of the same machine, it may be worthwhile to have production programs optimized at another installation if the programs will then execute faster at the original installation. Efficient coding means that a greater number of problems can be solved without resorting to machine language or going to a larger computer system, both of which are inconvenient for most operations.

A great deal can be said on how to make a program execute efficiently. The rest of the chapter is devoted to techniques that will produce programs that do precisely that.

The techniques described here are as machine independent and language independent as possible for optimizing the execution time and minimizing storage usage of compiled programs. The methods are machine independent because the improvements made in the program will cause it to run faster on a variety of computers. They are relatively (except where specified for a particular language) language independent in that they are applicable to high-level languages in general and that the optimizing techniques do not depend on the characteristics of any particular language. Several of these suggestions on execution will produce more noticeable results on some machines than on others. Even different models of the same machine can have different assembly instruction sets that will provide noticeable difference of optimization.

Some compilers do optimization for program execution. Two types of optimizations are done: (a) machine-dependent optimization and (b) machine-independent optimization. First, machine-dependent optimizations are totally dependent on the machine used. As a rule, these optimizations are not generally known or understood by the source-level programmer. They consist of methods of handling subscripts, register assignments, and analysis of machine instructions.

The second type of optimization is the machine-independent optimization that is done at the source language level. Although the compiler can optimize a program, the programmer can usually optimize better or at least help in the optimization. Many optimizations can be done only by the programmer, since they require a knowledge of the logic of the program. Other compiler optimizations that could be done are not done simply because they would require too much machine time. Thus the original programmers can do much to optimize their own programs.

The use of the optimizing techniques discussed here does not eliminate the need for an optimizing compiler, since the machine-dependent optimizing can seldom be anticipated or controlled at the source code level. Also, even the best optimized source program will be improved by an optimizing compiler. By using structured programming techniques, you can help an optimizing compiler. The reason is that the program flow is simpler (less GO TOs) and easier to analyze by the optimizer compiler.

Use an optimizing compiler.

OPTIMIZING A PROGRAM

Frequently, a particular production program must be optimized because it runs too long or it requires too much storage. Perhaps when the program was originally written, no one thought it would be used much, and no care was taken to make it efficient. Or possibly the program has been modified extensively and has become inefficient. Now the program is used quite often, and it consumes too much time, or possibly it is close to exceeding available storage. The result is that an effort is to be made to make it more efficient.

Before explaining a method to optimize a program, let us return to the subject of algorithm selection. If a program must be optimized, the algorithm used in the program should be carefully examined. The basic method chosen for the problem has a major effect on the speed and core usage of the program.

Perhaps a different algorithm should have been chosen, and optimizing the old algorithm will not provide the gain desired. The following discussion assumes that the original algorithm is a sound and reasonable one, but programmers who need to optimize their program should never make that assumption.

Segment the Program

The program to be optimized should be divided up into subprograms. If the program has been already divided into subprograms by the principles of structured programming, then the optimization is much easier. Once the subprograms are established, three items should be estimated.

1. What percentage of total time does each subprogram use?
2. What percentage of optimization is possible in each subprogram?
3. How many people-hours are necessary to achieve this goal?

The next three sections will discuss each question in detail.

Time the Subprograms

Once the program is divided into subprograms, each subprogram should be timed to determine what percentage of time is used in each subprogram. It is important actually to time each subprogram in order to establish which sections are the most time consuming.

If estimates or guesses are used to allocate time to each subprogram, mistakes will often take place and the optimization will fail. A superficial analysis will lead to the wrong subprogram being chosen for optimization. Once the actual time is established, the subprograms that use the most time should receive the greatest effort toward optimization. For example, perhaps the program is divided into four subprograms and the timing is

> Subprogram A   5%
> Subprogram B   60%
> Subprogram C   15%
> Subprogram D   20%

Here we can see that even if subprogram A were eliminated (which usually is not possible or desirable), we would save only 5% of the total program time. Thus the major optimization effort will probably be put into subprogram B, where the greatest saving is possible.

If it is not possible to obtain actual timings of the subprograms, another approach is to count the number of statements, preferably from an assembly listing of a higher-level language. Loops should be treated multiplicatively. Counting the number of statements will give a fairly good indication of the percentage of time required for each subunit, but actual timing is much better.

Most programs have one *critical point* that is responsible for using the majority of the execution time. It is not unusual to have a single small section of code responsible for better than 50% of all execution time. This section is obviously the first section to attempt to optimize.

After the first critical point is optimized, it is a good idea to re-analyze the program again, for now there may be a different critical point that also can be optimized. This process can be repeated as often as significant results are obtained.

Execution-Time Profiles

In the past, the actual timing of segments of a program was the best possible method available for examining the program for time-consuming waste. Today, execution-time profiles are available in COBOL, FORTRAN, PL/I, and ALGOL W.

It is commonly observed that designers do not make correct estimates about the critical regions for efficiency in time and space. As a result, the actual code should be implemented, and software tools used to locate the critical regions, otherwise these critical regions will normally never be known.

> *Profile your code.*

One side advantage of using execution profiles comes during testing and debugging. Since execution profiles give frequency counts, they can be used to uncover statements that have not been tested. A statement executed with zero frequency has not been tested. Similarly, statement frequency counts can be used to see if a particular statement was executed the exact number of times expected.

Estimate Possible Improvement

Once an accurate estimate of percentage total time is established, an estimation of possible improvement should be made. If a subprogram accounts for a large percentage of total time but little improvement is possible, then the resulting effort would be fruitless.

When estimating possible improvement, only the approximate magnitude of improvement is necessary or possible. Whether the possible improvement is 20 or 25% is unimportant. What is important is whether it would be 5 or 70%.

Determining the possible improvement is not a trivial task. Experience will probably be the best guide. This chapter suggests many techniques for writing an efficient program. Thus it is possible to look for statements that can be modified by using the suggestions given here. Careful examination of loops and input/output are always the most rewarding.

We can now establish a product that will indicate the possible improvement. If we have a subprogram that uses 50% of the total program time but offers only a 5% increase in efficiency, we would end up with a 2.5% (.50 * .05 = .025) total increase in efficiency. A different subprogram that uses 10% of total program time but offers a 50% increase in efficiency would result in a 5% (.50 * 10 = .05) total increase in efficiency. So the second subprogram should be chosen first for optimization, since the final result is largest. It is important that the product of % usage and % improvement be considered in order not to spend a great deal of time and effort optimizing the wrong subprogram.

Necessary Effort

Along with determining the possible improvement, we should estimate the amount of work necessary to accomplish this improvement. We can calculate a weighted sum for each subprogram as follows.

$$\frac{\% \text{ time } * \% \text{ improvement}}{\text{effort needed}}$$

The subprogram with the highest weighted sum would commonly be the first one selected for optimization.

The major advantage of careful selection of the subprogram to be optimized is that valuable resources (programmer and computer time) can be assigned where they will do the most good. If resources are assigned unwisely, a great deal of effort can result in little increase in efficiency. If there is not enough time or justification to redo the complete program, the most fruitful subprograms can be worked on.

There are two approaches to optimizing an already existing program: clean up and redesign. Both have advantages and disadvantages. The clean-up approach consists of correcting obvious sloppiness in the original program. In addition, any language peculiarities that lend themselves to optimization can be exploited. Many of the suggestions in this chapter will help improve the efficiency. The positive side of this approach is that it takes little time. The negative side is that by simply cleaning up the original program, the gain in efficiency is usually not spectacular.

The second approach is a redesign of the original program. If the program is divided into subprograms, redesign can be done on the subprogram that is most time consuming. Although redesign usually produces the best results, it is also the most costly.

Hopefully, a great deal has been learned from the first effort to write a program; and this information can be used during redesigning. Redesign is especially helpful if the program has been changed extensively. Often revisions will have changed the goal of the original program. Possibly the program has been in a constant state of revision for a period of time. Now the program's results seem to be accepted, and revisions will be less extensive and less frequent. Then using the knowledge gained and the new goals, redesign should produce perceptible savings in program time.

Optimization Steps

Let us summarize the previous points before turning to the code optimization techniques.

1. Optimize only if necessary. Don't optimize if it isn't necessary, since doing so may obscure the readability, or may add errors, or may waste much programming time.
2. If optimization is necessary, first try using an optimizing compiler. It may be all you need and should be tried first.
3. Locate the critical region to be optimized. It is a waste of time to optimize the wrong code.
4. Apply localized optimization to the critical region.

Too often people spend a great deal of time tuning code that is seldom executed. The rest of the chapter is devoted to the last step — that is, local optimization.

EXECUTION EFFICIENCY

Program efficiency during execution involves two resources. The first is the time that the program will take to run, and the second is the storage that it will require. Time has always been important to programmers, for most programs are charged by the amount of machine time required. Since many computer installations now charge for the amounts of storage used, it is a good possibility that storage considerations will increase in importance: otherwise storage is only important if not enough is available.

It is more difficult to optimize storage space than execution time. It is not unusual to optimize a program so that it will run 25% faster, but it would be unusual to optimize a program and decrease storage space used by 25%. This statement assumes that no serious blunders have been made in writing the original program.

Keep in mind, however, that if you should select a new and better algorithm and reprogram the problem, you might dramatically improve both execution time and storage space usage. The reason that it is so difficult to reduce storage space use drastically is that any savings occur in small amounts scattered throughout the program. In contrast, execution speed can be gained in large chunks simply by improving one section of code, such as a loop that is iterated numerous times.

But a small space saving is often needed desperately (to get the program to fit into the computer), whereas a small saving in time used is not too important..

We gain execution efficiency by doing as much as possible at compile time. Included are such items as initializing arrays and variables, calculations of constants, and storage allocations. Storage allocation at compile time usually increases storage usage at the expense of saving execution time.

Good programming practices will decrease both time and storage use, but some types of improvements in either one of these factors will often be detrimental to the other. Most of the techniques discussed here save both time and storage. If a technique causes a trade-off between time and storage, it will be mentioned.

In most cases, a small increase in efficiency is not worthwhile if it costs a great deal in programmer time, readability, reliability, generality, or convenience. In other cases, however, small increases in efficiency are worth a great deal of effort. One obvious example is in compilers where a great effort is expended to write very efficient programs. Since compilers are used over and over, a small increase in efficiency will pay large dividends. Another example in which efficiency is important is in program libraries. Since these programs are used often, small increases in efficiency will generally repay the computer installation many times over.

The approach in each case depends on a number of factors, such as cost of developing the program, how often the program is used, the relative speeds of different operations on the machine, and the way in which different statements are compiled.

A good program is a program that accomplishes the objective with a minimum of computer time. This situation is desirable because more jobs can be processed during a given time period. With the advent of multiprocessing (i.e., the processing of more than one job at the same time), the use of minimum storage is also desirable because each program in a multiprocessing environment must be allocated a region of core storage. The less core needed for each program, the more programs can be kept in core at one time and thus processed at the same time. In a multiprocessing environment core usage is as important as time usage, and so charges are usually made for both resources. Reductions in either core usage or time usage will reduce program charges. Since computer resources are quite expensive, consistently saving even small amounts on a program that will be used repeatedly may be well worth the effort.

In general, any effort to improve efficiency is reserved for programs that are used often. Although this is a productive approach, here is another one that will also save a great deal of computer time. Train yourself to develop a group of habits that will consistently provide you with more efficient programs. As a result, you will always produce more efficient programs and consistently save machine time.

STORAGE

Usually people do not worry about storage until they run out. Then it becomes apparent that storage is not infinite. The ideal situation is a fast machine with sufficient storage. This situation exists only for small jobs on large machines.

Shortage of computer storage is a common problem. Several years ago it was thought that the problem would be temporary, since storage was becoming less expensive. Predictions were that soon there would be enough storage for any problem.

This prediction overlooked three important facts. First, the size of problems has increased as storage has increased, a situation that illustrates the following rule: the size of programming problems increases to fill the machine storage available for use. The second trend overlooked was the proliferation of inexpensive minicomputers. Since minicomputers have become so common, the value of efficient programming has increased. This is true both for storage and for speed. And, finally, with the introduction of multiprocessing, no one program is allowed to occupy all of storage. Instead core storage is divided into partitions of varying size. So if a program is compact enough to fit into an available smaller partition, the turnaround time is faster and costs less.

An increase in the economical use of storage almost always causes an increase in programmer's time and execution time of the program. Thus if storage is not charged for, storage usage is of no concern unless there is not enough of it.

Program Overlays

A program overlay refers to the technique of bringing routines into high-speed storage from some other form of storage during processing so that several routines occupy the same storage locations at different times. Overlays are used when the total storage requirements for instructions exceed the available main storage. WATFIV FORTRAN is one of the few systems that does not allow overlays.

The program must be broken into logical units so that nonoverlapping units can serially be called into storage as needed. Program modules are usually used for overlays. Time is necessary to transfer the modules from the peripheral storage device, and so execution time is used. Overlaying conserves storage use, but costs extra programmer's time and machine time.

If a program can be overlayed, some thought must go toward placement of data. Each time that a new module is brought in from disk storage it is a fresh module. No data is saved from the last use of this module. For example, a module to produce headings might contain the page count, line counts, and special heading information. If this module was overlayed, the accumulated data would be lost after each overlay. The simplest solution to this problem is to remove all working storage from the lower-level modules and place it in the main calling module. This calling module would never be overlayed.

It should be remembered that the use of overlays results in access to a disk each time an overlay segment is needed. This situation is costly in execution time, so only use overlays when absolutely necessary. It is better to check to see if program size can be reduced and avoid the use of an overlay.

Several observations can be made about overlays to save time and storage. Segments should be approximately the same size. Total memory requirements are influenced by the largest overlay.

Do not "oversegment." Each overlay costs a small amount of nonoverlayable storage (segment dictionary), and a small amount of additional code is needed to make the overlay calls. Also, overlays take time. You should not execute a number of overlays for each transaction. It is well to keep in mind that every call on an overlay usually requires a disk read.

In order not to "oversegment," it may be desirable to place totally unrelated sections in the same segment to make the sizes fit well. We first establish the size of the largest segment and then check to see if some of the smaller segments can be combined in order to reduce overlay calls.

We can attempt to segment the programs in more than one way, and, using the same data, see how much time is saved or lost by a particular segmentation structure.

Virtual Memory

Another type of overlay is done by using virtual memory. If virtual memory is available on your computer, your program is automatically divided into fixed-length segments (called pages) by the operating system. Then the operating system transfers pages into main memory as needed. Thus the problem of organizing an overlay vanishes from the programmer's purview and is assumed by the computer system.

Programmers believe that they have a very large main memory at their disposal even though the computer may have a relatively small memory. But time is lost when a section of the program is needed for execution and it is not available in main memory. It must then be read from a storage device. The less often this condition occurs, the faster the program will execute.

There are a few things that the programmer can do to improve efficient execution when using virtual memory. The program should be written with subroutines. This step aids *locality* — that is, the degree to which during execution a program favors some subset of its program. Locally is a readily observed phenomenon in programs. Locality is improved by adhering to structured programming. First, avoid use of COMMON or global variables as they cause locality to deteriorate. Second, avoid use of GO TOs and labels. Both precepts will ensure good locality of your logic and data references.

Two other features that contribute to locality are loops and subroutines. Both will cause a program to execute repeatedly over a small set of the total program. The higher the degree of locality in a program using virtual memory, the more efficiently the program will execute because it will not need to call as many pages into memory. Thus when using virtual memory, keep items used with each other near each other.

The second method of increasing execution efficiency when using virtual memory is to group the subroutines together according to the order in which they are likely to call one another. This step will tend to decrease the number of pages that must be read into main memory.

There are several classical examples of very simple programs that can degrade performance on virtual storage. Here is a FORTRAN program that zeros a double-precision array.

```
        DO 15 K = 1, 512
          DO  15  L = 1, 20
15          X(K,L) = 0.0
```

Unfortunately, FORTRAN arrays are stored by column and each column requires a 4K page. Thus each execution of line 15 will reference a different page. The inner loop will zero an element in 20 different pages, and this will happen 512 times. The solution to this problem is simply to reverse the order of the loop (i.e., so the $K = 1, 512$ is the inner loop). Then the program will zero 512 elements in one page be-

fore requiring a new page. By making this simple change in the order
of the loops, we can decrease cost by 512 to one.

A similar situation occurs when processing several arrays inside
the same loop as follows.

$$DO\ 25 \quad K = 1,N$$

$$A(K) = 0.0$$

$$B(K) = 0.0$$

$$C(K) = 0.0$$

$$25\ CONTINUE$$

One element is referenced in each array for each iteration of the loop.
If the arrays are large or scattered in memory, a page fault could be
caused for each array for each iteration. So it is better to process
each array with a separate DO loop on a virtual machine. Try running
similar programs on your virtual storage machine.

Hints for Virtual Memory Users

1. Compile the program with an optimizing compiler, since less
   code will be generated.
2. Structured programs and use of modules will increase locality.
3. Remove exception routines, error-handling routines, and
   other low-use code from the mainline of the program in order
   to increase the density of reference of the most heavily used
   pages.
4. Initialize each data area just prior to its first use rather than
   initializing all at the beginning of the program.
5. Reference or store data in the order in which it is stored. For
   example, arrays are stored in columns, so complete all reference to a single column before moving to the next column.
   Nonarray data can be grouped together by rearranging the
   order of the declarations. Usually it is best to group together
   high-use areas.

The article by Morrison (in the References) has numerous suggestions for virtual storage systems.

Report and Column Headings

Heading lines are often space-wasting items. The common approach is to define the complete heading line as a literal. Another approach that saves storage when a majority of the heading is blank is to use code to accomplish the space fill. The cost is normally just a couple of instructions versus a large literal of blanks.

Heading routines are good routines to put in overlays, since they are generally quite wasteful of storage and are not needed on every transaction. The literals for the headings should be "stored" in the overlay segment, too.

Equivalence

Most computer languages have a command that allows two variables to share the same storage location. If a variable is used only in the beginning of a program and then a new variable is needed in another part of the program, these two variables can share the same storage locations, since they are used at different times in the program.

This type of command can be used to conserve storage because it is common to have variables that are only used in segments of the program. The equivalencing of arrays can save large amounts of storage and should be carefully considered for a program needing more storage. A trivial technique for reducing storage is to reduce the size of arrays. This step should be done before resorting to making two arrays equivalent in storage. And since equivalencing unrelated variables can be very confusing, it should be heavily commented.

Using Loops

Use of loops for repeated operations is one common method to conserve storage. Sections of programs often have similar sequences of operations. If programmers wish to conserve storage, they should look for similar sequences of coding that can be expressed in loops.

Loops require some extra storage because the initialization, the test procedure, the tally adjustment, and the constants must all be set up. Still, the reduction in total amount of storage is generally more than offset by the elimination of the duplicate instructions. Short loops that require an elaborate sequence of control operations can often be written by using straight-line coding rather than iterative coding. This is usually true only for very few iterations.

CALCULATION OF CONSTANTS

Programs are often more readable if expressions containing constants are used. But many compiler methods are used to do computations involving only constants. Some compilers will calculate all constant expressions at compile time and store the result. Other less sophisticated compilers store the constants and do the calculations at execution time. The latter method is inefficient if constant expressions are within loops. Examples of constant expressions are

```
TAX = INC - 3200/12
Y = SQRT(ABS(COS(2.30259 ** 1.839)))
INT = IRATE/365/12
B = 4.0 * A/3.0
```

All these expressions have constants, but caution must be used where the expressions are inserted. If constant expressions are not evaluated at compile time, then they should always be placed outside loops.

This process is commonly called *folding:* the process of executing at compile-time source program operations whose values are known so that they need not be executed at run time. Folding is also done with values that can be determined within blocks of coding.

INITIALIZATION OF VARIABLES

Variables that are initialized when they are declared save execution time. The reason is that the variables are initialized during the compiling step instead of the execution step. Initializing of variables when declared helps documentation and also avoids the error of not initializing a variable.

Most programs have some variables to be initialized. For instance,

```
PI = 3.14159
E = 2.71828
```

Since these variables never change in value in the program, they should be initialized in the declare statement.

PL/I

```
DECLARE (PI, E)
    REAL
    INITIAL (3.14159, 2.71828);
```

Two assignment statements are eliminated, thereby saving both storage and execution time.

Initialize variables at compile time.

ARITHMETIC OPERATIONS

Arithmetic operations are done at greatly different speeds. So it is helpful to know which operations are faster because sometimes it is quite easy to substitute one operation for another. Here are the mathematical operations listed in order from fastest to slowest.

Fastest   1. Addition or subtraction
            2. Multiplication
            3. Division
Slowest   4. Exponentiation

Some fast mathematical operations are easily substituted for a slower operation.

Addition is faster than multiplication, so for multiplications with small integer powers, addition should be substituted. Thus 3*I should be changed to I+I+I. If the expressions are not both integers, loss of accuracy can occur. The roundoff error with real numbers tends to accumulate instead of cancel. So for R real and I integer, I*R is more accurate than R+R+R+... (I times).

Rearrangement of equations can eliminate operations. For example, X = 2*Y + (A - 1)/P + 2*T can be changed to X = 2 * (Y + T) + (A - 1)/P, which eliminates one multiplication.

Since division is slower, multiply whenever possible instead of dividing. For instance, don't divide by five; multiply by 0.2 instead. Multiplication is usually at least twice as fast as division. Eliminate as many divisions as possible in your program and replace them with the reciprocal of the number.

Not A/5.0   Instead A*0.2

If you continually divide by some number, say X, in your calculations, replace it for its reciprocal.

Bad — X can be replaced by its reciprocal:

$$A = 1.0/X$$

$$\cdot$$
$$\cdot$$
$$\cdot$$

$$C = B + D/X$$

Use the reciprocal instead

$$RX = 1.0/X$$

$$\cdot$$
$$\cdot$$
$$\cdot$$

$$A = RX$$

$$\cdot$$
$$\cdot$$
$$\cdot$$

$$C = B + D*RX$$

This example substitutes one division for many divisions.

Another important consideration is the type of the power in exponentiation. Integers should be used whenever possible. For instance,

Slow   A**8.0   or   A**P   where P is floating point.
Faster A**8   or   A**I   where I is an integer.

Not only is the second method faster, it is also more accurate and will eliminate certain types of errors, since

$(-6)**I$ is allowed if I is an integer, but
$(-6)**P$ is usually not allowed

because if P was 0.5, this would be the square root of a negative number. So if using integer powers, make the exponent an integer form.

Slow   B = A**P where P is floating point
Faster IP = P
       B = A**IP where IP is integer

When integers are used for exponents, the operation is performed by repeated multiplication. When floating point exponents are used, it is necessary to call a special subroutine to take care of the operation.

The function for square root is generally quite a bit faster and more accurate than using an exponent. That is,

```
Slow   A**0.5
Faster SQRT(A)
```

Multiplication is much faster than exponentiation, so repeated multiplication should be used when the exponent is a small integer.

```
Slow   VOL = (4.0*R**3)/3.0
Faster VOL = (4.0*R*R*R)/3.0
```

Exponentiation normally requires a library subprogram. Thus repeated multiplication saves both core and time. Use the following when the exponent is a small-integer exponent.

```
X**2  should be  X*X
X**3  should be  X*X*X
X**4  should be  (X*X)*(X*X)
       or        (((X*X)*X)*X)
```

The last example contains a repeated calculation (X*X) that can be further optimized. The substitution of one operation for a faster operation is called *reducing the strength of an operation*.

Reducing the strength of an operation, however, can sometimes reduce the readability of a program, and so this fact should be considered. Also, some machine time is used in handling intermediate results when reducing the strength of an operation.

Fixed Point Arithmetic

Most computer languages allow integer arithmetic. Integer arithmetic can be used for any type of counting operation. Special arithmetic procedures for integers are used because many computing problems involve only integers (inventories, census information) and integer arithmetic is usually handled directly by a single machine instruction, whereas floating point arithmetic is performed by subroutines involving dozens of machine language instructions.

Some machines can execute 50 integer additions in the time required to execute one floating point addition. In this case, integer arithmetic should be used whenever possible, particularly when a great number of simple integer arithmetic operations must be done, such as with subscripts. Using the wrong form of subscripts can drastically slow down any program.

A few machines actually do floating point operations faster than fixed point operations. Generally these are the huge scientific computers that have special hardware features capable of handling point arithmetic operations.

Particular care must be taken so that internal switches, counters, and variables involved in numerous calculations are defined in a form that results in the most efficient calculations. This factor is mainly a problem in PL/I and COBOL, where it is possible to do arithmetic with variables that are actually character strings. When this situation occurs, numerous conversions are necessary for each calculation. Both storage and time can be saved by properly declaring the variables.

Mixed Data Types

Mixed data types result from using numbers that have different arithmetic attributes in arithmetic or logical operations. If you mix numbers that have different attributes, then conversions are often necessary to do the arithmetic. This situation can be minimized by declaring as many variables as possible to have the same attributes. Then less care need be taken to avoid mixing them, since all have the same attributes. Although mixed arithmetic is allowed to cut down errors and help the programmer, it should be avoided, since it uses both extra time and storage.

Avoid mixed data types.

Correct Mode

On some primitive compilers it is important to be careful about the type of constant used. For instance,

$$A = 0 \qquad \text{Inefficient}$$
$$A = 0.0 \quad \text{Efficient}$$

Several compilers require a conversion from an integer zero to a real zero at execution time in the example $A = 0$, whereas in the second case no conversion is necessary. A good compiler stores the constant in the correct form at compile time instead of execution time.

If conversion is necessary, it can be very time consuming inside a loop. For example,

FORTRAN

```
      DO 10  I = 1,1000
         A(I) = 0
 10 CONTINUE
```

The preceding statements could cause 1000 conversions. Instead use

$$A(I) = 0.0$$

to avoid unnecessary conversions.

A similar situation arises from

$$Y = 1/X$$

which might necessitate a conversion, whereas

$$Y = 1.0/X$$

would not. A simple method to avoid any problems is to write all constants in the dominant mode of the expression. Conversions of this type are usually necessary only on small compilers.

If when using COBOL, you do extensive arithmetic on DISPLAY fields instead of COMPUTATIONAL, severe inefficiences in storage space and time occur, at best 4-10 times slower. However, numeric fields that are not used in arithmetic operations should be defined as alphameric (X PICTURE).

Decimal Alignment

Programs that use fixed decimal variables can be made more efficient by careful selection of variable attributes. If efficiency is important, then studying the language manual for your computer will be necessary in order to ascertain when conversions are needed in arithmetic operations.

Decimal points must be aligned in COBOL and PL/I; so a programmer should carefully select the attributes used with variables. For instance,

```
WORKING-STORAGE SECTION.
77 A  PICTURE S999V99.
77 B  PICTURE S99V9.

.

.

.

PROCEDURE DIVISION.
   ADD A TO B.
```

Both time and internal storage can be saved by defining B as

```
77 B PICTURE S999V99.
```

Doing so eliminates the extra instructions necessary to align the decimal point.

Storage Alignment

Considerable time and storage can be saved by ensuring that variables are aligned properly in storage. In other words, certain types of variables should be aligned on a word or double word of storage. If they are not, the compiler generates the necessary instructions to move the items to a work area having the correct boundary necessary for computation.

In FORTRAN, if variables in COMMON are placed in order of decreasing size — that is, complex, double precision, real, integer — they will be aligned properly. In COBOL, COMPUTATIONAL variables should be aligned by use of the SYNCRONIZED clause. If arrays are not aligned, severe penalties in time and space can occur. Although these rules are true in general, you should consult the programming language manual for exact information on alignment.

Grouping

When using a series of mixed mode operands that are separated by operators of equal priority, group the operands of like mode together with logically redundant parentheses. For instance,

```
I Mode 1
A Mode 2
R Mode 3
I * A * I * R * A * R * I
```

should be written

$$((I * I * I) * A * A) * R * R$$

The grouping and parentheses help eliminate conversions that would otherwise have to take place.

Extra conversions can be avoided by converting from one mode to another once and then using the mode needed. For example, if I and A are variables that are used together and they require extra conversions, convert them once and use the correct form in all mathematical operations. For example,

Slow
```
B = A * I
C = (A + I) * 2.0
D = A * A/I
```

These statements use the variables A and I several times. It is better to convert I to A's mode once and then use the new variable. To illustrate,

Faster
```
AI = I
B = A * AI
C = (A + AI) * 2.0
D = A * A/AI
```

Here I must be converted only once instead of three times.

Use Assembly Lists

One of the easiest ways to check the efficiency of different operations is to request a printing of the assembly code generated for each instruction. Then a casual examination of the number of assembly instructions generated for each higher-level command will help demonstrate the relative efficiency of different methods of coding. Here is a program and its assembly listing.

0008			A = A + B	
0009			A = A + I	

Assembly

000190	A = A + B 8	LE	0,100(0,13)	A
000194		AF	0,104(0,13)	B
000198		STE	0,100(0,13)	A
000190	A = A + I 9	L	0,108(0,13)	I
0001A0		LPR	1,0	
0001A2		ST	1,156(0,13)	
0001A6		LD	0,152(0,13)	
0001AA		AD	0,136(0,13)	
0001AE		LTR	0,0	
0001B0		BALR	14,0	
0001B2		BC	11,6(0,14)	
0001B6		LCDR	0,0	
0001B8		AE	0,100(0,13)	A
0001BC		STE	0,100(0,13)	A

The second addition requires a mode conversion.

Repeated Calculations

It may seem obvious not to repeat any operations, but repeated operations usually sneak into many parts of the program, especially loops. The best solution to this problem is to do as many of the simple calculations near the beginning of the program as possible and then use them as variables throughout the program. This is called *eliminating redundant* instructions. Some compilers do it for you.

Here are some examples of repeated operations.

Bad	X = Y + A/B*C
	Z = W + A/B*C

Instead	ABC = A/B*C
	X = Y + ABC
	Z = W + ABC

These examples illustrate another fact about efficiency. That is, the second group of statements is longer, but it is more efficient and uses the least core. A smaller number of source statements does not prove that a program is more efficient timewise or corewise. In this example it is much cheaper to move ABC twice than to calculate A/B*C twice. Moves are very cheap.

Another example is

Inefficient

```
SIGMA1 = SIN(THETA) + SIN(THETA) ** 2
SIGMA2 = SIN(THETA)/3.0
```

Efficient

```
RHO = SIN(THETA)
SIGMA1 = RHO + RHO * RHO
SIGMA2 = RHO/3.0
```

Here SIN must be computed only once, whereas in the first example it is calculated three times.

The natural method of solving a problem often introduces redundant expressions. For example, the normal method for finding the roots of a quadratic equation is

```
ROOT1 = (-B + SQRT(B**2 - 4.0*A*C))/(2.0*A)
ROOT2 = (-B - SQRT(B**2 - 4.0*A*C))/(2.0*A)
```

But a more efficient (but less readable) coding is

```
D = A + A
DIS = SQRT(B*B - 4.0*A*C)
ROOT1 = (-B + DIS)/D
ROOT2 = (-B - DIS)/D
```

The amount of time or storage saved varies, depending on the machine. On some machines a very simple repeated expression will save almost nothing by being removed. But the more complicated the repeated expression is, the greater the saving. The saving also increases the more often the expression is used. On some small computers floating point operations are quite time consuming, especially if there is no floating point hardware. Here there is the possibility of large savings.

FUNCTION CALLS

Some programs call many intrinsic functions, such as SQRT, SIN, COS, and ABS. On some compilers it is possible to have some control over how the functions are handled. If we wish to reduce the execution time, it would be nice to have all functions end up as in-line code. If the goal is to reduce core usage, then it would be desirable to have just one copy of the code needed for the function and to have function calls made to this copy.

An examination of the assembly code should indicate whether your compiler provides in-line code or function calls. If only one copy of the function code is desired, usually an EXTERNAL statement can be used to indicate that functions are not to be put in in-line code.

Function calls can be reduced by storing the values. Generally there are many function calls in a program. If any of the function calls does not change arguments, then the values returned from the function should be saved to be used elsewhere in the program. Built-in functions like TIME or DATE are often used several places in the program, but DATE need never be called more than once in a program, since its value can be saved.

COMPILER OPTIMIZATION

Some compilers do optimization that eliminates repeated calculations, but there are severe limitations on how much optimization is done. The greater the amount of optimization, the larger the compiler and hence the slower the compiling. The programmer can at least help to optimize at the source language level. For example, compilers will not usually eliminate the following repeated expression.

$$A = X*Y + 2.0 + Y*X$$

Since the order is changed, the compiler would not normally determine that X*Y is the same as Y*X. Similarly, some compilers are not able to discover that 2.00*X is the same expression as 2.0*X or that the following contains a hidden repeated expression.

$$A = B*B*C*C$$

If reordered, the repeated expression becomes obvious.

$$A = (B*C)*(B*C)$$

A different type of repeated expression is

$$A = B - C$$
.
.
.
$$D = C - B$$

The two expressions on the right side of the replacement sign are the same except for sign. These examples illustrate the many difficulties an optimizing compiler has in locating all repeated expressions. Thus programmers should do their best to eliminate as many repeated expressions as possible.

Another limit on compiler optimization is that the compiler can optimize only a linear sequence of code that has one entry (the first command executed) and one exit (the last command executed). This situation is called a *basic block*. Thus the following group of code could be optimized.

PL/I

```
K = I/3.0*B;
P = 3 + I/3.0*B;
A = B*B + I/3.0*B;
```

The preceding statements must be entered at the first statement and exited at the last statement. But if a label is put on the second statement, the compiler can no longer optimize this code because it cannot determine the effect that an entry at the second statement will have. For example,

PL/I

```
         K = I/3.0*B;
LOOP1:   P = 3 + I/3.0*B;
         A = B*B + I/3.0*B;
```

The label LOOP1 prevents compiler optimization, but the programmers, with their superior knowledge of the logic of the program, know whether these three statements can be optimized.

A similar situation is a nonstandard subroutine or function call that will prevent compiler optimization because the compiler cannot know which variables are changed in the subroutine.

AVOIDANCE OF LOOPS

Whenever possible, avoid loops because time is spent in incrementing and testing the loop index. Subscripts can cause execution time to be increased by one-third. Small calculations can often be done without loops.

For example, polynomial evaluation by

$$POLY = ((A(1)*X + A(2))*X + A(3))*X + A(4)$$

is faster than

FORTRAN

```
      POLY = A(1)
      DO 1    I = 2,4
    1 POLY = POLY*X + A(I)
```

In addition, the initializing features of each language should be used to initialize arrays. The commands that will initialize variables are as follows.

Language	*Command*
FORTRAN	DATA
PL/I	INITIAL
COBOL	VALUE

These commands are the most efficient way to initialize a variable as they initialize during compilation instead of during execution.

One method of reducing loops is to collapse two or more into a single loop. Reduction of the number of loops is often possible by careful preprogramming analysis. Programs that have gone through extensive modification are especially susceptible to extra loops.

LOOP ORGANIZATION

When using loops, a great deal of time is spent in initializing and testing the loop index. Time can be saved by careful ordering of nested loops. To illustrate,

PL/I

```
DO K = 1 TO 20;              loop initialization occurs 1 time
   DO J = 1 TO 10;           loop initialization occurs 20 times
      DO L = 1 TO 5;         loop initialization occurs 200 times
                  .
                  .
                  .
         loop statements     useful statements occur 1,000 times
                  .
                  .
                  .
      END;                   loop closing occurs 1,000 times
   END;                      loop closing occurs 200 times
END;                         loop closing occurs 20 times
```

Here loop initialization occurs 221 times and loop closing occurs 1,220 times.

By rearranging the loops (which is not always possible), we can reduce the number of loop initializations and loop closings. For instance,

PL/I

```
DO L = 1 TO 5;               loop initialization occurs 1 time
   DO J = 1 TO 10;           loop initialization occurs 5 times
      DO K = 1 TO 20;        loop initialization occurs 50 times
                  .
                  .
                  .
         loop statements     useful statements occur 1,000 times
                  .
                  .
                  .
      END;                   loop closing occurs 1,000 times
   END;                      loop closing occurs 50 times
END;                         loop closing occurs 5 times
```

This example has 56 loop initializations and 1,055 loop closings. Thus the number of loop initializations and loop closings can be reduced by nesting the loops so that the outer loops have the least number of iterations.

LOOP OPTIMIZATION

When trying to make a program execute faster, loops are usually the most important factor. This point is obvious, since commands inside a loop may be executed many thousand times and any savings, no matter how small, will increase by a factor of thousands. Programs can be made more efficient by developing the programming habits illustrated in this chapter. But if programmers spend much time trying to improve the efficiency of their programs by improving a statement that is only executed once, it is like trying to lose weight by trimming your fingernails — you might make a little progress, but it won't be very noticeable.

So concentrate any extra effort in loops. Here is an example.

```
┌─ Loop A      --    100 iterations
│     ┌─ Loop B      --   100 iterations
│     │     ┌─ Loop C    --    100 iterations
│     │     └─ End  C
│     └─ End   B
└─ End   A
```

First, concentrate on loop C. Any savings, no matter how small, will be multiplied by $100 \times 100 \times 100 = 1,000,000$ — that is, a factor of one million. A very small improvement inside loop C would pay much higher dividends than a large improvement outside loop C. Then concentrate on loop B, and, finally, on loop A.

The computation within a loop should be minimized. Thus almost all the suggestions in this chapter should be applied to loops, particularly in the case of repeated calculations, unchanged subscripts, arithmetic operations, and data conversions.

Repeated calculations are the most common efficiency errors in loops. For example,

```
┌─ Loop A
│     ┌─ Loop B
│     │        X = Y * Z + C(I,J)
│     └─ End  B
└─ End   A
```

Here Y*Z will be calculated each time the loop is executed, which may be thousands of times. Instead the program should calculate Y*Z before the loop as follows.

```
YZ = Y * Z
```

```
┌─ Loop A

    ┌─ Loop B

        X = YZ + C(I,J)

    └─ End  B

└─ End  A
```

Now the quanity Y*Z is calculated only once, no matter how many times the loop is executed. Significant results in saving computer time can usually be achieved simply by checking loops that do many iterations and eliminating repeated calculations inside these loops.

This process is commonly referred to as removing *invariant* expressions from loops. Invariant expressions are expressions that are not changed within the loop. If at compile time we can remove a single multiplication out of a loop that iterated 1000 times at execution time, we can save 999 execution time multiplications. Removal of invariant expressions from loops incurs a small penalty in the necessary storage used for storing and retrieving the results of the expression.

Optimize inner loops first.

This example of repeated calculations makes use of the subscript for part of the calculation. For example,

PL/I

```
DO I = 1 TO 10;
    DO J = 1 TO 10;
        A(I,J) = B(I,J) + D/I + D/K;
    END;
END;
```

The expressions D/K and D/I are repeated calculations and should be removed from the inner loop. For instance,

PL/I

```
DK = D/K;
DO I = 1 TO 10;
      DI = D/I;
      DO J = 1 TO 10;
          A(I,J) = B(I,J) + DI + DK;
      END;
END;
```

In this calculation D/K is done once instead of 100 times. Also, the calculation D/I is done 10 times instead of 100 times. A move operation is substituted for a division operation. Moves are usually cheaper than arithmetic operations. There is still one expression that can be removed from the loop. Can you find it?

Some compilers do not process loop iterations as fast as expected because of costly loop-closing code. If true, the following may be improved.

FORTRAN

```
    DO 12 I = 1,1000
       A(I) = 0.0
 12 CONTINUE
```

An improvement can be made by

FORTRAN

```
    DO 12 I = 1,1000,2
       A(I) = 0.0
       A(I+1) = 0.0
 12 CONTINUE
```

which reduces the number of increments and loop closings by half. Notice that more core is required. This is called *unrolling* a loop.

Loops can often be combined. To illustrate,

PL/I

```
DO I = 1 TO 500;
    X(I) = 0.0;
END;
DO I = 1 TO 500;
    Y(I) = 0.0;
END;
```

146

An obvious method to reduce both time and memory is

```
DO I = 1 TO 500;
   X(I) = 0.0;
   Y(I) = 0.0;
END;
```

which is called *loop jamming*, or loop combining, or loop fusion. Loop jamming reduces loop overhead and storage space usage.

A final example of loop optimization that does the opposite of loop jamming is

ALGOL W

```
FOR I := 1 UNTIL 100
   DO
      IF (T) THEN X(I) := A(I) + B(I)
             ELSE X(I) := A(I) - B(I);
```

Here the IF statement must be evaluated for each iteration (100 times) even though the logical variable T cannot change within the loop. A more efficient method is

ALGOL W

```
IF (T) THEN
         FOR I := 1 UNTIL 100 DO
            X (I) := A(I) + B(I)
         ELSE
         FOR I := 1 UNTIL 100 DO
            X(I) := A(I) - B(I);
```

Now the IF statement is evaluated only once. This process is called *unswitching*. Execution time is decreased at the expense of core storage.

CONDITIONAL EXPRESSIONS

If the IF THEN ELSE construct is available, it can be used at some point during execution when a single variable must be checked for several values. The usual approach is

```
IF (A = 1) THEN MOVE C TO D.
IF (A = 2) THEN MOVE C TO E.
IF (A = 3) THEN MOVE D TO C.
                .
                .
                .
```

Here even if A = 1, all IF statements will be executed. By using the ELSE construct, the comparing can be terminated as soon as a TRUE condition is found. For example,

```
IF (A = 1) THEN MOVE C TO D
    ELSE IF (A = 2) THEN MOVE C TO E
        ELSE IF (A = 3) THEN MOVE D TO C
        .
        .
        .
```

In the preceding statement, as soon as a TRUE condition is found, the rest of the conditionals are skipped because of the ELSE

A further improvement (which may reduce readability) is to place the most likely condition to be TRUE first and place the rest of the conditionals in order. That is, if A usually has the value of 3, then that statement should be first.

```
IF (A = 3) THEN MOVE D TO C
    ELSE   ...
```

We would also place the rest of the conditionals in the order of their likelihood to be TRUE In this way, the conditionals will, on an average, be completed as fast as possible.

Conditional expressions are often a source of repeated expressions. For example, if the roots of a quadratic equation are to be calculated, here is the formula.

$$\text{Roots} = \frac{-b \pm \sqrt{b^2 - 4ac}}{2a}$$

The discriminant $(b^2 - 4ac)$ must be checked for a negative value, since we cannot take the square root of a negative value. To program it, we would probably do the following.

FORTRAN

```
    IF (B*B - 4.0*A*C) 25,10,10
10  ROOT1 = (-B + SQRT(B*B - 4.0*A*C))/(2.0*A)
    ROOT2 =...
                 .
                 .
                 .
                 .
```

The expression B*B - 4.0*A*C is a repeated expression, since it is used in the IF statement and in the solution for the roots. It would be better to calculate the expression before the IF statement and store the value as follows.

FORTRAN

```
    DIS = B*B - 4.0*A*C
    IF  (DIS) 25,10,10
10  ROOT1 = (-B + SQRT(DIS))/(2.0*A)
```

It is easy to place complicated repeated expressions inside conditional statements because it is common to have to check part of the calculation first.

LOGICAL EXPRESSIONS

Proper ordering of logical expressions can save time at execution on an optimizing compiler. Some compilers will stop evaluating the following expressions as soon as the result is known.

```
    A .OR. B .OR. C ...
    X .AND. Y .AND. Z ...
```

In the first expression, as soon as a TRUE value is encountered, the whole expression is true; whereas in the second expression, as soon as a FALSE value is encountered, the entire expression is false. A good compiler stops evaluation as soon as the result is known. By proper selection of the order of the variables in these expressions, time can be saved at execution. That is, in the expression

```
    A .OR. B .OR. C
```

the variable that is most likely to be true should be first. If C is usually TRUE and A sometimes TRUE and B is seldom TRUE, then the order should be

$$C \text{ .OR. } A \text{ .OR. } B \text{ ...}$$

In order to take advantage of evaluation optimization, the programmer should arrange the variables in a left-to-right order so that the leftmost variable would most frequently cause termination of the entire logical expression. A similar rule can be developed for a series of AND conditions.

Some compilers do not stop the evaluation as soon as the result is known. For instance;

PL/I

$$\text{IF } (A > B) \text{ \& } (C < D) \text{ THEN ...}$$

This expression can be rearranged to speed up execution as follows.

PL/I

$$\text{IF } (A > B)$$
$$\text{THEN IF } (C < D)$$
$$\text{THEN ...}$$

In the second example, it will not always be necessary to evaluate both comparisons, but greater care must be taken if ELSE clauses are used.

SUBSCRIPTS

Subscripts are costly both in machine time and storage, but they also are useful. Thus no programmer would be willing to stop using them no matter what improvement in efficiency would result. Several steps can be taken, however, to improve the efficiency of subscripting.

If a subscripted item is referred to more than once within the same statement or group of statements, assign the element to a variable. For example,

$$X = (A(I) + 1/A(I)) + A(I)$$

should be changed to

```
AI = A(I)
 X = (AI + 1/AI) + AI
```

The second example uses only one subscript evaluation, whereas the first needs three subscript evaluations. But an optimizing compiler would probably do this for you.

Next, be sure you are not using subscripts inside loops where a single variable could be used. Here is an example of a nested loop.

PL/I

```
DO I = 1 TO 10;
   DO K = 1 TO 25;
      B(K) = B(K) + A(I);
   END;
END;
```

In this nested loop, $A(I)$ must have its subscript calculated each pass through the inner loop, even though it does not change in the inner loop. A much more efficient program would be:

PL/I

```
DO   I = 1 TO 10;
     AI = A(I);
     DO K = 1 TO 25;
        B(K) = B(K) + AI;
     END;
END;
```

In the first program the subscript for $A(I)$ was calculated $25 \times 10 = 250$ times. In this second program the subscript for $A(I)$ is calculated only 10 times. Since it is time consuming to calculate subscripts, you should remove all unnecessary ones from loops and replace them by unsubscripted variables. Figure 3.1 contains another example of reducing subscript calculations.

Another characteristic of subscripts is that the more subscripts there are, the less efficient the program. That is, an array of $A(720)$ is much more efficient than an array of $A(12, 5, 12)$ Most individuals would rather work with an array of two or more subscripts if this has mnemonic meaning to the programmer. But if the programmer has a subprogram that uses multiple subscripts and the subprogram is heavily used, then a change to single subscripts is probably in order once the program is debugged. Some programmers use single dimensioning all the time and seem to feel that there is little loss of readability.

PL/I   Slow

```
DO I = 1 TO N;
    DO J = 1 TO M;
        A(I,J) = 0;
        DO K = 1 TO L;
            A(I,J) = A(I,J) + B(J,K) * C(K,J);
        END;
    END;
END;
```

PL/I   Faster

```
DO I = 1 TO N;
    DO J = 1 TO M;
        TEMP = 0;
        DO K = 1 TO L;
            TEMP = TEMP + B(J,K) * C(K,J);
        END;
        A(I,J) = TEMP;
    END;
END;
```

Figure 3.1. An example of reducing subscript calculations

To transform a two-dimensional N*M matrix into a vector of N*M elements, we can use one of the following methods.

1. When the first subscript is to vary the most rapidly, the Kth element is given by

$$\text{VECTOR (K) = MATRIX (I,J)}$$

where K = I + [N*(J - 1)] .

2. When the last subscript is to vary the most rapidly, the Kth element is given by

$$\text{VECTOR (K) = MATRIX (I,J)}$$

where K = J + [M*(I - 1)] .

Method 1 changes $\begin{bmatrix} a & b & c \\ d & e & f \end{bmatrix}$ into $[a \quad d \quad b \quad e \quad c \quad f]$.

Method 2 changes $\begin{bmatrix} a & b & c \\ d & e & f \end{bmatrix}$ into $[a \quad b \quad c \quad d \quad e \quad f]$.

Because these methods of changing a two-dimensional array to a one-dimensional array will reduce the readability of most programs, it should be used sparingly.

Another method for reducing the number of subscripts is to make two- or multidimensional arrays equivalent to a one-dimensional array. Very often it is necessary to set every element of a multidimensional array to zero. The normal method is

FORTRAN

```
DIMENSION A(2,3,4,5)
            .
            .
            .
DO 10 I = 1,2
    DO 10 J = 1,3
        DO 10 K = 1,4
            DO 10 L = 1,5
                A(I,J,K,L) = 0.0
10 CONTINUE
            .
            .
            .
```

which requires four subscripts and four loops. A much more efficient solution to the same problem is

FORTRAN

```
        DIMENSION A(2,3,4,5),B(120)
        EQUIVALENCE ( A(1,1,1,1),B(1) )
                    .
                    .
                    .
        DO 10 I = 1,120
           B(I) = 0.0
    10 CONTINUE
```

These statements set the four-dimensional array A equivalent to the one-dimensional array B. Then only one subscript and one loop are needed to zero the array. The preceding example has the advantages of storage conservation, faster compile, and much faster execution. The disadvantage is it reduces readability of the program, since a reader must notice that two arrays are equivalent. The reduction in readability can be a serious drawback if it contributes to confusion or makes modification of the program more difficult.

Complicated subscript calculations within a loop should be avoided. For example:

FORTRAN

```
        DO  6  I = 1, 10
            X(3*I+4) = Y(3*I+4) + C
     6 CONTINUE
```

Two complicated subscript calculations are made each time the loop is executed. Since both subscripts are calculated the same way, the subscript could be calculated once, set equal to a new variable, and then that variable used as follows.

FORTRAN

```
        DO  6 I = 1, 10
            IK = 3*I+4
            X(IK) = Y(IK) + C
     6 CONTINUE
```

Although an improvement, a greater improvement can be made by rewriting the loop incrementing.

FORTRAN

```
DO  6  I = 7, 34, 3
    X(I) = Y(I) + C
6 CONTINUE
```

Subscripted-variable references with constant subscripts generally do not need any programmer optimization. Most compilers calculate the address arithmetic for constant subscripts (such as $A(7)=$) during compilation so that no subscripting is necessary during execution.

Some languages, such as PL/I, allow array expressions. That is,

PL/I

```
DO I = 1 TO 100
   A(I) = B(I)
END:
```

can be replaced by

```
A = B
```

The complete array will be processed if the array name alone is mentioned. When you use array expressions, as in the example, the compiler will choose the most efficient method for handling the array.

Most compilers will generate code to input/output a whole array if just the array name (without a subscript) is listed in the I/O data list. Although it is the most efficient way to input/output arrays, it works only when the complete array is to be handled and when the order of array I/O is acceptable.

Subscript Mode

Every programming language has a special data type that is preferred for subscripting. This mode should be used whenever possible, since it will speed up the process. Use of the wrong mode for subscripts causes the machine to do several conversions for each subscript reference. The difference in efficiency is easy to measure. Simply execute a program twice, once with inefficient subscripts and once with correct subscripts. The difference in execution time is usually quite noticeable. Subscripts are normally most efficient when in binary form.

Use the preferred variable type for subscripts.

Subscript Form

Most compilers permit a wide variety of arithmetic expressions as subscripts. But some constructions of subscript expressions permit optimizations. The constructions that permit optimizations are

1. V integer variable
2. C integer constant
3. $V \pm C$ integer variable plus or minus an integer constant
4. $C * V$ positive integer constant times an integer variable
5. $C_1 * V \pm C_2$ positive integer constant times integer variable plus or minus a positive integer constant

Several of the earlier compilers (FORTRAN II) actually restricted subscripts to the preceding form.

The subscripts must be exactly in the forms shown above. An algebraically equivalent subscript will usually not permit the same optimization. That is, $A(I+3)$ may permit optimization, whereas $A(3+I)$ does not.

The foregoing subscript forms permit at least partial evaluation at compile time. For example, $A(2)$ can have the location calculated at compile time so that no subscript calculation is necessary during execution.

INPUT/OUTPUT

Input/output (I/O) is time consuming and should always be cut to a minimum. In other words, do not read anything in that can be calculated inside the program. In addition, make sure that each I/O statement transfers as much information as possible to or from a minimum of physical records. That is, two consecutive I/O commands to the same device can often be combined into one command. This step reduces the number of calls to the general I/O subroutines and supervisory requests. Also, don't forget to remove all excess I/O statements after debugging.

Each language has a most efficient way to read or write information. If a program is doing a great deal of input or output, considerable time can normally be saved by using the most efficient method of I/O. For example, unformatted I/O is generally faster than formatted I/O. Unformatted I/O can be used with tapes, disks, and cards if the data is to be written out and then reread by the same or a different program. Accuracy is also better with unformatted records, and less space is needed. Unformatted I/O is faster because it requires no conversions or formatting of data from internal to external form or vice versa. Unformatted I/O is more accurate because significant digits can be dropped when converting data from the internal machine form to the external formatted form.

Printed Output

Printed output should be reduced to the minimum necessary. Not only is it time consuming to print, but, in addition, large reports full of pages of numbers are seldom read by anyone. Instead print only what the user wishes to read. Apart from saving machine time, paper, and money, the computer can disregard all uninteresting results (which must be adequately specified) far more quickly than unwanted paper can be torn up and assigned to the wastebasket. From an efficiency point of view, it is almost always cheaper to write the extra statements to eliminate unwanted output than to print out unwanted output.

Computer paper is expensive, so don't print merely one number on a line when printing many lines. Program ecologically — print as much information as readable on each line. Old computer printouts can be used as scratchpaper. Also, computer cards and paper are high-grade material that can be profitably recycled.

Cards

When using cards, read or punch as few as possible. This situation is achieved by packing as much information as will fit on each card. Decimals can usually be eliminated, which means that more digits can be placed on the card.

But the format of information on the card is limited by the input source or what other uses the card is to have. If the physical card is not needed and volume is large, then tape or disk files should always be considered in place of cards.

Sometimes input can be greatly reduced. Here is a column of numbers that could be input.

$$10.0$$
$$10.1$$
$$10.2$$
$$\cdot$$
$$\cdot$$
$$\cdot$$
$$24.9$$
$$25.0$$

This approach wastes a great deal of machine time, since you could read the starting and ending value $(10.0, 25.0)$ and the increment (0.1) and the computer can calculate the intervening values.

Magnetic Tapes

If storing intermediate computer data that does not require physical form, such as cards, magnetic tape is usually cheaper. Magnetic tape can be used only for sequential files. A comparison of the cost of magnetic tapes and cards shows that as soon as you wish to punch over 4000 cards, a magnetic tape is cheaper. This fact, however, is only half the picture, since magnetic tape can be used over and over and cards can be used only once. Morever, cards are bulky, whereas magnetic tape is compact. The only time that cards should be used for output is when the volume is small, say less than 1000 cards, or when the physical card is needed for some other purpose.

A tape is much more efficient for storing or processing data. The slowest tape drives write about 4000 characters per *second*, whereas the fastest card punches punch only 400 characters per second. A magnetic tape can easily hold the equivalent of 200,000 cards.

Tapes can be used efficiently or inefficiently, depending on how the data is organized on the tape. Tapes are organized into records, blocks, and files. A *file* is the complete set of records processed in the job. A *block* is a collection of records. And the *record* is the data that is processed each time a read or write command appears in the program. If records are unblocked, then each time a record is read it is read from the tape. Reading the physical tape is slow and inefficient in comparison to reading from a buffer area. If records are grouped into blocks, the whole block is read and stored in a buffer at one time. Each write command in the program then puts a record in the buffer area. Once the buffer is full, a physical write (issued by the control program) records the block on the tape. Input works similarly — that is, blocks of records are read automatically from the tape, and each input statement of the program causes one record to be transferred from the buffer. The computer can transfer records from the buffer much faster than from the tape.

Here is how a block of records looks on a tape.

This block has n records. When the block is exhausted, a new block is read in automatically by the supervisor. Generally input/output is double-buffered, which means that two blocks are available. Thus blocks of records can be transferred to or from one buffer while the other buffer is being processed. The collection of records into a buffer area and the transfer of a block of records from or to the magnetic tape are handled automatically by the computer. All the programmer does is specify the record type, record size, and buffer size. If blocks are large enough, there should be no waiting for input/output, since one buffer should always be ready for use.

Each block is separated by interblock gap (IBG), which requires six-tenths of an inch of tape. This gap is required by the tape drives for proper reading. If you put unblocked card images on a tape with a recording density of 800 bpi (bytes per inch), this means that 80 characters would need 0.1 inch. Since the IBG needs 0.6 inch, Fig. 3.2 shows how the tape would look. Thus the ratio of IBG to data is

0.6 inch IBG

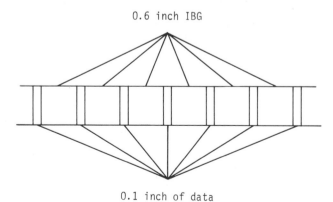

0.1 inch of data

Figure 3.2

6:1, which means that a great deal of time is spent reading the IBG. In contrast, if blocks are 1600 characters long (20 card images), there is only one 0.6 inch IBG for each 2.0 inches of data.

Efficiency is gained by using large blocks in sequential files. If only one record is in each block, then a block must be processed for each input/output statement. Since it is common to charge for input/output (I/O), the process can be quite expensive. Also, much time is wasted while waiting for new records to be processed. If ten records are included in each block, only one-tenth as much input/output must be done. And if 100 records are to be included in each block, only one-hundredth as many input/outputs must be done. This situation may lead the unexpecting to assume that very large blocks are always best, which is partially true.

> *Block input/output efficiently.*

Two problems prevent the use of infinite blocks: errors and storage. If you have an input/output error on a tape, you will often lose the whole block. If one record is involved, then the loss is not as serious as losing a block of 1000 records. So if tape I/O errors are common, use small blocks. Most tape I/O errors are caused by dirty tape drives, however, so it would be better to start keeping your tape drives cleaner.

Buffers

The second limitation is storage requirements. The larger your block size, the less time needed and the more storage needed. This is a case where execution efficiency costs storage. Each buffer requires storage. There is usually a maximum-sized block that can be read. On some computers it is 32,760 characters. If there are two buffers and your block size is the maximum, which may be 32,760 characters, then the buffers use 65,520 characters of storage. If your program is large or your computer size is small, then this block size would not be possible,

So what is an easy answer? Assuming that I/O errors are not much of a problem (and they shouldn't be if the tape drives are clean and maintenance is good), then a block size of 4000 characters would normally be a minimum. This would be 50 card images (50 × 80 = 4,000). Maximum would be whatever could be handled by storage.

In order to optimize the tape handling so as to avoid blocks that are too small or too large, an ideal situation is the following. Each time a block of data is being processed, some computing is done. That is, some calculations are done on the block. Thus ideally we always want a block of data waiting for computing. The computer can process a buffer while other computing is going on. So, if the amount of time necessary to do the computations on each block was just a little greater than the amount of time needed to I/O an old block, then, on a double buffer machine, a block of data would always be available. Also, block sizes would not have to be excessively large.

Thus, on a file where each record involves a great deal of calculation, small block sizes can be used. But on an inactive file or where little calculation is done, longer block sizes should increase efficiency.

Some machines allow for an increase in the number of buffers. For long jobs that have a great deal of input/output, try comparing the execution times for a few test runs, using different numbers of buffers and different size blocks in order to determine the most efficient combination.

The number of buffers to assign to each file can be established for each program. But since buffers require storage, there is often a limit to the number used. One major method of saving buffer space is to have more than one buffer use the same storage. This practice is possible only when two or more files will not be open at the same time. It allows one file to use a buffer area early in a program and another file to use the same area after the first file has been closed.

It is common in programming for one file to be used by several programs. We can adjust the number of buffers used for each program, but we cannot change the blocking factor for most file types (i.e., for sequential tape files), since the record size and blocking factor are already established. Therefore the system design phase must carefully consider block size in respect to memory requirements and speed of processing for each job in the system. Otherwise too much storage will be used, or processing might be quite slow.

Most systems are double-buffered. That is, two buffers are assigned to each file. If storage is desperately needed, the second buffer is available. This second buffer can usually be eliminated, a fact that will result in savings in storage and cost execution time because there will be no overlapping of I/O operations.

Disk Files

Stating how to organize disk files for efficient processing is more difficult than in the case of tape because there are many ways to do so. A few important principles can be given, however.

First, unformatted I/O should be used with disk files. Efficiency is improved in two ways. There is a space savings of disk space, and no conversion from internal (machine) data to an external (disk) representation is needed. Furthermore, unformatted I/O always provides the best accuracy in transferring data.

When using more than one disk file in the same job, do not place all the files on the same disk. Instead use different disks in order to allow overlapping of file processing. If two files are placed on the same disk, too much time is lost waiting for the disk arm to be correctly positioned. If possible, make sure that the disk files use different channels, too.

Sequential Files. For sequential disk files, the blocks of data should be close to but should not exceed the capacity of a track. If the program is so large that blocks of this size cannot be accommodated within the computer, an integral number of blocks should be fitted to a track. Disk space is needed for interblock gaps; so the smaller the blocks, the more disk space is used for the IBG. A table of opportune block sizes is usually provided by the manufacturer.

Thus sequential disk files are similar to sequential tape files in that larger blocks (but not greater than the track capacity) provide the most efficient operation. Transfer of numerous, very short logical blocks is undesirable.

If the processing is I/O bound, it may be more efficient to decrease the size of the block and increase the number of buffers used. Long jobs might permit some experimentation, using different combinations of block size and number of buffers to determine the most efficient combinations.

EXPLORE NEW COMMANDS

Once programmers have achieved a reasonable familiarity with their programming language, they should read the programming reference manual in detail. In reading the manual, try using some of the program language commands that you have not used in the past. You will probably discover that you have not been using many commands to their fullest capacity. A rereading of the reference manual will introduce fresh programming techniques, and, hopefully, some will result in more efficient programs.

WARNING MESSAGES

An often-overlooked technique for a sharp increase in compiling and executing efficiency is the removal of any conditions causing warning messages. Since warning messages do not prevent execution of the program, there is a tendency to ignore them, which is a serious error from an efficiency point of view. Time is lost each time a compile is done, and severe penalties of execution time or core usage can result.

In FORTRAN, for example, variables used in COMMON statements must be aligned properly. If they are not aligned, *considerable* execution time can be lost. A warning message is provided on this point that is often ignored.

The correction of any code to remove warning messages at compile time is probably the easiest and most profitable method to increase execution efficiency. Thus programmers interested in efficient execution should first check to see if they can remove any compile warning messages. Warning messages are often given on alignment problems and conversions.

LOAD MODULES

Load modules are compiled programs. Load modules should be used for all production programs. Once a program is debugged and tested, a load module can be created for future runs. Load modules on disk are the most efficient. They save time by eliminating the compiling and linking steps each time the program is executed. Recompiling a source program for each production run is wasteful and usually unnecessary.

Use load modules.

MODULES

Since the purpose of this chapter is to cover program efficiency in full, one of the main disadvantages of using modules, as far as efficiency is concerned, should be listed. I believe, however, that the multitude of advantages (readability, maintainability, debugging, testing) of modular approach outweigh any disadvantages of less efficient program execution.

Modular design aids writing, debugging, testing, and modification and thus can save a great amount of programming and machine time at the writing stage. This is an important factor, since some programs spend more machine time at the writing than at the production stage.

Subroutines can be programmed, debugged, and tested individually. As a consequence, machine time can be saved because long programs increase in compiling time faster than linearly.

A disadvantage when using subroutines is that subroutines can cost core storage. Subroutines cost storage and time because linkage instructions are necessary to coordinate the calling program with its subroutines. Some COBOL compilers generate a fixed overhead of 1K core for each subroutine. But the space penalty is easily made up if the subroutine is called from more than one place in the main program; otherwise the subroutine would have to appear in several places.

Strictly from an efficiency point of view, a subroutine that is called from only one place in the main program could be handled more efficiently by being coded at the place called from instead of by using a subroutine. Coding in line eliminates the linkage instructions and thus saves time and storage.

You must decide if your primary interest is saving time or storage, since this is a situation in which the saving of one resource results in using the other resource. If the primary interest is in saving execution time, then subroutines should not be used and the coding should be done in line. But if the primary consideration is saving storage space, tasks that would appear more than once in the program should be considered for subroutines.

If the subroutine must pass an argument list, extra time and storage are needed. Argument addresses must be passed from the calling main program and then linked in some fashion to the instructions that will use them. All this takes time and storage.

If the argument list can be eliminated or reduced, considerable savings will result. The normal method for reducing or eliminating argument lists is to use the command that places these variables in a common storage area where all the subprograms can find the variables.

Therefore when a variable in a subroutine always corresponds to the same variable in the main program at every call of the subroutine, the variable should be placed in the named common area. But when a variable in the subroutine corresponds to different variables at different calls from the main program, the variable must be part of the argument list. If an argument is normally a constant, it can be assigned to a variable that can then be placed in common. There is a tendency to place all variables in an argument list. It should be avoided, since the common storage is much more efficient. Both storage and time are saved by using common storage.

Another method to reduce the number of items in a parameter list is to combine several to form a contiguous area. For example, a module for doing heading routines may have a number of items passed as parameters, such as date, page count, and heading labels. If these items are combined into a single data area, the number of parameters can be reduced. Languages like PL/I and COBOL have data structures available that make it easy to combine items into one item.

COMPUTER LORE

Each computer and compiler has some efficiency lore — that is, information, if known and used, that will make a program compile or execute more efficiently. But information of this type is usually very machine dependent and often is available only from assembly listings.

An example in FORTRAN for one rather popular computer is that if statement numbers are evenly distributed over their range, the program will compile faster. This situation occurs because, for its internal use, the compiler places statement numbers in tables and these tables are divided into strings that are searched many times during compilation. If the number of entries in each string is about equal, the average time required to find a statement number is reduced.

Statement numbers are assigned to five strings in the statement number table according to the last digit in the statement number. Statement numbers ending in 0 or 1 are placed in the first string, those ending in 2 or 3 are placed in the second, those ending in 4 or 5 are placed in the third, and so on. Thus statement numbers that are evenly distributed will decrease compilation time.

A similar situation occurs with variable names. Names are assigned to a string according to the length of the variable name. Names that are one character long are assigned to the first string, names two characters long are assigned to the second string, and so forth. Thus if names are fairly evenly distributed over the different strings, less search time will be needed to find each name.

These comments on computer lore are simply to illustrate that if efficiency is very important, you must not only know the general rules in this chapter but also learn some of the lore of your computer and its compiler and operating system.

CONCLUSION

It seems evident that the writing of efficient programs will continue to be important in the foreseeable future. Indeed, such writing has assumed a renewed importance with the availability of minicomputers. The development of storage-efficient programming can mean the difference between being able to run a program in a straightforward manner or having to segment the program for an overlay, resorting to assembly language, looking for a larger computer, or not solving the problem. Programs that do not use computer time efficiently can rapidly absorb all computer time, thereby reducing the number of problems that can be solved.

Programs written in high-level languages are often written only once, then patched, repaired, added to, and thus inflated to the point that available storage is not enough. In the past, if a program could not reside in core because of its size, the solution was always to get larger equipment. But it has been observed that no matter how much core is available, there is never enough. Instead a few techniques, such as those discussed in this chapter, once learned will continue to pay dividends in faster and smaller programs. Otherwise a computer installation will find itself continually plagued by programs that are too slow or too large.

PROGRAMMING MAXIMS

If it doesn't work, it doesn't make any difference how efficient it is.

Establish efficiency goals at the design stage.

Readability is usually more important than efficiency.

Use an optimizing compiler.

Profile your code.

Initialize variables at compile time.

Avoid mixed data types.

Optimize inner loops first.

Use the preferred variable type for subscripts.

Block input/output efficiently.

Use load modules.

EXERCISES

Chapter Review

1. What is the most important factor in writing an efficient program?

2. What type of programs should be optimized? What type should not?

3. Why is an optimizing compiler still necessary even if the programmer does optimizations?

4. What are the definitions of
   (a) program overlay?
   (b) folding?
   (c) reducing the strength of an operation?
   (d) eliminating redundant expressions?
   (e) collapsing a loop?
   (f) removing invariant expressions?
   (g) unrolling a loop?
   (h) critical region?
   (i) locality?

5. When is it less efficient to use a loop than to use straight-line coding?

6. How should nested loops be arranged to reduce loop initializations and testings?

7. What areas of a program are usually the most productive for optimization?

8. Put the arithmetic operations below in order of fastest to slowest.
   (a) Division   (b) Square root
   (c) Addition   (d) Exponentiation
   (e) Multiplication   (f) Subtraction

9. Code the following in the most efficient manner.
   (a) $B = \dfrac{4A}{3}$

(b) C = P**0.5
(c) Y = $5x^4 + 3x^2 - 2x + 2$
(d) T = COS(THETA) - COS(THETA)**2.0
(e) PUT = COST/2 * 4 * K
(f) T = P/2 + (6 - R)/4 - T/2
(g) Y = 6 + T**5.0
(h) T = 2 * PI/4
(i) IF (A < B) OR (C > D) THEN X=4
                           ELSE Y=0;

Problems

10. Is there an optimizing compiler available for your programming language? If so, what type of optimizations are made?

11. What compiler options are used at your installation to speed compilation during debugging?

12. What compiler options are used at your installation to speed program execution?

13. Are there compiling options on your compiler to minimize storage usage in object programs at the expense of execution speed? Is it possible to maximize execution speed at the expense of storage?

14. Select two different commands in your programming language and develop timing tests to see which command executes faster.

15. Obtain an assembly listing of one of your high-level language programs. Examine the assembly listing to see which program statements generate the most code.

16. Describe an efficient algorithm for finding all the factors of a number. For example, the factors of 12 are 1, 2, 3, 4, 6, 12. If you are not positive that it is the most efficient algorithm, program it.

17. *Chess players.* Describe an algorithm for placing the maximum number of knights on a chessboard so that no knight can capture another.

18. In your programming language, what steps can be taken at compilation to speed up execution?

19. What are the most efficient types of variables in your programming language for subscripts?

20. What are the most efficient types of variables in your programming language for numerous noninteger calculations?

21. How does your compiler handle this expression?

$$B = 3.0 / 4.0 * B$$

Is the constant expression calculated at compile time or execution time? A look at the assembly code will usually tell you the answer.

22. How do you do a program overlay in your programming language?

23. Is there an equivalence method in your programming language? How would you set up two arrays so that they use the same storage locations?

24. In your programming language, how can you initialize variables (arrays) at compile time instead of execution time?

25. Does your compiler store constants in the correct form so that conversions are unnecessary during execution?

26. On your computer, how long does each of the following operations take? (Look up the machine instructions.)
    (a) Integer addition
    (b) Real addition
    (c) Integer multiplication
    (d) Real multiplication
    (e) Real division

27. Obtain an assembly language listing of a high-level language program. See if you can determine which statements seem to be inefficient.

28. Does your computer use double buffers for input/output? Can you request more or fewer buffers? If yes, try changing the number of buffers and see if it will change the time used by a program.

29. Find a program that needs optimizing and try to optimize it by using the techniques discussed in this chapter.

30. Can you think of techniques for optimizing your program that are not discussed in this chapter? If so, send me a list of your new techniques.

Programs

31. Write a program to read a positive integer N and then sum all the integers from 1 to N.

32. *Compound interest.* Assume that $100 is to be deposited for 55 years at 6% compounded quarterly. Program this problem.

33. Assume that I, J, K, and L are positive integers less than 20. Write a program to find the values that satisfy the equation

$$I^3 + J^3 + K^3 = L^3$$

Your program should be both readable and efficient. Compare your solution to someone else's solution.

34. Sort problems are good tests of algorithm selection and efficiency techniques. Read N numbers and then sort the numbers in ascending sequence and print the sorted numbers. If you have a function that generates random numbers, use it to generate 1000 random numbers and sort these numbers. Compare your program to another program to see which one is the fastest. For information on sorting algorithms, I refer to Donald E. Knuth, *The Art of Computer Programming*, Vol. 3 (Reading, Mass.: Addison-Wesley, 1973).

35. *Table searching.* Generate a table of 1000 random integers between 1 and 10,000. Write a program that reads a positive integer less than 10,000 and then determines if the number is in the table. You can organize the table and searching any way you like.

36. *Diagonal matrix.* *A diagonal matrix has zeros everywhere except in the principal diagonal. Write a program to store and multiply two diagonal matrices.

37. *Symmetric matrix.* A symmetric matrix is identical with its transpose. That is, for any element $a_{ij} = a_{ji}$. Write a program to store and multiply two symmetric matrices. Is your program efficient?

38. *Triangular matrix.* A lower-triangular matrix has all zeros above the principal diagonal. That is, $a_{ij} = 0$ if $j > i$. Write an efficient program to add two large lower-triangular matrices.

39. *Tetrahedral matrix.* A tetrahedral matrix is a three-dimensional triangular matrix. After you figure out what one looks like, write a program to store and manipulate the elements efficiently.

40. *Tridiagonal matrix.* A tridiagonal matrix has zeros everywhere except in the three central diagonals — that is, the superdiagonal, the diagonal, and subdiagonal.

$$a_{ij} = 0 \quad \text{if} \quad |i - j| > 1.$$

Write a program to add two tridiagonal matrices efficiently.

*On these matrix problems, first figure out an efficient way to store the matrix.

41. *Repeated elements.* Assume that you have a large rectangular matrix. Some of the columns in the matrix are identical. Devise a method for storing the matrix without storing any identical columns more than once. Then assume that two of these matrices are identical in size, and add the matrices. Do not assume that the two matrices have the same columns repeated.

42. *Sparse matrices.* Assume that you have two very large matrices (i.e., 1000 by 1000 elements each) and that most of the elements (95%) are zero. Devise a technique to store the arrays efficiently. Then write a program to add arrays and multiply arrays.

43. If the preceding problems are too easy, try a sparse symmetric matrix or a sparse triangular matrix. Is a sparse symmetric, triangular matrix possible? Careful.

44. Write a program that finds the smallest and largest value in a vector of size n. What is the minimum number of comparisons that are necessary for a vector of size n?

45. Write a program that reverses the order of items in a vector. What is the minimum number of moves needed for a vector of size n?

46. Does the system you use allow you to read the clock? How do you use the clock and what sort of time can you get (time of day, elapsed time, cpu time)? Does the clock give you misleading results? Can you measure the execution time of a routine?

47. *Armstrong number.* An n-digit number is an Armstrong number if the sum of the nth power of the digits is equal to the original number. For example, 153 is a three-digit number and

$$153 = 1^3 + 5^3 + 3^3$$

A four-digit Armstrong number is

$$1634 = 1^4 + 6^4 + 3^4 + 4^4$$

Find all the two- three- and four-digit Armstrong digits. Write an efficient program.

Projects

48. Wolf Island is a 20 by 20 plot populated by rabbits, male wolves, and female wolves, all acting wild. In the beginning a few of each kind of the inhabitants are scattered about the island. Rabbits

are rather stupid; at each time step they move with equal probability to one of the eight squares in their neighborhood (except as restricted by the coastline). One-ninth of the time, therefore, they simply sit still. Each rabbit also has a probability of 0.2 of becoming two rabbits. Each female wolf also moves randomly unless there is a rabbit on one of the eight neighboring squares, in which case she gives chase. If she and the rabbit end up on the same square, she eats it and gains one "fat." Otherwise she loses 0.1 "fat." Zero-fat wolves are dead. Each male wolf behaves like the females unless there are no rabbits nearby, then if there is a female on one of the eight neighboring squares, he gives chase. If a male and female end up on the same square with no rabbits to eat, they produce an offspring with a random sex.

Program the ecological simulation suggested and watch the population counts over several time periods. (Thanks to Bill McKeeman for this problem.)

49. The previous simulation is inherently unstable (Wolf Island is destined to be a desert). Add a hedgerow (an area forbidden to wolves) and observe the results.

50. *Keyword search.* You have a list of books and article titles. Your program must accept keywords and search to see if any titles contain the keywords and then print those titles. You have so many titles that you cannot keep all titles in core at one time. You can organize the search and titles any way you wish, but if the program is too slow, the project will have to be dropped and you will become unemployed.

51. *Phone number search.* Your telephone company gets many requests from you know who for an address and name, given a telephone number. They have been handling the requests manually but have just hired you because you said you could do it efficiently on a computer. Start with a small list of telephone numbers, but plan the system so that it could become rather large. People can be either added or deleted from the file.

52. Write a program to read five poker hands. That is, given five (or seven) cards in each hand, indicate which hand is the best (a pair, two pair, flush, etc.).

53. *Tower of Hanoi.* The Tower of Hanoi consist of three pegs A, B, C on a board with n squares of varying size. At the start, all squares are stacked on peg A in order of size with the largest square on the bottom. Your program is to indicate how to move the squares from peg A to peg B one at a time with the restriction that no square is ever placed on a smaller square. Peg C can

be used as needed. How many moves are needed for a stack of n squares?

54. *Pick up sticks.* Write a program to play pick up sticks. The program should read the following data.
    (a) The number of sticks.
    (b) The number of sticks in each stack.
    (c) The maximum number of sticks that can be removed in any single move.
    A good solid program should be able to win against a mere mortal.

55. The board game shown has pegs in all the holes except the center hole. You can jump one peg at a time, and each time a peg is jumped it is removed from the board. The goal is to end up with only one peg, in the middle hole. Although a little difficult, a program could be written to play the game successfully.

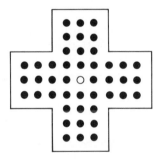

56. *Soma cube.* *All of you have probably tried this game. It is a 3 by 3 cube of seven pieces. Once you take it apart, it is difficult to put back together. Write a program to put the Soma cube back together. You should get a Soma cube and try it before attempting to write a program. Calculate how many different solutions there are.

57. *Instant insanity.* The puzzle consists of four colored cubes. The solution is achieved when the cubes are aligned so that each of the four colors appears on each side of the stack. Write a program to indicate how to arrange the colored cubes.

58. *Eight queens problem.* Given an 8 by 8 chessboard and eight queens that are hostile to each other, find a position for each

*In the next three problems solutions cannot be found unless an efficient algorithm is used. For a discussion of these problems see W. M. McKeeman, "A Formal Model for Space-Filling Puzzles," *Machine Intelligence*, 8, D. Michie and T. Elcock, eds., 1977.

queen such that no queen may be taken by any other queen. That is, every row, column, and diagonal contains at most one queen. Find all the solutions.

59. On the problems below, you must program an efficient algorithm and decide how much effort to put into the problem. The solution may be very difficult or even impossible.
    (a) Find two integers m, n such that $m^2 = 2n^2$.
    (b) Find some integer solutions for x, y, z, where $x^3 + y^3 + z^3 = 1$. Two solutions are

$$x = y = 1 \qquad z = -1$$
$$x = y = -4 \qquad z = 5$$

    (c) Find all solutions of the equation $x^3 - y^2 = 18$, where x, y are integers.
    (d) For n, x, y, z integers and $n > 2$, is there a solution for $x^n + y^n = z^n$?
    (e) Generate a map so that more than four colors are needed to color the map in order that no two contiguous districts shall be of the same color.
    (f) Write a program to generate some interesting mazes with only one path.

For similar problems and a solution to the four-color problem, see *Scientific American* "Mathematical Games," by Martin Gardner, April 1975.

REFERENCES

Aho, Alfred, John Hopcroft, and Jeffrey Ullman, "Design of Efficient Algorithms," *The Design and Analysis of Computer Algorithms.* Reading, Mass.: Addison-Wesley, 1974.

Allen, F. E., "Program Optimization," *Annual Review in Automatic Programming*, Vol. 5. New York: Pergamon Press, 1969.

Cohn, Laurence S., *Effective Use of ANS COBOL Computer Programming Language.* New York: John Wiley & Sons, 1975.

Ignalls, Daniel H. H., "FETE: A FORTRAN Execution Time Estimator." Available from National Technical Information Service, Springfield, Va. 22151. Document number PB–198 510, 1971.

Knuth, Donald E., "An Empirical Study of FORTRAN Programs." Available from National Technical Information Service, Springfield, Va. 22151, 1970.

Kreitzberg, Charles B., and Ben Shneiderman, *The Elements of FORTRAN Style.* New York: Harcourt Brace Jovanovich, 1972.

Morrison, J. E., "User Performance in Virtual Storage Systems", *IBM System Journal*, No. 3, 1973.

"Optimization and Efficient Performances," *IBM System/360 Operating System PL/I (F) Language Reference Manual.* IBM Corporation.

"Programming Considerations," *IBM OS FORTRAN IV Compiler Programmer's Guide*, C28-6817.

"Programming Techniques," *IBM OS Full American National Standard COBOL.* C28-6456.

Rustin, Randall (Ed.), *Design and Optimization of Compilers.* Englewood Cliffs, N.J.: Prentice-Hall, 1972.

Samet, P. A., "Detailed Analysis of a Program — An Instructive Horror Story," *Software — Practice and Experience*, April–June 1975.

Zelkowitz, Marvin V., and William G. Bail, "Optimization of Structured Programs," *Software — Practice and Experience*, January–March 1974.

4

Program Debugging

Few occupations offer greater opportunities for making errors than programming. These errors are called *bugs*, and the art of locating an error once its existence has been established is called *debugging*. Thus a known error must exist before you are debugging; otherwise you are testing.

One measure of programmers' proficiency is their ability to find and correct their own bugs. Beginning programmers cannot locate and correct their bugs, but experienced programmers can. All programmers have program bugs.

Programmers are often trained in programming but seldom in debugging. Since debugging a program takes longer and is much more difficult than writing the original program, it is unfortunate that more time is not spent in showing how to debug. Estimates of the amount of time spent debugging verge from 50 to 90%. Writing a program is like writing a report. Both require a first draft (before bugs) and a final draft (after bugs). Seldom is the first draft the final draft in writing or programming.

Little information is available on how to debug a program. Debugging is commonly called an art to avoid the difficult task of teaching it. The process depends on the environment — that is, the machine, the language, the operating system, the problem, and even the individual program.

It is certainly true that each language, compiler, and machine lends itself to certain types of bugs or errors. The simplest example is syntax errors, which are very language dependent. Very little information is available on the relationship between a language and the number and difficulty of bugs.

This chapter covers the subject of source language debugging. For those who like to read dumps and do arithmetic in hexadecimal or octal, I offer my warmest encouragement. But one of the major reasons for using source language is to be able to avoid learning machine language. Machine language debugging has the disadvantage that it is machine dependent. Thus changes of computer due to new models or a new job can make all machine language information useless. It is my belief that skills learned should be as resistant to technological changes as possible, that is why it is more valuable to learn how to debug programs in source languages than in machine languages. Machine language and memory dump debugging are desirable tools only as a last resort after all other methods have failed.

The advantages of source language debugging are

1. It is not necessary to know machine language.
2. Output can be printed in readable form along with identifying labels.
3. Techniques from the source language can be used to debug the program.

DEBUGGING VERSUS TESTING

Many programmers confuse the debugging and testing stage of checking out programs. If a program is obviously not working correctly, then it is being debugged. So debugging always starts with some evidence of program failure. If the program seems to be working correctly, then it is being tested. Frequently, after tests have been run, the program will fall back to the debugging stage. Testing determines that an error exists; debugging localizes the cause of the error. Hence there is overlapping of the two stages. Programming time should be allotted for both stages in order to emphasize that each one needs to be done.

Beginning programmers often believe that the program only needs to be debugged. That is, once the program works for one carefully selected group of data, they believe it will work for all other data. Consequently, they are surprised when, after using and believing the results for several runs, the program produces obviously incorrect output. All previous output is then of questionable veracity.

Generally there are two approaches to debugging: either a great deal of programmer time is spent trying to avoid and detect bugs manually or the machine is used to do most of the detecting of bugs. The choice of the alternatives is governed by the amount of machine time available. There is a natural tendency (due to human laziness) to try to push most of the debugging work off on the machine. It is always best, however, to avoid bugs.

There is, nevertheless, another approach to debugging. In this approach, debugging overlaps the writing stage of programming. Some programmers prefer to write a few lines of code and then attempt to execute them to see if they work properly. Programmers who program this way are writing, debugging, and testing as they program. It would be interesting to determine which method of programming is most productive.

This step-by-step approach allows us to ferret out errors as we code. The advantage is that the code is still fresh in our minds and so errors are easier to spot. The approach is similar to dividing a program into subroutines.

DEBUGGING IS THE NEXT HURDLE

It is probable that debugging will be the next hurdle to be crossed in computing. Until the late 1950s hardware was the limiting factor in computing. Everyone was trying to squeeze his or her program into 4K of memory and have everything ready when the next read was available. Then the software epoch began. Today, with ALGOL, FORTRAN, COBOL, PL/I, and similar languages, sufficient software is available.

The present bottleneck is debugging. At present we have machines that are big and fast enough to execute most useful programs, as well as software varied enough to get these programs written.

Some people have assumed that as computer languages and compilers became more sophisticated, bugs would disappear. A few characteristics are ignored with this assumption. Logic errors cannot be discovered by compilers because that situation assumes that the compiler knows what you want to do. If the compiler did know, it could also write the program.

Programs have increased in size and complexity, thereby keeping approximately a constant level of bugs.

The First Bug

A story about the first program bug goes as follows. Early in the history of computers, when the Whirlwind I at MIT was first switched on, it failed to run. A frantic check of the wiring and hardware failed to indicate anything wrong. Finally, in desperation it was decided to check the program, then a small strip of paper tape. Thus the error was discovered — the programmers' Pandora's box, a plague of bugs descends on future generations of programmers.

ERRORS IN PROBLEM DEFINITION

A common situation is that once the program is written, the user discovers that the results are not the desired results. This situation can occur because the programmers and the users did not understand each other or because the users did not really know what they wanted. If the incorrect program does help the user discover what is wanted or if it shows the programmers what the users actually want, then all is not lost.

Sometimes, only when incorrect results are generated can the original problem be carefully redefined. Bad program definition results in a program correctly solving the wrong problem. Usually the entire program must be reprogrammed. Insist on a new time schedule when the program must be redone. Don't allow the incorrect program to use all the resources (programming time, machine time, etc.). A new program is to be written and thus a new schedule is required.

When writing a program for someone else, a warning sign that the program may not be the desired one is a feeling that the problem is not clear. In order to avoid an "incorrect" program, it is best to write down a description of what the program should do, along with a sample. Writing a description of the desired program forces those wanting the program to organize their thoughts enough to describe it accurately. Oral instructions on specifications are notoriously undependable and often lead to violent misunderstandings.

INCORRECT ALGORITHM

Once the problem is correctly defined, the programmer searches for an algorithm or method that will solve the problem. Unfortunately, the programmers may choose an incorrect algorithm or a poor algorithm, in which case they must repeat the whole process.

An example of an incorrect algorithm is an iterative method for solving an equation that diverges when another method would correctly calculate the answer. An example of a poor or badly chosen algorithm is one that correctly calculates the answer but does it very slowly. Unfortunately, often it is not possible to know that a bad algorithm was selected until after it has been tried. But some time and thought should go into algorithm selection in order to avoid redoing every program. Quite a few books are available on programming techniques, and some have programming algorithms in them. Readers who wish to avoid incorrect algorithms should familiarize themselves with books in their own fields.

ERRORS IN ANALYSIS

Errors in analysis consist of either overlooking possibilities or incorrectly solving the problem. The overlooking of possibilities includes such items as not considering negative values or small or large numbers.

Incorrectly solving the problem is normally a major or minor logic error. Here are some possibilities.

1. Not initializing variables
2. Incorrect termination of a loop
3. Incorrect indexing of a loop
4. Omitted loop initialization
5. Interchanging of two or more paths after leaving a decision statement.

The best way to debug is to minimize the need for it. A good functional design followed by a fairly detailed flowchart or synopsis will result in better coding.

Flowcharts will help prevent many errors. In addition, they can be used for reference while debugging to see if errors have occurred. A technique to check a flowchart for correctness is to take the problem definition a second time a few days later and redraw the flowchart. Then the first and second flowcharts can be compared to see where they differ. This step may seem a waste of time, but errors at this level can be catastrophic later, requiring major program revision.

GENERAL ERRORS

After an appropriate algorithm has been selected for solving a particular problem, errors can still occur during programming, regardless of the programming language used. Some are listed below.

1. Lack of knowledge or misunderstanding about the language or machine can cause errors. An example is the programmer who uses a command or function that performs differently than expected. This situation can be the result of a systems change of which the programmer is unaware.
2. An error in programming the algorithm. Perhaps the program instructions are inconsistent with the series of events required by the algorithm; examples are logic errors or coding errors, such as putting a minus sign where a plus sign is needed.
3. Syntax errors also occur.
4. Syntactically correct statements may cause execution errors; examples are division by zero or negative square roots.
5. A fifth general error is a data error caused by anomalous data. A mathematical operation performed on an alphabetic piece of data is a typical example.

With the exception of syntax errors, all these general errors are discoverable during testing that results in the program reverting to the debugging stage. Table 4.1 summarizes the errors discussed so far.

Table 4.1 Common Programming Errors

1. Error in problem definition	Correctly solving the wrong problem.
2. Incorrect algorithm.	Selecting an algorithm that solves the problem incorrectly or badly.
3. Errors in analysis.	Incorrect programming of the algorithm.
4. Semantic error.	Failure to understand how a command works.
5. Syntax error.	Failure to follow the rules of the programming language.
6. Execution error.	Failure to predict the possible ranges in calculations (i.e., division by zero, etc.)
7. Data error.	Failure to anticipate the ranges of data.
8. Documentation error.	User documentation does not match the program.

The last error could be either a programming error or an error in the documentation. One other type of error is usually called a glitch. A *glitch* is a hole or incomplete feature of a computer program. It is a commonly used computer term to describe a program problem in which the program is awkward, clumsy, or does not apply. Thus a program can still work and match the specifications, but the original specifications were incomplete.

PHYSICAL ERRORS

Here are eight physical errors that can cause program bugs.

1. Missing program cards or lines
2. Interchanging of program cards or lines
3. Additional program cards or lines (i.e., failure to remove corrected lines)
4. Missing data
5. Data out of order
6. Incorrect data format
7. Missing job control (monitor) statements
8. Referring to the wrong program listing.

Careful handling of card decks can help prevent these errors. If the missing or out-of-sequence program lines do not generate syntax errors, they can be difficult to locate.

Programs should always be consecutively numbered. This step helps to prevent or discover most of the physical errors involving program decks. Program decks that are sequence numbered also facilitate the locating of cards during debugging.

Data should be carefully edit-checked and echo-printed to avoid data errors. Echo-printing means printing all data that is read.

PROGRAM DECK MARKING

All program decks should be marked with a wide ink marker (Magic Marker, etc.). Each subroutine should have separate markings as follows.

1. Mark first card on the face with FC.
2. Mark last card on the back LC.

3. Mark program name on the tops of the deck.
4. Mark diagonal or cross strips on the top of the deck.

This practice makes identification and location easy during debugging. It will also help indicate shuffled decks.

SIMPLE CODING

Simple, straightforward coding is a great help when debugging. It is easier to avoid and detect errors if the program is written in an orderly and logical manner. In the early stages of writing a complicated program, do not hesitate to rewrite sections if it will simplify the program. Programming tricks should be completely avoided. The more "tricks" used when programming, the more difficult it is to debug your own program. Moreover, tricky programs are impossible to debug by someone who did not write the original program.

My final mention of simple coding will only refer you back to Chapter I on programming style. Many of the suggestions of program style can make your program more readable and easier to debug.

CORRECTNESS

Programs are logically correct only in a relative sense — that is, relative to a certain class of data. A program to find the largest common divisor of two input numbers is correct only if the two numbers are integers. If input is either zero or fractional, then the program would not operate correctly. So, the domain of data over which the program will operate correctly must be carefully defined. Program statements are needed to verify that the input data stays within the necessary domain of definition.

For a program to be acceptable, it must be correct. There are two ways in which a program may be incorrect: (1) if the syntax is incorrect and (2) if the program provides incorrect answers. Syntax correctness means that variable names must be correctly formed, arithmetic and logical operations must follow the syntax rules, and so forth.

SYNTAX ERRORS

The compiler's discovery of syntax errors is the most important and most taken-for-granted stage of debugging. The greater the number of errors discovered and corrected at this stage, the easier all later debugging and testing will be. The beginning programmer assumes that all syntax errors are discovered at this point. The more experienced and cynical programmer knows that many subtle "syntax" errors will not be discovered by the compiler. The trend has been to provide more of these diagnostics and to make them more specific about the error that they are reporting.

If a syntax error is defined as "anything that violates the language specifications," then many syntax errors are not discovered. An uninitialized variable, a branch into the middle of a DO loop, and an out-of-range subscript are merely a few of the errors commonly missed. Results in these operations are undefined. If such statements are compiled, they will cause the program to act in mysterious ways that can be quite difficult to detect. The absence of syntax error messages is a necessary, but not sufficient computer condition for a correct program.

Detecting syntax errors is important because these errors are certain to cause trouble in the execution. Moreover, the compiler requires that syntax errors be corrected before the execution of the program is attempted.

Examples of syntax errors are

1. Required punctuation missing
2. Unmatched parentheses
3. Missing parentheses
4. Incorrectly formed statements
5. Incorrect variable names
6. Arithmetic operators used incorrectly
7. Misspelling of reserved words.

Another variety of syntax errors involves the interaction of two or more statements. Some examples are

1. Conflicting instructions
2. Nontermination of loops
3. Duplicate or missing labels
4. Not declaring arrays
5. Illegal transfer.

If a compiler does not carefully analyze the interaction of two or more commands, it often misses some of the foregoing errors. For example, some compilers will not warn programmers if they attempt to transfer illegally into a DO loop.

Other errors that are often discovered by the compiler when checking syntax include

1. Undeclared or incorrectly declared variables
2. Typing errors
3. Use of illegal characters.

Most syntax errors are language and machine dependent; so there is little that can be said in detail about correcting individual syntax errors. A few general hints can be given, however.

One hint for correcting syntax errors is that when a great many errors are generated, simply correct the obvious errors and rerun the program. Some syntax error messages are spurious — that is, caused by other syntax errors — so a great deal of time should not be spent trying to understand a syntax error message if the error is not immediately obvious. Spurious error messages are particularly prevalent when something serious has been omitted in the program, such as variable or array declare statements.

Another is don't hesitate to read the program language manual. When trying to correct nonobvious syntax errors, a reading of syntax rules for the particular command will usually indicate the error.

The compiler used greatly affects the amount of debugging needed. A good debugging compiler can often reduce debugging time by half. A *debugging compiler* checks for more errors than a regular compiler. Syntax is more carefully examined, and the interaction of commands is checked. More importantly, numerous checks are done during execution of the source program. Uninitialized variables, out-of-range subscripts, and illegal transfers are flagged during execution. All this additional checking requires extra time, however, and so execution time is generally much slower.

FORTRAN users have long had the benefit of the debugging compiler WATFIV. Long experience with it has proven that debugging time can be significantly reduced with a good compiler. In addition, bugs are removed early in program construction.

Nevertheless, these compilers must be purchased; they do not come supplied with the computer. My opinion is that it is difficult to spend too much on a good debugging compiler. When you consider that 70% of the programmer's time and a high percentage of machine time are spent debugging, then a good debugging compiler will soon pay for itself.

The University of Waterloo (Waterloo, Ontario, Canada N2L 3G1) supplies two debugging compilers, COBOL WATBOL and FORTRAN WATFIV. Cornell University has a PL/I compiler called

PL/C, and IBM has the PL/I Checkout compiler. Finally, there is ALGOL W from Stanford University. Thus all major programming languages have a debugging compiler.

Use a debugging compiler.

Errors the Compiler Cannot Detect

There are many errors that the compiler cannot detect when the statements used are correctly formed. Examples of undetectable errors are

1. Omission of part of the program
2. Branching the wrong way on a decision statement
3. Using the wrong format for reading data
4. Incorrect values in loops, such as the initial value, increment, or terminal value
5. Arrays too small or incorrect array subscripting
6. Failure to consider all possibilities that may occur in the data or in the calculations.

Here is an example showing why subscripting errors cannot be discovered during compilation. If an array has ten elements and subscripts are calculated by using variables, then the array bounds may be exceeded. But they are exceeded during execution. For instance, given an array of $A(10)$ and

$$I = 4 * K$$
$$\cdot$$
$$\cdot$$
$$\cdot$$
$$A(I) = \ldots$$

Whenever K is greater than 2, the array subscript will be incorrect, but this fact cannot be discovered at compilation.

Other errors that cannot be discovered during compilation include incorrect mode of arguments in the call statements. That is, a subprogram expects to get an integer argument and is passed a real number. This type of error cannot be discovered at compilation because each subprogram can be compiled separately. Thus the compiler cannot check to see if the mode of the arguments of the subprogram is compatible with the mode of the arguments in the calling program. This type of error can be caught during execution if information about type of variables is supplied by the compiler, or it can be caught on a compile and execute by a good debugging compiler.

If an error passes undetected by the compiler, the object program will, nevertheless, be compiled from the source program. Then the object program will cause an abnormal end at some point during execution. If no abnormal end occurs, the result will be an output that is incorrect, and no indication will be given of this fact. Program testing is used to discover any errors the compiler did not locate.

Other errors that can be caught by the compiler (but seldom are) are

1. Unused labels
2. Undefined variables
3. Variables that are declared but never used
4. Incorrect type of function argument
5. Incorrect type of a format item.

Such errors can all be discovered at the compilation stage. Other errors can be discovered only during execution. Some compilers generate code (such as checking subscript ranges) that will check for certain errors during execution. The more checking that is done, the less work needed in removing bugs.

TYPES OF DEBUGGING

Debugging starts after all syntax error messages are eliminated. Use simple test data to start the debugging. If the test data produces correct results, continue testing. If the program does not produce correct results, five situations are possible.

1. The program did not compile, but there are no syntax errors.
2. The program compiles, executes, but produces no output.
3. The program compiles, executes, but terminates prematurely.
4. The program compiles, executes, but produces incorrect output.
5. The program does not stop running (or infinite loop).

Case 1: Compilation Not Completed

This situation is rather rare and indicates a catastrophic error someplace in the program. System error messages usually appear in this situation. If so, they can be used to help locate the error. Generally, however, a great deal of experience is needed to interpret these messages.

If you have not had experience with a particular system, *abend* (stands for *ab*normal *end*), it is often difficult to ascertain what has caused the error. If you do not know what a particular abend means, ask around and find out if anyone else does. A good method to gain experience with system abends is to keep a notebook of past abends and their causes. Since most abends occur rarely, it is easy to forget what the problem was earlier unless a written record is kept.

If no one is available to help you and you can't fine the error yourself, the best approach is to try to isolate it. We do so by breaking the program into smaller, executable segments and attempting to compile the smaller segments. Keep segmenting the program until a segment will compile. Then start adding segments until the program stops compiling. The last segment added is the section with the error in it. Either careful inspection of the error section or segmenting of the error section should help indicate the statement that is preventing compilation. This is an undesirable method, so use it only as a last resort. The help of a knowledgeable friend is preferable.

Case 2: Execution but No Output

The program executes but does not produce any output. Some progress has been made but not much. This type of error can be caused by a logic error or a system error. An example of a logic error would be a program that starts execution and then branches to end of job before producing any output. Such an error can be located by using the techniques suggested in the discussion on locating errors.

The system error is caused by some fatal error that stops the operating system from allowing execution to continue. The interruption of your program execution can be generated by the computer hardware, operating system, or your compiled program. Generally a system error code is provided. Hopefully, the system gives some indication of what the error is. But system error messages are usually quite cryptic. Also, normally there is no indication of *where* the error is. If some program output is provided, then there is at least a little indication of where the error is, and it is simply a matter of narrowing down the error location either by debugging traces or by debugging output, both of which are covered in a later section.

Here are examples of errors that can cause system errors.

1. Division by zero
2. Branching to a data area and attempting execution

3. Array subscripts incorrect
4. Numeric underflow or overflow.

Locating the error in Cases 1 and 2 can sometimes be extremely difficult. One approach is to reprogram the segment, using an alternate method to achieve the same result. This step may be the simplest way to overcome the error if the error is not obvious. A similar solution is to make several copies of the malfunctioning section. Next, vary the coding and rerun the program. Repeat this process until the error disappears or can be isolated.

Case 3: Terminates Prematurely

The program now compiles, starts execution, provides some output, but then terminates before it should. We have progressed beyond the first two errors and are usually quite relieved to be obtaining some output.

Since some output is being produced, regular debugging techniques can be used. Errors that stop the program execution prematurely and then provide a system error message are *blowups* or *cratered*. They are so severe that execution cannot continue. This type of error can be located by using the techniques suggested in the section on locating errors.

Case 4: Incorrect Answers

The program runs but produces incorrect answers. Experienced programmers always consider themselves lucky when this stage is reached. It probably indicates that the program is basically sound and that the logic is almost correct. The rest of the chapter will be devoted to helping debug this type of error.

Case 5: An Infinite Loop

This error is normally not too difficult to find. If you cannot spot the loop immediately, simply add print statements before and after suspected loops. Do not put print statements in the loops; otherwise thousands of lines of output will usually appear. The print statements will provide output that will indicate which loop is entered but never exited.

GENERAL HINTS

When using cards punch the program all in one-color cards, usually manila. Then punch all debug cards in a different color so that they can easily be removed once the debugging is finished. Statements inserted for debugging should be on a line all by themselves, also to facilitate removal. Use columns 73–80 to type some message such as DEBUG or REMOVE in all debugging lines. Or use a comment or note to indicate that the debugging line is to be removed after debugging. Then the source listing will clearly indicate which lines are to be removed after debugging.

Do not let any one routine become too large. There is a direct nonlinear relationship between the number and difficulty of bugs and the size of a routine. As the routine increases in length beyond 50 statements, the number of bugs and the difficulty in locating them increase exponentially. [But very small routines cause too much interaction between routines.]

Think about the debugging stage when writing the original program in order to avoid writing a program that is impossible to debug or test. Develop at least a rough flowchart before starting to program. This flowchart will help to organize your thoughts.

During debugging it is often helpful to have a list of variables and constants used in the program. This list is usually supplied by the compiler. It can be used to indicate typing errors, since extra variable names will be available from it.

Isolate problems and fix one at a time. If you make several changes and new trouble arises, you won't, as a rule, know which change caused the new error. Also, you won't learn what corrected the old error. After you get an error corrected, look it over so that you will remember the problem and not make the same error again. If the error causes very unusual output, you should attempt to remember the type of error so that next time you will know what causes that type of error.

Make changes at the source level only. Never patch a program in machine language. Program patches destroy the documentation of a high-level language and are prone to introducing errors.

Don't blame the computer. Computers and their compilers are quite reliable today. If the computer stops working, it is usually immediately obvious to the machine room staff. Computers don't make small mistakes, only big ones.

Realize that there will probably be mistakes. Even good programmers make mistakes, but they realize that there will be mistakes, find them, correct them, and get all the bugs out of their program.

Amateur programmers take for granted that there are no mistakes, or they leave some bugs in that result in either consistent or occasional spurious output. Quite often, by explaining to someone what you are *trying* to accomplish, you can discover an error.

When debugging, it is common to rerun a program many times. So care should be taken with output, or the many runs will add to the confusion. All output should have the date and the time on it. Discard uneeded output in order to avoid confusion. But remember that attempts at correcting one error can often introduce new errors. Then you usually wish you could get back to a previous stage where the errors were less serious.

In general, it is necessary to save some of the previous outputs. One solution is to take all old program listings away from your desk and stack them, one on top of another, in a different location. By storing old program listings in a different location, you will remove them and hence avoid confusing them with current runs, but will still have them for reference if needed. Then you can recycle the old program listings at your leisure.

If you have saved dated output, it is easy to back up. Always save the most recent program run or two because programs can easily be lost, dropped, become out of sequence, or otherwise damaged. Then a previous run is worth a lot. If you wish to be very careful, you can occasionally copy your source program. This step provides a ready backup if one is ever needed.

After correcting one bug, examine output carefully to ensure that other bugs have not been introduced. This advice is particularly apt when changing the logic of the program. Modifying the logical structure of a program might correct one error but will frequently introduce new ones.

UNDEFINED VARIABLES

A common source of program errors is undefined or uninitialized variables. Every variable that is used in an output statement or on the right side of an equal sign in an arithmetic statement or in a logical statement must have been computed on the left-hand side of an equal sign, used in an input statement, or inputted as subroutine parameter. That is, you can't use variables that have not been defined by input or computing.

Here are some programming statements.

```
A = 1
B = B + A
```

If B has not previously had a value assigned to it, B is an undefined variable. What actually happens in most languages is that the old bit pattern left over from previous operations at the storage location assigned to B is used for the present value of B. Thus the value of B is a random number and anything may happen. A good debugging compiler will locate undefined variables.

One certain sign of undefined variables is to run the same program and data (with *no changes* in the program or data) and get different results on the two runs. This bug causes the program to violate the rule of determinacy. *Determinacy* is defined as the behavior of a program that is reproducible in separate runs given the same input data. Quite often a program will be used for a long period before it becomes obvious that there are undefined variables. Perhaps the undefined variable has usually had a zero assigned to it, or it was given a value that didn't cause an obvious error.

There are two ways to get undefined variables:

> By not initializing a variable before it is used.
> By typing error.

The first type has already been discussed. Programmers must be careful not to use a variable before it is defined.

The second type of undefined variable results from typing error. After programs are typed, they should always be verified and desk-checked to eliminate typing errors. Careful selection of variable names will help eliminate typing errors. Names like the following are dangerous.

> KO is this KO (zero) or KO (letter)
> K1 is this K1 (one) or KI (letter)

The letter O and the number zero are most difficult to locate if interchanged in variable names. Other typing errors are discussed in the typing section.

STORAGE MAP

Most compilers have an option called a *storage map*. A storage map is a table of names that appear (or are implied) in the source program. One way to use a storage map is to scan the list for unfamiliar variable names. The variable names are in alphabetic order; so you might notice there is one variable name, VI but also one V1 which is typing error (punched 1 instead of I). The storage map would help you locate unfamiliar names.

The names are usually provided by type (i.e., integer, real, character, etc.). Some storage maps provide a separate list of functions, subroutines, arrays, and constants. The storage map for the IBM PL/I compiler also indicates which variables were explicitly declared and which variables were implicitly declared.

A storage map is generally requested by job control commands. Each compiler has different grouping and style for its storage map. Storage maps are especially useful when modifying someone else's program because they allow you to get a complete list of all variables used in the program.

CROSS-REFERENCE LIST

A *cross-reference* list indicates where each variable is used in a program. In addition, some cross-reference lists will indicate every place a label, function, or subroutine is referenced. This type of information is often very useful when modifying a program.

Some bugs can also be discovered by a cross-reference list. If a variable is declared but never referenced in the program, this fact might indicate a misspelled variable name. In addition, a label that is never referenced might indicate an error. Cross-reference lists are commonly requested by job control language commands.

TYPING ERRORS

Typing errors in source programs can cause bugs that are difficult to locate. Several steps can be taken to reduce the number of such errors.

1. Standard coding forms should be used for the programming language. The use of regular lined paper contributes to errors due to wrong columns and makes paragraphing difficult.
2. Use a legible writing device, preferably a soft lead pencil. Soft lead pencils provide readable code and are easy to erase.
3. Code in block letters — not script.
4. Insist that all keypunched programs be mechanically verified.

Certain types of typing errors continually cause programmers a great deal of trouble. The following characters are often mistyped.

1 number
I letter
| or
/ Slash
' quotation mark

_____

¬ not
7 seven
> greater than

_____

L letter
< less than

_____

O letter
Q letter
∅ zero (strokes in opposite
   direction)

_____

S letter (tails on the letter)
5 five

Ƶ letter
7 seven
2 two

_____

U Make the u round on
   the bottom plus a tail
V

_____

4 four (close the top of
   the four)
+ plus

_____

D put tails on the letter D
O letter

_____

G letter
C letter
6 close the number

_____

_ break character
− minus

Careful attention should be paid to these characters so that symbols are not interchanged.

DESK CHECKING

Several things can be done while the program is being keypunched or as a break from the monotony of punching the cards or typing the program into a terminal. First, review the problem statement, design documentation, algorithms, and flowchart. Convince yourself that the problem is completely understood and that your program will actually solve it. Even though you have already done so, now would be a good time to review the design while the program is fresh in mind. In addition, have a colleague who has not worked on the project review everything; it never hurts to have an unbiased mind check things over.

As soon as the program is keypunched and verified, the cards should be listed. At many installations this step is done automatically as part of the keypunch routine for source decks. It allows the programmer to desk check for keypunch errors or missing cards. Even a casual desk check of the source cards will generally eliminate some errors and thus reduce compiling and debugging time.

It is best to do desk checking right after the keypunching because the program is still fresh in your mind. A desk check a week later, after becoming hopelessly involved in debugging, means that the original program is no longer so fresh as to make you notice a missing or a mispunched card. A few minutes of desk checking can save endless hours of debugging.

There is a tendency to take the attitude that the compiler will catch all typing errors. The compiler will catch only typing errors that cause syntax errors.

Desk check first.

After the program is compared to the keypunch sheets, it should be compared to the flowchart. A command-by-command inspection, while using the flowchart, should eliminate some early bugs. Sometimes it is useful to have a friend (does anyone have such a friend?) compare your program to the flowchart. If small subroutines are used, this job does not seem so arduous; instead of checking one large program, individual tasks can be checked.

Two kinds of error usually indicate undefined variables: UNDERFLOW and OVERFLOW. These words mean numbers that are either too small or too big. Today's computers allow for such a wide range of numbers that almost any calculation can be handled without an underflow or overflow. Unless you know that you are using very small or very large numbers, an overflow or underflow error normally indicates an undefined variable in the program.

One of the best ways to avoid undefined variables is to initialize as many as possible when declaring them. This process avoids an error caused by omitting the initialization, improves documentation by exhibiting the initial values in one location, eliminates assignment statements, and thus increases execution efficiency. (This type of initialization is commonly done at compile time instead of during execution).

ATTRIBUTES

It is good policy to declare all attributes even if there is a default. The explicit declarations help to document the program. If you do not declare attributes of the variables, the defaults could change, thereby causing a significant effect on the execution of production programs.

Explicit declares of all attributes also have the advantage of making the programmer cognizant of what the attributes are. It is especially important to declare all user-supplied functions and parameter lists to ensure that they have the desired attributes. Explicit declares of all variables will eliminate one type of common program bug. Also, it is advisable to check to see that data types of all variables in a given expression are consistent. Mixed data types in a single expression can result in subtle errors.

INPUT/OUTPUT ERRORS

One of the first steps in debugging should be the printing of all input. A great many program errors are caused by incorrect reading of input. If input is read incorrectly, much time can be lost looking for a program bug when the whole problem is due to bad data.

Bad data can be caused by typing errors, misunderstandings, or incorrectly specified input formats. By printing input, the programmer can scan the printout and see if input is being read correctly. Inspection of the data records will help locate typing errors but will not pinpoint input format errors. I almost always print my input because through experience I have learned that printing the input is the only way that I can be sure input is read correctly.

Input should be printed immediately after it is read. The immediate outputting of all input is called *echo checking*. If you delay the echo checking until later in the program, it is possible that the program will never get that far or that the storage locations used for input numbers are altered during execution of the program.

Echo check input data.

In addition, output should be labeled so that it is easy to determine which values belong to which variables. FORTRAN has a NAMELIST command and PL/I has a PUT DATA command that do this easily for you. The DISPLAY or EXHIBIT command in COBOL can be used for easily printing debugging values.

In modules or subprograms your input is the parameter values of the module. They should be printed because if they are being received incorrectly, all debugging activity will fail until this situation is discovered.

Output errors can cause programmers to believe that they have a program bug when the error is simply incorrectly specified formats. The most common error is too small output fields or completely incorrect output fields. These errors are usually obvious if the programmer has seen them before. A little bit of experimenting, using too small or incorrect output specification, will illustrate what this type of error looks like.

PSYCHOLOGY OF PROGRAM BUGS

Each type of program bug has a certain character or "psychology." Experienced programmers can often look at a cryptic system error message and say "Oh, that is probably an overrun array subscript" or something similar. Such knowledge comes from experience, but the process can be greatly accelerated by writing small programs to cause obvious errors. Then you can look at the output and observe the "psychology" of that particular type of bug. This technique can also be used to clear up incomplete, missing, or incorrect documentation.

NUMERICAL PATHOLOGY

If calculations are done by using a desk calculator, the observant operator can notice any major arithmetic faults. In using a computer, however, most faults are hidden from view. In addition, calculations are done at a million calculations a second; so it is impossible to trace all of them. A few of the errors are sufficiently gross (division by zero, overflow, underflow), that the hardware warns the user of trouble.

Most of the trouble occurs because real numbers are stored only with a limited number of digits. The result of calculations can be disastrous even in logically correct programs that have been used with no noticeable error for a long period of time. A new set of input may produce obviously incorrect results. The problem occurs because the computer uses only a set precision for real numbers. For example,

$A = 1.0/3.0$ Provides the value 0.3333333
.
.
$B = A*3$ Provides the value 0.9999999

The unwary programmer may use the above in a logical test as follows.

$$\text{IF } (B = 1) \ldots$$

Another serious error can be caused by

$$I = B$$

where I is an integer and B is real with the value 0.9999999. The result stored in I will be zero because of integer truncation.

A similar type of error occurs with addition and subtraction. Assume that you have a machine that does arithmetic with four decimal digits. Data

$$X = 999.0 \quad Y = -1000. \quad Z = .001$$

and the equation

$$X + Y + Z + 1.0 =$$

ordered as follows.

$$((X + Y) + Z) + 1.0 =$$

$$((999.0 - 1000.) + .001) + 1.0 =$$

$$(-1.0 + .001) + 1.0 =$$

$$-.999 + 1.0 \quad = \quad .001$$

Reordered, we get a different answer.

$$X + (Y + Z) + 1.0 =$$

$$999.0 + (-1000. + .001) + 1.0 =$$

999.0 + (-1000.) + 1.0   (loss of precision because of only four places.)

$$11.0 + 1.0 \quad = \quad 0.0$$

Thus the dangerous situation is one in which you subtract two almost equal numbers. It is easy to lose all significant digits. This process is called *cancellation*. The above happens in a four-place example but could just as easily happen on a computer with more places. Often the lost digits are the most important, especially if there are none left.

LOCATING ERRORS

Locating an error in a program is often quite difficult. Some of the reasons for wanting to locate an error are

1. Not sure if the program started to execute.
2. The program started to execute but terminated prematurely, either with or without a system error.
3. The program started to execute but got caught in an endless loop, as indicated by the program taking too long.
4. The program provided incorrect answers.

Any of these errors requires the programmer to trace the flow through the program. Generally TRACE statements are available to do so, but TRACE statements have disadvantages that are mentioned in the section on debugging aids.

If the bug appears unlocatable and subtle, we can rerun the program and see if the bug is repeatable. Most bugs are repeatable and if nothing else, this step shows you that the bug is still there. Nonrepeatable bugs can be caused by operator error, hardware error, power fluctuation, or operating system problems. If the bug is not repeatable, at least some record of it should be kept because nonrepeatable errors often surface at random times. An undefined variable can cause a nonrepeatable error. Thus these nonrepeatable errors should be kept track of, perhaps by adding a note to the documentation and filing the bad output, so that they will be available for later reference.

Locating an unknown place in a program means basically setting up a search strategy. In some cases (e.g., when a systems error message is the only output), we have little information concerning the location of the error. Otherwise the programmer has some knowledge (e.g., when some output is available) of where the error is. If the exact location of the error is known, then normally it is simple to correct the error.

Sometimes it is useful to exclude unlikely sources of error. You start with a known error or bug. First, you must decide if it is a hardware bug, an operating system bug, a compiler error, or a bug in your own program. Most bugs are in your own program unless you are working with new hardware or new software.

Next, if you have accepted the bug as being in your own program, you can exclude parts of your program. Perhaps input routines look all right, since you print some of the input. Generally you can eliminate a few other routines similarly and narrow your search down to two or three probable candidates. Then you start your investigation there. The main point is to avoid a random approach that inexperienced programmers attempt.

One hint that can be made is that when looking for a bug, eliminate the simple cases first. For example, if you believe the error is in one of three subroutines and it will take 10 minutes to check out routine A, 2 hours to check out routine B, and 3 days to check out routine C, then it makes sense to check out the simple routines first, since a payoff is possible for a small amount of time. (Human nature usually suggests this procedure even though it is not verbalized.)

The goal is to keep narrowing down the error location until found. Thus parts of the program may have a zero probability of the error being there, whereas other sections may have a high probability of containing the error. The goal is to find the error — that is, to increase the probability of finding the location of the error until it is 100%.

The general method for tracing your own program is to put between five and ten output statements in the program. One output statement should be at the beginning of the program and another at the end. The rest of the output statements should be spaced at fairly regular intervals throughout the program.

It is best to avoid putting debug statements inside loops. Instead put the debug output statements immediately before and after loops. If debugging output statements are put inside loops, they will produce output each time the loop is executed, which could easily be thousands of times.

My favorite output statement for tracing program flow is to print statements as follows.

DEBUG 1
DEBUG 2

That is, the first debug statement should print the word DEBUG plus the number 1. The next debug statement will print DEBUG and the number 2. The word DEBUG indicates that it is a debugging statement and is to be removed after debugging is complete.

Once these statements are placed in the program, the position of the error is easy to locate.

Suppose that we had placed ten debug statements interspersed throughout the program. Then our output might look as follows.

```
DEBUG 1
DEBUG 2
DEBUG 3
DEBUG 4
```

Since DEBUG 4 is the last statement printed, we know that the error is between the statement that prints DEBUG 4 and the statement that prints DEBUG 5 If inspection of these statements does not produce the error, then we can take all ten debug statements and put them in the program between the statements where DEBUG 4 and DEBUG 5 were. The process will eventually lead to the error.

Once you find the error statement, you are often not finished. The statement that causes the error is usually elsewhere. For instance,

$$C = B/A$$

This statement would cause trouble when A had the value zero. So the next step is to trace the previous statement to determine why A has the value zero.

So two factors are involved in locating an error, *point of detection* and *point of origin*. The point of detection is the location where the error manifested itself or where it became apparent. This is the first point that must be located. In the preceding example the point of detection is the statement that uses zero for a divisor.

The point of origin is the location where the error condition was created — that is, in the above example, where A assumed the value zero. The real error takes place at the original point, not the detection point. The detection point is simply the starting point in the search for the error origin point.

In addition to using the computer to find the error, another often-overlooked method exists — reading the program listing. This approach works best if the error has been isolated to a small area. Studies have been done in which two groups were told to locate a bug. One group used the computer and one group did not. The noncomputer-using group found the bug as fast as the computer-using group.

Debugging Output

Debugging output consists of statements that are used to print results of calculations for debugging purposes. The first debugging statements needed are the echo printing of all input data. Next, information is needed that will indicate the progress of numeric calculations. Finally, output statements are needed that will indicate the logic flow of the program.

If large amounts of computations are involved, a wrong answer will seldom provide enough information to locate the error. Variables that are printed out during debugging should be clearly labeled so that it is evident which variables are being printed. It should not be considered unusual to have a great deal of the program devoted to debugging aids. And all the debugging aids put in the source program should be designed so that their removal will not cause bugs in the program. Since it is common to compile a program 10 or 20 times while debugging, it pays to provide debugging output early to reduce the number of compiles necessary.

The aids actually provided by the programmer are generally the most helpful and effective. It is usually easier to put these aids in while writing the program than to add them later during the debugging stage. It is trivial to remove debugging aids once the program is completely debugged and tested.

Typically, people do not introduce enough debugging aids at the writing stage. The reason is that we really never know how necessary these aids will be until completely bogged down at the debugging stage. A good question for deciding if debugging statements are needed is: If the program is incorrect, in this block of coding will there be enough output to locate the errors?

We forget that more programmer time is spent at the debugging stage than at all other stages. And on many programs more machine time is spent debugging than on the production runs.

Introduce debugging aids early.

Strategically placed output statements will provide both an arithmetic and a flow trace of what happened during the execution of the program. Generally the earlier a number of debugging statements can be put into the program, the less the number of debugging runs that will be required.

After debugging is completed, all the debugging statements must be eliminated. The best method of doing so is to change them to comments to suppress output. Then the debugging statements will be available if needed later. Otherwise if a bug appears later or a program modification is required, the debugging statements would not normally be available. Changing the debugging statements into comments allows them to be carried along with the program as documentation and makes them readily available.

If using a terminal system, it is possible to label the debugging and testing lines so that the editing system can automatically remove these lines. For example, if using FORTRAN, you could start all lines you want to remove with statement numbers 9XXXX. Then direct the editing system to remove these lines.

Finally, if the test lines are changed to comments, they provide an important part of the documentation, indicating the specific tests that were done.

IBM PL/I allows the programmer to specify the left and right margins for program source statements by using the SORMGIN option. The normal margins, when using card input, are SORMGIN=(2,72). This margin feature can be used to switch a program from the debugging/testing version to the production version automatically.

Here's how. Use SORMGIN=(4,70) for the debugging and testing version of the source program. Use SORMGIN=(2,72) for the production version. Then for all debugging and testing statements that you wish removed before production use, simply place the /* in columns 2-3 and a */ in columns 71-72. Since they are the comment delimiters, this step allows automatic conversion of debugging and testing statements to comments.

Selective Printout

Frequently, it is desirable to print some information selectively during debugging. This situation arises when only certain cases are to be checked or when a nonselective printout would provide too much output, such as putting a print statement within a loop.

An example of a statement to do selective printing is

```
IF (X .LT. 0.0) WRITE ...
```

This statement would print out data only when X is less than zero. The following could be used to check an index and selectively print debugging information.

```
IF (I .GT. 10 .AND. I .LT. 15) WRITE ...
```

This statement would provide printout only when $I = 11,12,13,$ or 14.

The example below takes advantage of integer arithmetic.

```
IF (I / 5 * 5 - I .EQ. 0) WRITE ...
```

The expression

$$I / 5 * 5 - I$$

will equal zero only when I has a 5 as a factor (i.e., $I = 5,10,$ $15,\ldots$) because of integer arithmetic. This technique can be used to print data every nth iteration. The above can also be done with a MOD function, if available.

Selective printouts can also be used to check to see how many iterations are taken on iterative routines as follows.

$$IF (N .EQ. 1000) WRITE \ldots$$

This statement will indicate when N has reached 1000, which may indicate an infinite loop. It is much safer than putting a nonconditional output statement inside a loop.

A very useful type of statement is

$$IF\ DEBUGGING\ THEN\ \ldots$$

where DEBUGGING is a logical variable with either a true or false value. This type of construct allows you to turn your debugging (or testing) statements on or off for the whole program by setting just one logical variable to true or false. If this method is used, debugging statements can be left in the program for later possible use. Simply set DEBUGGING to false. Some compilers (i.e., PL/I) have conditional-compilation features. These features can be used to conditionally turn debugging and testing aids on and off.

Logic Traces

Output statements can be used to indicate the flow of execution in the program. This type of output statement is normally put in subroutines or after program decisions are made. Thus the completion of the various stages of the program will be recorded by printing suitable chosen messages. An example of output might be

```
ENTERED SUBROUTINE MAXNUM.
EXITED SUBROUTINE MAXNUM.
ENTERED SUBROUTINE FIXNUM.
LESS THAN ZERO BRANCH TAKEN.
ONE THOUSAND ITERATIONS.
```

The first three output comments indicate which subroutines are being executed. The fourth comment indicates that a particular branch was taken. The last output comment indicates how many iterations have been executed. Output statements should indicate both desirable and undesirable conditions.

Debugging output statements can be easily removed when the program is accepted as correct or changed to comments so that they can be used later if needed. It is usually easier to include these debugging statements when the program is being written than to wait until the program has been tried and found to fail. Logic flow statements will help the programmer discover bugs that might stay hidden otherwise.

One very simple aid to debugging that is often overlooked is that all programs should print out a final message indicating that the program reached normal completion. Just before stopping execution, print

```
NORMAL END OF JOB.
```

Otherwise it is easy to overlook the fact that the program did not complete execution. At the same time the program can print program summary information, such as how many good and bad transactions were processed.

Failure

What do you do when you can't find the bug? In general, it doesn't help to spend days poring over the same problem without a break and without getting some assistance. There are two obvious things to do. First, you can go home, or have a relaxed lunch, or do something else for awhile. Even though you stop looking for the bug, your brain will still be thinking about it. Often after a good night's rest it is much easier to find yesterday's elusive bug.

The second suggestion is to find a debugging partner — that is, someone you can go talk to about the bug. Frequently, it is useful to have someone else *listen* while you attempt to describe the problem and logic of the program. The solution of the problem often appears to the programmer when trying to explain the trouble. The debugging partner may even have some suggestions. This is a situation in which you should develop the habit of actively listening to the partner without telling him that he is wrong. If you do not want to accept the advice, that is your business.

A debugging partner should be used sparingly and considerately, since he or she is busy, too. And a partner should not be asked to go through a hexadecimal or octal dump or do line-by-line checking; that is your job. Instead the partner is someone who will listen to your problem, and you should be willing to reciprocate.

DEFENSIVE PROGRAMMING

Defensive programming (also called *antibugging*) refers to the practice of writing a program so that when a bug appears it will be obvious to the programmer and 'easy to locate. It is often not apparent when a bug appears on most programs, and the bug may go undetected for months or years.

We antibug by building debugging aids into the program. Debugging aids that are built into the original program are called *bug arresting*. They are used to preserve the evidence that permits bug identification by locating the specific fault. The normal approach to debugging is to discover an obvious bug and then attempt to backtrack. However, generally there is no trail to backtrack. So you must put in several debugging runs to attempt to locate the bugs.

Here are several reasons why people do not antibug.

1. Assuming too much confidence in oneself. We do not put debugging statements in when writing the program because we overestimate our chances of not having any serious bugs. Somehow even long experience fails to shake this false belief.
2. Assuming too much confidence in others. Since dependable old Joan said her subroutine would give us clean data, we don't check it even though her data has been full of trash before.
3. Assuming that bug-arresting code will require too much core or slow the program down. The main factor usually slowing things down is that you can't get the program working.

The first two assumptions are generally false. Moreover, even if the program works perfectly, the debugging aids are normally necessary to prove it to yourself.

Never assume that data is correct. Operator error, incorrect data formats, last minute program changes, keypunch errors, and similar factors, will all cause data problems. Also, do not take the attitude that if someone else gives you bad data, it is their fault. If your program or subroutine accepts bad data and blows up or, even worse, processes the bad data, it is *your* fault. And if your subroutine accepts bad data and passes it to some other subroutine, then your subroutine fails to pass correct data and you compound the error. It may be that your subroutine is the best place to catch the error.

The third reason given (efficiency) for not antibugging is of doubtful validity. A few extra statements to prevent or locate bugs will not cost much in machine time during execution. Furthermore, these instructions will obviously save you and the machine time while debugging. If it is necessary to remove the error-arresting routines because of machine or storage efficiency, this step can easily be done later.

It is easier to put in bug-arresting statements when originally writing the program. If you wait until the bugs appear, you may have easily forgotten some of the details of the program and insert the error checking incorrectly. And the later insertion requires a compilation, which requires time, too.

Most manufacturer-supplied subroutines check input parameters. Square root or logarithm routines check to ensure that the argument is positive. Similarly, arguments are checked to make sure that a magnitude is not exceeded. This checking is done each time the supplied routine is used and is considered well worth the trouble. It should be imitated when implementing your own subroutines. Usually there is an acceptable range for your parameters also.

Defensive programming has several principles.

1. *Mutual suspicion.* Each module assumes that any data passed to it may be incorrect and should be checked.
2. *Immediate detection.* It is best to detect the error as soon as possible, since doing so simplifies locating the source of the error.
3. *Error isolation. Fire walls* are used to isolate errors in one part of the system so that the error cannot cause damage in other parts.

Ideally, the printouts from the debugging aids could be used to verify that the module did receive the expected input, that it did perform its operations correctly, and that it did provide the correct results to the calling program. These checking statements should be independent in that their removal would not affect the module.

Another useful debugging statement is a counter that keeps track of how many times a routine is entered or how many times a loop is iterated. Such counts are useful when debugging because they provide clues to the progress of the computation and indicate areas of code that are heavily used, which may justify optimization.

The program can monitor the behavior of critical data variables during execution. A check can be provided to ensure that data does not fall outside its maximum and minimum. This is called a *data filter*. In addition, relationships between variables can be monitored to detect incorrect computations. Some old operating systems used data filters to examine the status of the operating system; if an error was found, the following message was printed out "If this prints, call a system programmer." By then, of course, the programmer who wrote the message was gone and no one knew what to do. Hopefully, you can do a little better.

Next, what do you check for or how do you check your program?

1. *Data type.* Check alphabetic fields (name fields) to ensure that they are alphabetic (no numbers). Check numeric fields (ZIP code) to make sure that they are numeric.
2. *Range checks.* Make sure positive numbers are positive.
3. *Reasonability checks.* Certain variables should not exceed some constant or other variables. Calculated taxes and deductions should not exceed calculated pay and so on.
4. *Total checks.* Cross totals, hash totals, transaction counts should be included and verified by the program when possible.
5. *Automatic checks.* Use all automatic checks, such as overflow, underflow, and file label checking.
6. *Length check.* If a data value must have a certain length, check the length (i.e., ZIP code).
7. *Dog tags.* A dog tag is an item that must appear in a field or record. For example, a certain type of record may always have the code MST in columns 73–75. This fact should be verified.
8. *Check digits.* Items like part numbers can have a check digit added to it so that the fact that you have a legal part number can be verified.

Such coding is also called *redundancy code*, since it is like redundancy hardware (similar to using parity bit in hardware). Remember that the bug you catch or prevent is one less to look for later. "Garbage In, Garbage Out" (*GIGO*) is a common phrase used in computer centers to describe what happens when input data is bad. A good program should catch the "garbage in" so there is no "garbage out."

Check input for reasonableness.

ASSERTIONS

A number of new experimental programming languages have an *assertion* feature. The assertions allow us to establish conditions that must be true for correct execution of the program. Frequently, there are two types of assertions. The first type is global assertions, which are located with the declaratives. For instance, we could declare N an integer number, with the assertion that it must always have a positive value.

The second type of assertion is located in the code and allows us to assert certain values at this point of execution. An example would be that weekly pay must be less than $2000. If any assertion is violated, the program stops executing and indicates the errors. The last type of assertion can easily be included in a program by using an IF statement. In some languages a programmer can specify assertions that result in checking code being produced when the compiler is in debug mode; otherwise assertions are treated as comments.

ERROR CHECKLIST

Most programmers have certain errors in coding that they tend to make over and over. They may include using illegal subscripts, writing conditional jumps the wrong way, counting from one when counting should start at zero, and so on. These types of errors are particularly common if the programmer habitually programs in two or more languages. Since each language works differently, it is easy to confuse them. What you should do is keep a list of your own common errors. This list can then be used as a checklist while debugging. Tables 4.2 and 4.3 list many common programming errors.

Table 4.2 A Catalog of Bugs (A Classification of bugs by type)

These are not syntax errors but bugs that would still be present after syntax checking is complete.

Logic
1. Taking the wrong path at a logic decision.
2. Failure to consider one or more conditions.
3. Omission of coding one or more flowchart boxes.
4. Branching to the wrong label.

Loops
1. Not initializing the loop properly.
2. Not terminating the loop properly.
3. Wrong number of loop cycles.

Table 4.2 (Continued)

4. Incorrect indexing of the loop.
5. Infinite loops (sometimes called closed loops).

Data
1. Failure to consider all possible data types.
2. Failure to edit out incorrect data.
3. Trying to read less or more data than there are.
4. Editing data incorrectly or mismatching of editing fields with data fields.

Variables.
1. Using an uninitialized variable.
2. Not resetting a counter or accumulator.
3. Failure to set a program switch correctly.
4. Using an incorrect variable name (that is, spelling error using wrong variable).

Arrays
1. Failure to clear the array.
2. Failure to declare arrays large enough.
3. Transpose the subscript order.

Arithmetic Operations (see also Variables)
1. Using wrong mode (i.e., using integer when real was needed).
2. Overflow and underflow.
3. Using incorrect constant.
4. Evaluation order incorrect.
5. Division by zero.
6. Square root of a negative value.
7. Truncation.

Subroutines
1. Incorrect attributes of function.
2. Incorrect attributes of subroutine parameters.
3. Incorrect number of parameters.
4. Parameters out of order.

Input/Output (see also Data)
1. Incorrect mode of I/O format specifications.
2. Failure to rewind (or position) a tape before reading or writing.
3. Using wrong size records or incorrect formats.

Character Strings
1. Declare character string the wrong size.
2. Attempting to reference a character outside the range of the string length.

Logical Operations
1. Using the wrong logical operator.
2. Comparing variables that do not have compatible attributes.
3. Failure to provide ELSE clause in multiple IF statements.

Machine Operations
1. Incorrect shifting.
2. Using an incorrect machine constant (i.e.; using decimal when hexadecimal was needed).

Terminators
1. Failure to terminate a statement.

Table 4.2 (Continued)

2. Failure to terminate a comment.
3. Using " instead of ', or vice versa.
4. Incorrectly matched quote.
5. Terminate prematurely.

Miscellaneous
1. Not abiding by statement margin restrictions.
2. Using wrong function.

Table 4.3 Special Bugs

There is another category of bugs that will be called special bugs here. They are sophisticated errors (i.e., difficult to locate).

Semantic Error
These errors are caused by the failure to understand exactly how a command works. An example is to assume that arithmetic operations are rounded. Another example is to assume that a loop will be skipped if the ending value is smaller than the initial value. In IBM FORTRAN DO, loops are always executed once.

Semaphore Bug
This type of bug becomes evident when process A is waiting on a process B while process B is waiting upon process A. This type of bug usually emerges when running large complicated systems, such as operating systems. This is called the *deadly embrace*.

Timing Bug
A *timing bug* can develop when two operations depend on each other in a time sense. That is, operation A must be completed before operation B can start. If operation B starts too soon, a timing bug can appear. Both timing bugs and semaphore bugs are called *situation bugs*.

Operation Irregularity Bugs
These bugs are the result of machine operations. Sometimes unsuspecting programmers do not understand that the machine does arithmetic in binary; so the innocent expression

$$1.0/5.0*5.0$$

does not equal one. This error shows up when this test is made.

```
A = 5.0
    .
    .
    .
B = 5.0
    .
    .
    .
IF (1.0/A*B .EQ. 1.0) . . .
```

Table 4.3 (Continued)

Then an unexpected branch takes place, and probably an endless loop results.

Evanescent Bug

Another bug that generally doesn't appear until production phase is the *evanescent bug*. This is a bug that appears and then may disappear for several months. This includes the bugs that will not reappear even when identical data and program are rerun through the same machine. An example of a bug of this type is a program switch that has not been initialized but usually is correct due to the tendency of the machine to have a zero in that particular location.

Another variation is that when debugging tools are added, the bugs disappear. The author once spent 2 months trying to locate this type of bug and failed. My solution was to rewrite the program.

Recovery Bug

A *recovery bug* refers to what happens when there is a hardware or system software failure. That is, if the system collapses for any reason (power failure, disk crash, etc.,), we do not want files to disappear or become damaged.

Overload Bug

This bug will only appear when internal tables, queues, buffers, or other storage areas fill up or exceed their capacity. It affects real-time and on-line systems and may not show up for several years until usage taxes the system. For example, in a time-sharing system, what happens if all the users are trying to access the disk at the same time?

PROGRAM DIMENSIONS

In debugging there are two dimensions to be traced: space and time. The space dimension is storage space in the computer. The time dimension is the computation cycles completed during execution. In general, the time dimension is the longest and most important. Debugging aids concentrate on allowing the programmer to trace both dimensions. Debugging aids are stethoscopes necessary to isolate the cause and location of an error.

DEBUGGING AIDS

A repertoire of debugging aids is a welcome source of help during debugging. But they seldom relieve programmers from constructing their own debugging aids. In an interesting book, *Software Tools*, by Brian W. Kernighan and P. J. Plauger, many programs are described, some of which can be used as debugging aids. The most effective debugging aids seem to be those that are written into the program while writing the original program. In this case, the error areas can be pinpointed by the programmer.

There are several debugging programming aids.

1. Dumps
2. Flow trace
3. Variable trace
4. Subroutine trace
5. Subscript checks
6. Display

A *dump* is a record of information at a given time of the status of the program. It is usually provided in machine language and is of limited use for several reasons. The major reason is because it is difficult to relate the dump to your program. It requires the programmer to understand machine language and to be able to relate the machine language to the high-level language. In addition, if the compiler optimizes high-level code, it becomes even more difficult to use the dump even if machine language is known. A highly optimizing compiler may entirely rearrange the operations in a program, thus making a dump almost useless. Since the information provided in a dump is not in a form where it can be used, there has been a trend to provide debugging aids that give debugging information in a form more appopriate for use. The paper by Gaines cited in the References discusses different types of dumps.

A *trace* is a record of the path of execution of the program. It can be used to see if the program is being executed in the same sequence as the programmer intended and if the variables have the desired values stored in them. There are usually three types of traces. The first type traces the flow of control of the program. That is, it usually prints statement labels as they are passed during execution. The second type prints variable names and values. Every time a variable changes in value, the variable label and its new value are printed. A third type traces subroutine calls. This type becomes very useful in a program that calls many subroutines. Every time a subroutine is called, the name of the subroutine is printed; and when a return from the subroutine is executed, a return message prints.

Traces will often provide all the information needed to locate a bug in a program. Their weakness, however, is that they can easily provide too much information — that is, thousands of lines of output. The second disadvantage is that because of the great amount of information monitored and provided, they are normally quite costly in machine time. A full trace can easily increase execution time by a factor of 10 to 40 times.

So in order to overcome these difficulties, flow traces are usually designed so that they can be turned on and off. That is, they can be turned on just for the section of the program that needs to be traced and turned off for the other sections.

Variable traces are designed so that instead of printing out all variables, only a selected list of variables is monitored and printed.

ALGOL W has some very sophisticated tracing options. Here are a few.

1. A postmortem dump of all the program's variables if execution terminates abnormally, else nothing.
2. The above plus counts of how often each statement was executed.
3. The above plus a statement-by-statement trace of each value stored.
4. The above plus a trace of each value fetched.

In addition, a logic trace or trace of flow of control can be requested. An upper limit can be set on the maximum number of times that any statement is to be traced. That is, if an upper bound of four is requested, no statement will be traced more than four times. The postmortem dump may seem unexceptional until we note that all debugging outputs are in terms of the source language. All variables are given by the same name and format as declared, branches are given in terms of program labels, and, in statement tracing, the original source statements, as well as the values of the pertinent variables, are printed out as each is executed.

A *subscript* check monitors the validity of all subscripts used with the named arrays by comparing the subscript combination with the declared bounds of the array. If the subscript falls outside the declared range, an error message is printed. It is usually possible to monitor all or just some arrays.

A *display* debugging command allows the user to select the exact place in the program where the variable value is to be printed. This allows a much more selective printing than the variable trace. In addition, the display command generally prints the variable name with the variable value, which provides labeled output automatically.

Both IBM COBOL and PL/I have extensive error-checking facilities. Such error-checking facilities allow the programmer to check for arithmetic errors (division by zero, overflow, underflow, etc.,) end of files, and other conditions. COBOL has the USE command and PL/I has the ON SIZE ERROR command, which allows program monitoring of serious errors. IBM FORTRAN has an Extended Error Handling Facility that allows some control over errors. The Digital Equipment Corporation PDP 11 has very extensive error-handling routines in its BASIC-PLUS. Other compilers also have different types of error-handling routines that are often quite useful.

> *Find out which debugging aids are available.*

ON-LINE DEBUGGING

Many programs are created on line and so there is an opportunity to use on-line capability to facilitate debugging. Most techniques used for debugging on a batch system can also be used on a time-sharing system, but because of the interactive characteristics of a time-sharing system, there are some additional hints and aids.

First, it is amazing how many people attempt to debug without a correct listing of their program. This practice is particularly common when people use a CRT screen. I have seen people sit at a terminal changing program lines frantically and getting nowhere. In this situation, little progress will be made until a program listing is obtained so that you can see what you have.

Time-sharing systems often have special debugging aids, which are listed below. Not all on-line systems allow the following debugging techniques. If the program under test is interpreted, these features are easier to implement than if the program is being executed from machine code. Here are some of the desirable features.

1. *Breakpoints.* We wish to be able to stop the execution of the program and have the program frozen and control returned to the on-line user.
2. *Error breakpoint.* We wish the program to return control to the user whenever the program attempts to do anything illegal, such as square root of a negative number or exceed an array bound. In addition, we would like a precise error message, indicating the problem and line number.
3. *Examining and modification.* Once the program has stopped execution due to a breakpoint or an error, we need the ability

to examine or change any variable. What is desired is a simple way to print variables or assign new values to a variable.

4. *Restarts.* We want to be able to restart the program at any statement in the program. Thus we can restart after the breakpoint or at some other point.

5. *Program modification.* We need to be able to delete, insert, or modify lines of the program. These changes should be immediately effective so that debugging can be continued.

Some time-sharing systems have all these features, such as BASIC-PLUS for the PDP 11. Users having these debugging aids can speed through debugging quickly. Obviously, as the growth of on-line use continues, language interpreters and the foregoing debugging aids will become more common.

Although on-line debugging aids are helpful, some studies have found that debugging is accomplished faster by short periods of on-line debugging interspersed with desk checking. The reason is fairly obvious. If you can find the bug readily, then it can be fixed quickly during on-line debugging. But if the bug is difficult to locate, get off the terminal and do some desk checking. Otherwise you may start making random, not-well-thought out changes that could introduce new errors.

MODULES FOR CHECKING PROGRAMS

Occasionally a module can be used to help debug a program. If elaborate printing of variables is desired, a module can be used at several places in a program to provide this feature. Use of a debugging module also simplifies the removal of debugging statements. Special debugging modules are often useful when testing out single modules before they are combined.

AUTOMATIC CHECKS

During debugging many of the possible automatic checks should be used. Included are division by zero, arithmetic overflow, arithmetic underflow, string range, and subscript range checks. Some compilers allow these options to be turned off or on because they require considerable execution time. The preceding checks, besides indicating a specific error, often indicate a serious logic error.

GETTING IT RIGHT, FIRST

If you believe that you can write programs correctly, you will. If you believe that your program will have errors in it, it will. Many programmers accept the fact that their program will be riddled with errors and that half their time will be spent debugging. Because of this belief, that is what happens.

On the other hand, if you feel that you can write a program correctly the first time, you will no longer accept this carelessness and will concentrate on removing all errors before the first compilation. Here are some suggestions on writing error-free programs.

First, after writing some code, check it. How many times have you keypunched or typed some code at a terminal and then attempted to execute it to see what it would do? All along you had no confidence that the code would work correctly. Not surprisingly, you then find some typing or logic errors and resubmit the program several times until all obvious errors disappear.

A careful perusal of the code before submitting the job would have eliminated several runs. This willingness to accept so many errors is particularly damaging to your ability to write correct programs. Since you expect the program to be incorrect, you do not even try to get it correct the first time.

Instead let's lay out a plan for getting it right the first time.

1. Get the logic correct by a process of top-down design, stepwise refinement, and walkthrough checking.
2. Get the syntax right the first time. You already know most of the syntax for your programming language. But if in doubt, look the syntax up, just as you would look up spelling in a dictionary.
3. Get the typing right. Scan the typing as you type, and when finished, check it all over one more time. Many typing errors cannot be found by the compiler; they then turn into bugs.

If you take these steps and concentrate on what you are doing, you will probably find that your programming is improving by an order of magnitude or more immediately.

Get it right the first time.

Past studies of programming have shown that many programmers spend half their time debugging. Debugging is obviously too expensive; so get the program right the first time and there is no need for debugging. The desirable situation is to prevent errors from entering the program in the first place.

Which program would you be more confident of: (a) one that you test, uncover ten errors, and correct them or (b) one that you test and find no errors? If adequate testing was done, we would be more confident of the last program. So the best approach is to put no errors in the program and then there will be none to shatter our confidence in the program.

BEBUGGING

How do you know when you have found all the bugs? There is no easy answer. In fact, there is little to even tell us how we are doing. One method of evaluation is called *bebugging*. In bebugging, a program is seeded with random errors. Then our success in finding the artificial bugs is used to judge how well we are doing in finding the other bugs. That is, if we put 100 bugs in a program and after a few days of debugging 50 of the artificial bugs are found, we could estimate that we have found 50% of the bugs in the program.

We could use this information to predict how many real bugs remain. If we had discovered 30 real bugs along with the 50 artificial bugs, we could predict that there were probably around 30 more real bugs, since we had only found half the artificial bugs.

This procedure can be used to predict how many bugs have been found, but it is more difficult to predict how long it will take to find most of the bugs (i.e., 95%). Finding bugs is not a linear process. In fact, it tends to be a curve with an infinite tail. So if you have found 95% of all the bugs, it may take twice as long to find the next 1 or 2%. Interested readers are referred to Gilb's *Software Metrics* for a discussion on measuring software quality.

It is useful to keep records of the number of errors found versus time needed. This information can be plotted and used to predict how long it will take to complete a project to a certain reliability level. Another useful record is to keep track of which modules have the most errors. People involved in maintenance programming have noticed that a great deal of maintenance is often spent on just a few modules. The best place to look for an error is near the site of the last one. It is best to rewrite modules that are very error prone. If trouble-prone modules are identified early, they can be rewritten, saving a great deal of maintenance programming later.

TIME NEEDED FOR DEBUGGING

There is a continual tendency to underestimate the time needed for debugging. Here is a formula that I have used. Figure out how much time is needed for programming, double it, and call it one unit. Then a projected timetable might be

Task	Units
Planning	1
Writing	1
Debugging	4
Testing	1

It is generally agreed that debugging always takes the most time. The question is: How much more? Try this schedule and see how it works. Then adjust it to your own needs. If you are able to reduce the debugging time but your program continually blows up during production runs, then you are cheating.

PREVENTING BUGS

Debugging is often the largest program development cost. Thus effort should be made to prevent bugs. A few rules, if followed, will help eliminate some of them.

Avoid questionable coding. Assume that advance features won't work unless you know they work. Use the simplest statements. Don't try to fool the compiler or the system. Compilers and operating systems are very complicated, and it is not unusual to find a loophole in one where you can violate a language syntax rule and still get correct results. The only problem is that since you did violate the syntax rule, the computer manufacturer is under no duress to allow your trick to work on future releases or updates of the computer language or operating system. So an operational program with tricky coding in it may not run under new releases of the language. This type of bug can be difficult to find a year or two after you wrote the original program.

Avoid dependence on defaults. All programming languages have some language defaults that the compiler assumes. The use of these defaults saves work for the programmer but can be dangerous because computer manufacturers occasionally change the defaults. In addition, the programmer may assume that a wrong default is being used. IBM changed a default size for one variable type in PL/I on one of its frequent language releases, and many PL/I programs became inoperable. Also, different machines have different defaults; and if it is desirable to maintain portability of your program, it is best to avoid using too many defaults.

Never allow data dependency. Never allow your program to depend on whether the input data is in a special form or within a restricted range. Instead check the data at input time to ensure that it is correct. Data always follows Murphy's law: "Anything that can go wrong will." Data errors can be caused by ignoring input instructions, typing errors, or input/output errors. If data is not checked at input, the program will periodically be found to have mysteriously blown up. After laboriously tracing the error, it will be shown that it was the fault of the input data. But the program and the programmer will still gain a reputation for unreliability.

Always complete your logic decisions. If data is to have a 1 or 2 code, don't check for a 1 and, if false, assume a 2. This practice overlooks the pathological cases that will often be present. Always check for the 1; then if not true, check for the 2. If neither 1 nor 2, then program the pathological case — usually an error message or halt. If there are N possible conditions, your program must check $(N + 1)$ conditions to check for the error condition: that is, check the N conditions and the error condition.

Operator independence. Never assume that the operator will do anything correctly, because if the job is run often enough, something will surely go wrong. First, don't ask the operator to do anything that the program can do. For instance, don't ask the operator to type in the date if you can get the same information from the operating system. Secondly, check everything that the operator does. Have the program verify all data and files for correctness. It is easy for an operator to mount an incorrect tape or for someone else to provide job control statements that point to a wrong file.

CONCLUSION

The listings of possible errors in the chapter will probably not teach anyone how to debug a program, but they can be used as a checklist of what to check next when you are stuck while debugging. This might be called the entomology of program bugs: the study of bugs by observation.

The principal approach to debugging is to provide enough information in printed form so that the program error can be located easily. An expert programmer knows where to put the debugging statements, whereas a beginning programmer has no idea where to start and thus uses a great deal of personal time and machine time debugging. It is a rare program that doesn't need debugging statements.

As Gruenberger nicely puts it: "When debugging is completed, the program definitely solves some problem." Chapter 5 discusses how to ensure that the program solves the problem that was intended.

PROGRAMMING MAXIMS

Use a debugging compiler.

Desk check first.

Echo check input data.

Introduce debugging aids early.

Check input for reasonableness.

Find out which debugging aids are available.

Get it right the first time.

EXERCISES

Chapter Review

1. Define the following terms.
   - (a) Abend
   - (b) Determinacy
   - (c) Storage map
   - (d) Cross-reference list
   - (e) Echo checking
   - (f) Cancellation
   - (g) Bug arresting
   - (h) Fire walls

(i) Mutual suspicion   (j) Assertions
(k) GIGO   (l) Deadly embrace
(m) Breakpoint

2. Build a list of programming errors that you continually encounter. This is called a bug diary.

3. Discuss the advantages and disadvantages of the debugging techniques covered in this chapter.

4. What are some other debugging techniques besides the ones mentioned here?

5. When should a TRACE be used and when should you write your own trace statements?

6. What debugging aids would you like? How many are available to you?

7. Look at Table 4.1. Is the table complete? Can you think of any changes that should be made?

8. Using Table 4.2 as a starting point, add to the catalog of bugs to develop your own personal catalog.

9. This chapter listed a few errors that the compiler cannot detect. Think of at least five other types of errors that the compiler cannot detect.

10. What are the space dimension and the time dimension in a program? How is each dimension traced when debugging?

11. Name some of the reasons that subroutines simplify debugging.

12. What is the difference between syntax errors and execution errors? List seven syntax errors and seven execution errors.

Problems

13. Set up a bulletin board and post short program segments that have a difficult-to-locate error. To start, use some of the programs listed in these exercises. Ask people to try to figure out the error and to contribute their own error programs. If your installation has a newsletter, put some of the errors in the newsletter.

14. *Input editing.* A file of punched cards is assumed to have the following fields.
    (a) Columns 1–9   A Social Security number.

(b) Columns 10-30.   A person's name.
(c) Columns 31.   Sex, 1 or 2.
(d) Columns 32-50.   A street address.
(e) Columns 51-68.   City and state.
(f) Columns 69-74.   A ZIP code.
(g) Columns 75-80.   Employee birth data, MMDDYY.

Describe exactly how the data should be edited to verify valid input data. Could you do this easily in your programming language?

15. If someone handed you a copy of *just* the output of one of your programs (i.e., with the program listing and other items removed), how would you answer these questions:
    (a) What version of the program was actually used?
    (b) What set of data was actually used?
    (c) Did the program actually complete execution or did it blow up and stop right before it ended?
    (d) How many records were processed?

    How could you supply this information in your programs? Can you think of situations in which it would prove useful?

16. Some syntactic errors are local (in a single statement) and others are global (the error can be detected only by examining more than one statement). An example of a global error is a GO TO statement directed to a missing label. Find examples of local and global syntax errors.

17. *Bebugging.* When debugging your program, have someone else introduce two bugs into your program (called bebugging). Then you know that there are bugs, and the length of time necessary to find these bugs can be used to estimate how you are doing finding the other bugs.

18. Think of a bug that appeared after a program became a production program. What debugging tools could have located this bug? What could you have done to prevent the bug or discover the bug before the program went into production?

19. We should become familiar with our own bugs. One way to do so is to adopt a bug diary. A *bug diary* is a little notebook in which you describe your own program bugs. After awhile it may provide interesting clues to your proclivity for certain type of bugs. This information can be useful when debugging other programs.

20. What checks (like checking subscripts) would you like your compiler to develop code for during execution?

21. Which of these debugging aids is available on your compiler? compiler?
    (a) Flow trace
    (b) Turn flow trace off and on
    (c) Variable trace
    (d) Selective variable trace
    (e) Subroutine call trace
    (f) Dumps
    (g) A display command that labels output with variable names

22. If your compiler has a subscript range checker, would it detect an error for $A(4,2)$ if the array was declared with dimensions $A(3,4)$

23. Is there a debugging compiler available for the programming language you code in? Does it offer enough advantages so that it would be worth obtaining?

24. If you use a language that has blocks (i.e., DO, BEGIN), does the compiler indicate the level of nesting for the blocks?

25. Develop a personal list of error messages and their probable cause while working on your own programs. Here are two examples.

Error Message	Probable Cause
Time exceeded	Infinite loop
Overflow	Undefined variable

26. Which of these checks are done during compilation by the compiler you use?
    (a) Sequence check source decks
    (b) Unused labels
    (c) Unused statements
    (d) Unused variables
    (e) Truncation in moves
    (f) Statement which transfers to itself
    (g) Transfer into the middle of a DO (FOR) loop
    (h) Variable type and format specification match
    (i) Function arguments wrong type
    (j) Attempt to use a nonrecursive subprogram recursively
    (k) Attempt to use a subroutine as a function or vice versa

(l) Incorrect number of subscripts
(m) Illegal bit strings
(n) Correct attributes in comparisons
(o) Assignment compatibility

Arrange them in order of importance to you. What other checks would you like done by your compiler? Would it be logically possible to provide these checks?

27. Which of the following checks are provided during execution by the compiler you use?
    (a) Using an uninitialized variable
    (b) Illegal subscript
    (c) Real overflow
    (d) Real underflow
    (e) Integer overflow
    (f) Exponent overflow
    (g) Exponent underflow
    (h) Division by zero
    (i) Indetermine, that is, $0**0$
    (j) Correct number of subroutine arguments
    (k) Correct attributes of subroutine arguments
    (l) Character string range errors
    (m) Conversion errors
    (n) Bound checks on statements where bounds are critical

    Arrange these checks in order of importance to you. What other checks would you like provided by your compiler? Would it be logically possible to provide these checks?

28. Does your compiler provide the following options for debugging?
    (a) List all variables in alphabetic order (*storage map*)
    (b) List all constants used
    (c) List of variables showing attributes (*attribute table*)
    (d) List of functions used
    (e) List of subroutines used
    (f) List each variable indicating all statements that use it (*cross-reference table*)
    (g) List all statements that reference each label

    Arrange the preceding options in order of importance to you. What other options would you like to have available? Would it be logically possible to provide these options?

29. What is a glitch? Do you know of any examples of a glitch? Ask some other programmers what a glitch is.

30. Many tricks can be used in programs. Here is one.

```
DIMENSION X (25), Y(20)

DO 10 I = 1, 45

   X(I) = 0.0

10    CONTINUE
```

This example will zero both array X and Y since they are stored next to each other. But doing so invites trouble if either X or Y is ever changed in size, since this code hides the fact that Y is zeroed. This trick can be done in many programming languages. Try it on yours. Find some other programming tricks. When, if ever, are they justified? What trouble could they cause a later programmer trying to modify the program?

31. *Programs that modify themself.* There are commands in most programming languages that allow you to modify the source program during execution. Here are some examples.

FORTRAN

```
ASSIGN 16 TO I

         .

         .

         GO TO I
```

COBOL

```
PARAGRAPH-1.

   GOTO BYPASS-PARAGRAPH.

   .

   .

   ALTER PARAGRAPH-1 TO PROCEED TO PARAGRAPH-OTHER.
```

Both modify the source program during execution. Someone reading the program has a difficult time figuring out what branch was taken during execution. This type of statement is heavily condemned by programming experts. Do you agree that these commands should be eliminated from the programming language? When is this type of command necessary?

32. When you locate the next difficult-to-locate bug in one of your own programs, analyze how the bug entered your program. Write a short description of the bug and trace its inception.

33. A common statement goes as follows. The number of bugs in a program is proportional to the number of labels it contains. What do you think about this statement? Could it be true?

34. When looking for a bug, keep a log of what you do to locate the bug. In time you may be able to ascertain what your debugging strategy is. If this type of research interests you, look up John D. Gould, "Some Psychological Evidence on How People Debug Computer Programs," *International Journal of Man-Machine Studies*, No. 7, pp. 151–182, 1975.

35. Pretend that you wish to redesign a computer so that X = Y is *true* not only for exact equality but also when the two values differ only in the least significant digit represented. Do you think this would be a good idea? If you did the above, does

$$a = b \text{ and } b = c \text{ imply that } a = c?$$

Give some examples in which equality will occur under the preceding conditions. Give some examples in which equality will not occur.

Programs

36. Write a small program (less than 50 lines of code). Have a contest with others to see who can generate the most compiler error messages in one program.

37. Write a small program (less than 50 lines of code) that will compile successfully with no syntax errors but that will force the program to abnormally abort before execution is completed. A trivial technique to do so would be to cause a division by zero. How many different ways can you get your program to abort during execution?

38. Take the foregoing program, give it to someone else, and have that person find the error.

39. Take a small program and modify the program in a subtle manner so that the answer is obviously incorrect. Then trade it with someone else and see if that person can find your error.

40. Write a small program, misspelling some reserved words. How many different types of error messages can you create this way?

41. Write a program that uses an array but that does not declare the array. How many different types of error messages appear? Do any of the error messages indicate the problem?

42. Write a program to obtain as many *different* compiler error messages as possible. Next, classify the types of error messages. For example,
    (a) The error is discovered and error message correctly identifies the error.
    (b) The error is discovered, but a misleading error message is printed.
    (c) No error is present, but an error message occurs.
    Are there any obvious errors that do not produce error messages?

43. *Psychology of bugs.* Write programs to do the following to see what happens in your programming language when programming errors below are made.
    (a) Divide by zero.
    (b) Cause underflow and overflow.
    (c) Overrun an array. First, overrun it just a little. Then try it again, overrunning the array by a lot. For example, declare an array of 10 elements. First, try zeroing 11 elements and then try zeroing 1000 elements. What happens?
    (d) Have a subroutine call itself if recursion is not allowed.
    (e) Pass too few and too many parameters to a subroutine.
    (f) Pass wrong type of arguments — that is, real when expecting integer.

44. Let $F2 = 1.36103$. Then do this calculation

$$F2 = (F2*1.66673)/1.66673$$

in single precision 100 times. What answer should print out? Try it for 1000, 10,000, and 100,000 times. What answer prints? The answer will have truncation errors if the precision is only seven places. For computers that have greater precision, try longer constants.

45. Determine exactly the largest value that an integer can have in your computer. Determine the same for the smallest integer.

Do the same for real numbers. On real numbers you must determine separately the mantissa and exponent. Write a program to check this out.

46. Use logical statements to test the following comparisons on your computer. Use real values for X and Y.
    (a) Does $X^0 = X^{0.0} = 1$ for all X?
    (b) Does $SQRT(X) = X^{0.5} = X^{(1.0/2.0)}$ for all X?
    (c) Does $X = X^1 = X^{1.0}$ for all X?
    (d) Does $X*X = X^2 = X^{2.0}$ for all X?
    (e) Does $X*X*X = X^3 = X^{3.0}$ for all X?
    (f) Does $X/Y*Y = X$ for all X, Y?
    (g) Does $\sin^2 X + \cos^2 X = 1$ for all X?
    (h) Does $1000* (1.0/5.0) = \Sigma_{i=1}^{1000} (1.0/5.0)$?
    Think of some other "logically true" statements to check.

47. Write a program to do the following:

$$Y = A + B + C$$

where $A = -2{,}500{,}000.00$, $B = 0.01$, $C = 2{,}500{,}001.00$. Is the answer correct? If not, why? Could you rearrange the calculation so it would be correct?

48. Use logical statements to test the following comparisons on your computer. Use real values for A, B, and C.
    (a) Does $A + B - A = B$ for all A, B?
    (b) Does $A(B - C) = AB - AC$ for all A, B, C?
    (c) Does $(A - B)/C = A/C - B/C$ for all A, B, C?
    (d) Does $(A + B) + C = A + (B + C)$ for all A, B, C?

49. Write a program to do each of the following.
    (a) Sum 0.1 ten times.
    (b) Sum 0.01 one hundred times.
    (c) Sum 0.001 one thousand times.
    (d) Sum 0.0001 ten thousand times.
    (e) Sum 0.000001 one million times.
    Print the maximum significant digits. How close are the results to unity? Why are some results not exact?

50. Program the evaluation of $\Sigma_{n=1}^{100} (1/n^3)$ by adding forward and also by adding backward. Which sum is likely to be nearest the exact answer?

51. Many mathematical functions have an inverse function available. But because of truncation error, sometimes the inverse operation does not provide the original value. Write a program to

see if the following functions will always return the original value for random values of X.

(a) Y = SQRT(X)   then X = Y*Y
(b) Y = LOG(X)   then X = EXP(Y)
(c) Y = SIN(X)   then X = ARSIN(Y)
(d) Y = COS(X)   then X = ARCOS(Y)

Can you think of any other functions to test this way? In each of the above, can you notice any trend? That is, do large numbers (or numbers near PI) produce more problems than small numbers or vice versa?

52. Write a program to evaluate each of these sums.

(a) $1 - \dfrac{1}{2} + \dfrac{1}{3} - \dfrac{1}{4} + \dfrac{1}{5} - \cdots - \dfrac{1}{10000}$

(b) $-\dfrac{1}{10000} + \dfrac{1}{9999} - \dfrac{1}{9998} + \cdots - \dfrac{1}{2} + 1$

(c) $\left(1 + \dfrac{1}{3} + \dfrac{1}{5} + \cdots + \dfrac{1}{9999}\right) - \left(\dfrac{1}{2} + \dfrac{1}{4} + \dfrac{1}{6} + \cdots + \dfrac{1}{10000}\right)$

(d) $\left(\dfrac{1}{9999} + \dfrac{1}{9997} + \cdots + \dfrac{1}{3} + 1\right) - \left(\dfrac{1}{10000} + \dfrac{1}{9998} + \cdots \right.$

$$\left. + \dfrac{1}{4} + \dfrac{1}{2}\right)$$

Notice that all of them are the same sums. Why do the answers differ? Which answer is correct?

53. Real constants must be converted from base 10 to machine base before being stored. On some compilers different results will occur between read constants and set constants when too many significant digits are involved. Try a program like this:

Any Language

```
         A1 = 1111111111.111
         READ   A2
         WRITE   A1, A2
         END
     $DATA
     1111111111.111
```

Write a program similar to the above and try different large values. Are the results printed for A1 and A2 always the same?

54. When using subroutines, one particularly nasty bug presents itself in various languages. Here is a FORTRAN example.

```
        CALL SUBA (2,K)
        WRITE (6,10) K
        I = 2
        WRITE (6,10) I
   10   FORMAT (1X,I5)
        STOP
        END
        SUBROUTINE  SUBA(L, M)
        L = L+L
        M = L
        RETURN
        END
```

(a) Trace through the program and figure out which values will print out.

(b) Punch the program and submit it to run. Does the answer that you thought should print actually print?

(c) If the answer is different than the expected answer, what happened? How can you prevent this type of bug?

55. Here is a program and the printed results.

(a) Trace through the program and figure out what the results should be. Is the printed result correct?

(b) If not, why not? If you cannot find the error, keypunch the program and debug it.

```
FACTOR: PROCEDURE OPTIONS (MAIN);
 /* FIND FACTORIAL OF 5 */
    FACT: PROCEDURE(N) RECURSIVE;
            IF (N>1) THEN RETURN (N*FACT(N-1));
                ELSE RETURN(1);
    END FACT;

    M = 5;
    X = FACT(M);
    PUT DATA(X);
END FACTOR;
```

Printed result:

$$X = 5.00000E+00;$$

56. An assignment statement that would assign two different values

simultaneously to the same variable would be undesirable. It might look like

$$(A,A) = (2,3)$$

Can you think of ways to do this in your programming language? Here is one way.

```
CALL  SUBA (A,B,A)
PRINT A
STOP
END
SUBROUTINE  SUBA (X,Y,Z)
    X = 1.0
    Y = 2.0
    Z = 3.0
    RETURN
END
```

What value do you expect will print from the preceding code? Program the above in your favorite programming language.

57. What value will print from the following program?

```
     A = 2
     CALL SUBA(A,A)
     WRITE(6,10) A
10   FORMAT(1X, ' A=', F5.1)
     STOP
     END

     SUBROUTINE SUBA(A,B)
         A = A + B**3
         IF ( A .LT. SQRT(B) ) B = 5.15
         RETURN
     END
```

If you cannot agree on the result, program the problem in your favorite programming language.

58. Here is a program and the printed results.
   (a) Trace through the program and figure out what the results should be. Is the printed result correct?

(b) If not, why not? If you cannot find the error, keypunch the program and debug it.

```
LOOP: PROCEDURE OPTIONS (MAIN);
    DECLARE X(10) DECIMAL FLOAT;
    DO Y = 0.1 TO 1.0 BY 0.1;
        I = 10*Y;
        X(I) = Y;
    END;
    PUT EDIT ((X(I) DO I = 1 TO 10)) (SKIP, F(8,2));
END LOOP;
```

Printed result:

```
        0.20
        0.30
        0.40
        0.50
        0.60
        0.70
        0.80
        0.90
        1.00
    29312.00
```

Projects

59. It was said earlier that debugging is easier if we use small routines. How small should the routines be? We could make each separate statement a separate routine. As the number of routines increases, the number of interfaces increases and probably the number of errors. Can you establish any guidelines for an ideal number of routines and program size? This problem is much more complicated than it looks.

60. Write a program that accepts a source program and then lists any unused statements, unused labels, and undefined variables.

61. Research the types and kinds of debugging aids for your programming language that are available at your installation. (Obvious aids are debugging compilers, cross-reference programs, execution-time profilers, and debugging systems.) Then prepare documentation, in the form of a handout, that describes the available debugging options for your installation.

62. In any programming language it is possible to develop a list of *do*'s and *don't*s for avoiding program bugs. Develop a list for your programming language, using this chapter as a starting point. Pass your list around and see if you can get any consensus. Then send me a copy of the list.

63. A cross-reference program is described in this chapter. Write a program to provide a cross-reference for your source programming language.

64. A lazy (and smarter) way to do the preceding assignment is to research which type of cross-reference program is available for your programming language. If you find one, check it out and make it generally available to users at your installation.

65. Vendor-supplied software always has bugs. In fact, there are often large lists of known bugs with suggestion fixes or dates of expected fixes. These lists are never called Error or Bug Lists. IBM calls theirs "Early Warnings" or "Programming System Memorandum." DEC calls theirs "The Software Dispatch." Find one of these bug lists and survey them for several lists to see if the number of bugs is increasing, decreasing, or staying the same. If you can find out the number of instructions in some vendor-supplied software packages, you can calculate the ratio of "bugs per instruction" by dividing the number of bugs into the number of instructions and computing it for different software items.

66. Certain features in a programming language introduce frequent errors, called *characteristic* errors. Each programming language has its own characteristic errors. For example, in ALGOL all variables must be declared, but in FORTRAN this step is not necessary. To illustrate,

$$MISTAKE = MISTEAK + 1$$

In FORTRAN two separate locations will be assigned to the variables MISTAKE and MISTEAK, and the error will be undetected. In ALGOL, since all variables must be declared, the compiler would point out the error. Find some characteristic errors for your programming language.

67. *Standardization of diagnostic and error messages.* Every nontrivial program usually generates some errors in syntax or semantics. Today's compilers will detect most of these common errors, but no two compilers will display and flag them in the same manner. Compare the diagnostics of two compilers. You can

either compare two compilers for the same language or compare two different languages. Then develop some rules for standardizing diagnostic messages in regard to context and form. Also, determine how and where diagnostics should be generated.

68. *Debugging systems.* Examine some debugging systems. Examples are the DEBUG statements in IBM COBOL and the "AT" statement in IBM FORTRAN. Several other available debugging languages are mentioned in Rustin's *Debugging Techniques in Large Systems* (see References). In addition, survey the commercially available packages to determine which similar features are available in most debugging systems and which extras are available in some of the systems. Figure out which package would be best for you. Develop a checklist of what would constitute a good debugging system.

69. *Error-handling routines.* Examine error-handling routines presently available in compilers. Examples are the "ON" statement in PL/I and the "ON ERROR" in DEC PDP-11 BASIC. These error-handling routines allow the user extensive freedom in handling error conditions that arise during program execution. Survey the field of error-handling routines and see if you can find any general agreement on useful ones.

70. Develop some statistics on which types of language features are most bug prone. One way to do so is to examine a large number of discarded program listings and categorize the bugs.

71. A program can be written to read a source program and indicate possible coding errors. Examples of coding blunders are
    (a) Undeclared variables
    (b) Unreadable code
    (c) Unused variables or labels
    (d) Variables used only once
    Develop a list of coding blunders that a program could locate. You might try to write a program to flag these errors. A previous exercise lists some of these types of errors.

72. A more subtle error of the above type is the following.

T = arithmetic expression

.

.

.

some statements that make no reference to T and are a proper set of code.
T = (another arithmetic expression)

Since T is reset without ever being used, this example is an error. Would it be of value for a compiler to check for this type of error for programmers? For this type and for the errors discovered in the previous problem, develop a priority list of which errors should be checked for by a compiler and the practicality of checking for them.

73. *Foreign debugging.* In foreign debugging someone else besides the original programmer debugs the program. One advantage is that the original programmers usually try extra hard to make their program clear and documented when they know someone else is going to debug the program. This factor will make the program easier to maintain. On some program problem in this book, exchange programs with someone else and then debug each other's program. Next, write a short description of how the experiment worked.

74. *Limits of your compiler.* Many commands within your compiler have limitations. These limits are normally so large that you will seldom encounter them. For example, one popular compiler will allow about 400 parentheses in *one* statement before objecting. An interesting exercise is to find other limitations on your favorite compiler. Here are some suggestions.
    (a) Maximum number of parentheses in one statement.
    (b) Maximum size of a one-dimensional array. Maximum dimensions of an array.
    (c) Maximum length of literal or bit constant.
    (d) Maximum length of a single statement.
    (e) Maximum length comment or maximum number of consecutive comments.
    (f) Maximum number of nested DO loops (or blocks or IF THEN ELSE).
    (g) Maximum number of subroutines (or nested calls to subroutines).
    (h) Maximum number of arguments in a subroutine.
    (i) Maximum number of recursive calls.
    Can you think of any other restrictions of this type? (*Hint:* Examine the list of error messages for your language compiler.)

REFERENCES

Barron, D. W., "Programming in Wonderland," *Computer Bulletin*, 15, 1971.

Boar, B. H., *Abend Debugging for COBOL Programmers.* New York: Wiley–Interscience, 1976.

Brown, A. R., and W. A. Sampson, *Program Debugging.* New York: American Elseveir, 1973.

Gaines, R. Stockton, *The Debugging of Computer Programs.* Princeton, N.J.: Institute for Defense Analysis, August 1969.

Geller, Dennis, "Debugging Other Languages in APL," *Software — Practice and Experience,* Vol. 5, No. 2., April–June 1975.

Gilb, Tom, *Software Metrics.* Cambridge, Mass.: Winthrop Publishers, Inc., 1977.

Halpern, Mark, "Computer Programming: The Debugging Epoch Opens," *Computers and Automation,* November 1965.

IEEE Symposium on Computer Software Reliability. New York: IEEE Computer Society, 1973.

Kernighan, Brian W., and P. J. Plauger, *Software Tools.* Reading, Mass.: Addison-Wesley, 1976.

Poole, P. C. "Debugging and Testing," *Advanced Course in Software Engineering.* New York: Springer-Verlag, 1973.

Rustin, Randall (Ed.), *Debugging Techniques in Large Systems.* Englewood Cliffs, N.J.: Prentice-Hall, 1971.

Satterthwaite, E. "Debugging Tools for High Level Languages," *Software — Practice and Experience,* Vol. 2, 1972.

Shooman, M. L., and M. I. Bolsky, "Types, Distribution, and Test and Correction Times for Programming Errors," *Proceedings of 1975 International Conference on Reliable Software.* New York: IEEE, 1975.

Weinberg, G. M., *The Psychology of Computer Programming.* New York: Van Nostrand Reinhold Co., 1971.

Testing shows the presence,
not the absence of bugs.

Dijkstra

Testing should be a consideration
throughout the entire development
of the program.

5

Program Testing

If program testing is conducted in a laissez-faire manner in which the tester rambles around with no set direction, then program testing is an art. If the program tester carefully selects the required test data, carefully plots the points to be tested, and carefully executes the tests, then program testing is a science.

Planning and coding a program are skills that can be learned. It is time for program testing to shift now from testing as an art to testing as a science. If a laissez-faire approach to program testing is used, there is no way to prevent duplicate testing, no way to control testing so that areas with the highest payoffs are covered, no way to evaluate how complete testing is, no way to determine when testing is completed.

Testing is one of the most critical areas of system development and often causes the most trouble and most lost time. It is a distinct step from debugging. Debugging is the removal of syntax errors and obviously incorrect coding. Once they are removed and the program produces some correct results, then the testing stage commences. The main reason for insisting that there are two separate steps is to ensure that both steps are done and that both steps have time allotted to them.

Never assume that the program is correct simply because it is accepted by the computer, completely compiled, and numerical results achieved. All you have done here is obtain some results — not necessarily the correct results. Many logic errors may still exist. The requirement is not to produce answers but to produce *correct* answers. Thus you must usually check out the results by hand calculations. Once all debugging is completed, even the experienced programmer will still have an error for every 20 or 30 statements written. These errors can range from the catastrophic to the trivial, from complete errors in logic to small coding errors. A debugged program is one for which we have not yet found a set of test data to make the program fail.

BEGINNING PROGRAMMERS

Beginning programmers do not realize that programs are wrong until proven correct. An untested program generally is a source of future embarrassment when it produces obviously incorrect results. Then if the program has been used and believed for a period of time, all previous results of the program are of questionable veracity. It is at this stage that programmers learn that they had not tested the program, only debugged it. Amateur programmers work on a program until it provides results, not always correct results, and then the program is abandoned for a new project.

ROBUSTNESS

The goal of program testing is to ensure that the program solves the problem that it is supposed to solve and that it yields the correct answer under all conditions. The latter requirement is usually called the *durability* or *robustness* of a program. A program that stops producing correct results easily is not durable or robust. Programs tend to become more robust the longer they are used because, as they are used, failures are discovered and corrected.

A program can appear to work for months and even years before it becomes apparent that there is a major error in some part of it. There is a theory that big programs are never completely error free. Testing should never be skimped to save money or time. An incorrect program is worth less than no program at all because of the false conclusions it produces. It may inspire others to make expensive errors. The expense of reprocessing a year's transactions because of an incompletely tested program will forcefully demonstrate that adequate testing is desirable.

A robust program should be able to survive cross-eyed keypunchers, cretinous data control clerks, and retarded operators. If you assume that anything that can go wrong will and program accordingly, you will have a robust program.

Although it is impossible in an exact sense to specify completely how to test programs, several hints and guidelines can aid in the task of program testing. This chapter discusses some helpful testing techniques.

GENERAL HINTS

The most important hint about program testing is that some thought should go into the testing phase while the program is being written. Constant attention should be paid to the question: How will I test this segment? If you write a routine and you don't know how you will test it, the routine should be rewritten or broken into modules. The ultimate result of a program that is difficult to test is that it is never completely tested, and sooner or later it will fail during a production run.

Programs are not written to be tested. Programs are written to be efficient, to be readable, to be portable and so on, but they certainly are not written to be tested. Design in testability. Do a carefully controlled job of program design, emphasizing clarity and simplicity, keeping in mind the question: If this routine were coded in this way, how could I satisfy myself that it works as intended?

Programs should be reassembled for each test, immediately prior to the test. Load modules should not be used because source code will normally be in a state of flux. Use of load modules can easily lead to confusion, for it is difficult to ascertain which load module matches which source version.

If cards must be added to the source program to aid testing, punch them on a different color from the rest of the program. Also, keypunch TEST in columns 73–80 of each test line. Then you will have two reminders to remove these test source lines.

Control over the quality of the code produced should be established early. The code should be checked by experienced personnel to detect loose code, poor programming practices, and deviation from program specifications. Early catching of potential errors benefits the original programmer and helps to avoid large problems during testing.

The program should be coded in a language suitable for the problem programmed. This factor will permit easier testing. Selection of a good algorithm for solving the problem will also aid testing.

HOW MUCH TESTING

Beginning programmers always wonder how they are to know when a program has been tested enough. This is a difficult question, and many seasoned programmers have discovered that they stopped testing a program too soon.

One observation is that before testing is completed, every instruction should have been executed at least once. Test data should try every error condition possible. Each branch should be tested. Thus on a two-way or three-way branch they would all be tried at least once. If you have some special routines to handle unusual input data, each routine should be tested at least once. All classes of input should be used as test data. Although this is not a sufficient test, it is at least a necessary one. These are called *leg tests* (a test is sent through each leg in the logic of the program).

Program sections that interact heavily will need to be tested by using data that will cause the interactions to be tested thoroughly. If there are a large number of factors that influence the dependent quantities, complete testing can be difficult. Care must be taken so that data is such that errors that do not affect the results of a particular case are not hidden.

The temptation to drop the program as soon as it does not look incorrect should be avoided. A half-tested program can prove quite embarrassing to the programmer because it will still have to be tested later on after it has produced some disconcerting results.

Since it is seldom possible to test all the possibilities of a large program, where does testing stop? This factor depends on the value of the program. Considerations include:

1. the importance of accuracy,
2. how often the program is to be used, and
3. how long a period it will be used.

A program that is to be used once or twice would probably be tested less than a program that is to be used daily for many months. But the overriding consideration is the need for accuracy. In many cases, a small risk of inaccuracy is tolerable, considering the cost of trying to be certain. In reality, we are seldom certain anyway.

The sheer number of tests frequently is of little significance itself. Programs do not wear out. That is, if a program will add some numbers correctly once, it will add a group of similar numbers correctly again. Similarly, sheer quantity does not guarantee that all cases have been tested. If you process 100 records for test data from normal input data, 90 of them will be the same — that is, test the main logical sequence of the program. The last 10 will probably test only 2 additional cases. So the 100 records processed are actually only 3 different test cases.

Another reason for not using large volumes of test data is that no one is going to spend the time to examine 1000 test cases to see if they are correct. So nothing is gained.

Too often a large number of test cases merely proves that the program is good at doing the same thing with different numbers. Instead we wish to prove robustness. We want each test run to check something not checked by previous runs. The goal is to strain the program to its limit. Doing so requires a good imagination and a suspicious nature.

Use a minimum number of test cases.

EXHAUSTIVE TESTING

Exhaustive testing is prohibited by cost and schedule and usually unrealizable. On any normal program it is impossible to test all possible cases. For instance, suppose that we have a small program with two input variables and one output variable as shown in Fig. 5.1. If we can test the program for all possible assignments of X and Y, then we could determine the program's correctness. But even for this simple program, doing so is impossible. If numbers are stored in 32 bits, there are 2^{32} possible assignments for X and Y and

$$2^{32} \times 2^{32} = 2^{64}$$

assignments for the pair X, Y, which could take 50 billion years to test if the program executed in one millesecond.

So it is always impossible to check out all possible inputs, but is it possible to test all possible program paths? For example, if you

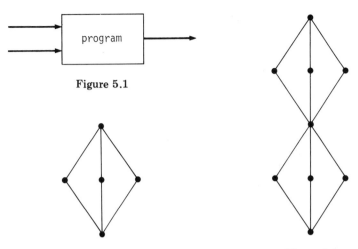

Figure 5.1

Figure 5.2   Figure 5.3

have the diagram shown in Fig. 5.2 there are three unique paths, but by using two of them as shown in Fig. 5.3, there are nine unique paths (find them). If the code for Figure 5.3 is executed twice, there are 9*9 possible paths. And if the code was part of a loop that is executed ten times, there are 9^{10} possible execution sequences. So exhaustive testing is impossible even in this simple example. Finally, if you did use the computer time necessary to check all possible paths or inputs, there is no way anyone could possibly hand check all of the results.

Not only is it almost impossible to test even a simple program exhaustively, but, in addition, only a limited number of all conceivable input cases will ever be executed during the lifetime of any program. It is necessary to select a small set of test cases that are significant, since any randomly selected set of test cases is insignificant.

Since exhaustive testing is impossible, test wisely.

SPECIFICATION VERSUS PROGRAM TESTING

Program testing is the process of guaranteeing that the program works in all cases in which it is supposed to work. Two types of testing should take place. 1) We must test to prove that the problem specified was programmed; 2) we must test to learn whether the program works correctly.

Specification testing is impossible if the problem specifications are not complete, clear, and consistent. The results to be obtained over the input domain must be completely stated. Clearness means that all parties must understand what is to be accomplished. Consistency means that no ambiguities are allowed. If the program specifications are complete, clear, and consistent, a program tester can treat the program as a "black box" (without knowing anything about the coding) and test the final program.

One way to test specifications is to have the problem originator provide the test data, together with the correct answers. This step ensures that the problem originators know what they want and also provides a check on the programmer's understanding of the problem.

Some testing can be done before any of the program is coded. A "hand simulation" of the logic of the specifications can be done. Some errors may be discovered in this way before coding has started and thus be easy to correct.

Two extremes are possible in considering program testing. One is to examine the code and use it as the basis for testing. However, if the code does not match the specifications, the tester would never discover this fact. So the tester must use the functional specifications in developing tests. The opposite approach is to use only the specifications and treat the code as a black box. But suppose that you are told to develop test data for a program that reads an integer value that is a radius of a circle and that the program calculates the area of the circle. Devise test cases for this program, treating the code as a black box. (A *black box* is something that accepts an input and returns an output, and you have no idea how it does so).

Suppose, next, that I claimed to write the program as follows. If radius is one, then the area is so and so; if the radius is two, then the area . . . . Would your previous test cases test this program adequately? The point is that in order to test a program adequately, you must use both the program specifications and the actual code.

EARLY TESTING

Early testing is essential. As each stage of the program development passes, the cost of testing and correcting errors increases by an order of magnitude. An error found during the design stage costs a negligible amount to correct. An error found during unit testing of a single module is not difficult to fix but costs more than the previous type of error. An error found when the entire program is being tested will often involve several people and require communication between groups. This situation easily costs an order of magnitude more than previously found errors.

An error found in a production program involves costs that increase by another order of magnitude or more. Users are involved, a temporary fix is necessary, and reruns of jobs may be needed. In addition, a great deal of communication is required between programmers and remote users.

Start testing early.

The solution is early testing. The earlier an error is discovered, the less it will cost to fix. Testing should start when the project begins, at the design stage. Testing, at whatever level, may result in a complete redesign of part or all of the system.

Testers should be brought into the project during the design phase for two major reasons. First, testers can help clarify the design specifications. Testers look at the specifications from an entirely different point of view than do the developers. Consequently, they can frequently find flaws in the logic of the design or incompleteness in the specifications. In doing so, they help to produce a better product and actually speed up progress of the project.

The second reason for bringing testers into the project at the design stage is the magnitude of work that they must do. Test cases must be prepared along with the expected results. These test cases and expected results must be recorded in some media for easy processing. This work can and should be done while the program is being developed. If top-down testing is done, the test data will be needed very early in the project.

DESIGN TESTING

If we do not know what the program is supposed to do, no amount of testing can ensure that the program is almost correct. Much time during testing can be saved by starting with good problem specifications. The final testing phase is not the place to find holes in the design. By then a great deal of work has gone into the program, which may have to be scrapped if the original design is incorrect. Instead the problem specification should be tested before it is set into code.

A test of the problem specifications is as follows. Can the testing group take the problem specifications and develop an adequate set of tests to check out the program, treating the program as a black box and only using the problem specifications? In general, the first time this question is asked the answer is no, and, in this case, the problem specifications should be redone. If the test group cannot understand the problem specifications, it is probable that no one else can either. Sometimes it happens that when the designers try to do a better specification, they discover that they cannot. This situation indicates that the entire problem is not well understood; it is also a warning signal of impending trouble if they proceed without clearing up the problem specifications.

Several studies have suggested that nearly half of all software errors in a large project occur during the design stage. Consequently, here is the most profitable place to attempt to reduce errors. Program errors can enter because of the inexperience of the developer or because of fuzzy goals on the part of the group wanting the software. Whatever the reason, it is important to eliminate errors at the beginning.

Structured Walkthroughs

The first test should be the *structured walkthrough* of the design by a group of people. Frequently, serious errors can be discovered at this stage. The purpose here is not to redesign the program but simply to check for possible errors. If errors are found, then the designers should redesign the program and the cycle can be repeated. It is not unusual for this cycle to be repeated several times. Remember that errors caught at this stage are inexpensive to correct. On the other hand, if the same error goes undetected until final program checkout, the price of correction is high. So the right attitude should be maintained about finding errors at this stage. The goal is obviously not to critize the designers but to help obtain a clean design. Also, obviously, if the attitude of the group becomes negative, it is that much harder to get everyone to cooperate. For this reason, supervisors are usually excluded from the structured walkthrough process. If the atmosphere can be kept nonfault finding, everyone, including the designers, will be eager to find errors.

Hand test the design first.

Design testing should concentrate on the higher levels only: that is, verify the correctness of the overall flow of the system and the interfaces between modules. When a design is accepted, we want only errors that can be corrected by changing a single module. Errors that affect many modules should be found during design testing.

Another common way to test the design is to write a first version of the system in APL or BASIC. Although this process involves some extra work, the extra work is repaid many times over if the design can be refined.

> *Try a simple first version to test out the basic design.*

The developer should arrange and schedule the structured walkthrough. Four to six reviewers are needed. Those attending usually include other people working on the project, such as testers, designers, and documenters. The reviewers should receive review material 4 to 6 days prior to the walkthrough and should go over the material and come to the session prepared to discuss any problems discovered. The session should have a definite goal in mind and should be restricted to a maximum of 2 hours. If more time is needed, a later session can be scheduled. A moderator keeps the session moving and compiles a list of all errors, discrepancies, and inconsistencies. These problems are not solved during the session. The developer will solve them later and report back on what was done.

To begin, reviewers comment on the general completeness, accuracy and quality of the product being reviewed. Then the developer gives a brief walkthrough of the software product step by step. Test cases can be walked through and examined by the group. After the meeting, the moderator distributes a list of all discovered problem areas to the members of the group. The developer must resolve all such problems and tell the reviewers what corrective action has been taken.

A limit should be placed on the numbers of errors found. That is, if there are more than 5 or 10 errors, the structured walkthrough should be stopped and the process repeated once a major overhaul is done. There is no reason to waste everyone's time locating 20 or 30 errors. If so many errors exist, the entire project may need to be redone, and piecemeal corrections will not help. Hughes and Michtom's *A Structured Approach to Programming* has a good section on structured walkthroughs.

TESTING METHODS

As a rule, program testing is done in stages, starting with the unit testing of a single module (sometimes called debugging) and ending with the final system testing. If the testing does not proceed in some organized fashion, there is little chance of developing reliable software. Organized testing normally proceeds in one of two directions: the traditional bottom-up testing or the newer top-down testing.

Bottom-Up Testing

This is the traditional way to test programs. It involves writing the lowest-level modules first and testing them. Next, we program and test the next higher levels. This sequence is repeated until the program is completed.

Bottom-up testing is now in disfavor with the advocates of top-down design and top-down coding. The main criticism of the bottom-up approach to testing is that serious design and interface errors do not appear until near the end of the project. Then major revisions that ripple through the code may be needed.

Another disadvantage is that test harnesses, or module drivers, and new test data are needed to test each routine as the routines are combined. This process may itself require a good deal of code.

Top-Down Testing

Top-down testing complements top-down design, structured walkthrough, and top-down coding. If top-down techniques are used, the main program is coded first. Program stubs are used to fill in for uncoded lower modules. This skeleton program can then be tested even if there are no lower routines. It can be executed with no data; this will check out all of the job control language, which often is not trivial. The next step might be to add a module that will produce some input. It can be the input module or a substitution module until the real input module can be coded. Then the skeleton can be tested with some simple input.

Advantages of Top-Down Testing

As the skeleton is fleshed out with new modules, more test data must be added. Thus the test data grows with the rest of the program. Test data is added as lower modules are added. This process also allows the pooling of test data instead of having separate test data for each module.

Another advantage of top-down testing is that the main logic of the program is tested early and continually as new modules are added. In bottom-up testing the program is built and tested from the bottom up; therefore the main logic is tested last. Errors in the main logic can cause all lower levels to be scrapped, thus resulting in a great loss of work. Top-down testing usually catches serious errors earlier.

A common situation is to have two groups of programmers building two separate systems that must interact or mesh at the top. In the bottom-up approach, the last feature tested is the meshing of the two systems. In the top-down approach, the interaction of the two systems can be tested early before the lower modules are completed.

Still another advantage is that testing is distributed. Ideally, testing is distributed throughout the project. As modules are added, they are tested. In the bottom-up approach, on the other hand, all testing is generally saved until the end of the project. Frequently, pressure to finish the project is intense at this time, and so testing is sometimes skimped on, with the normal disastrous results when the untested system collapses.

Try top-down testing.

Furthermore, top-down testing also produces early results. Such results have many advantages. Early results occur because some of the program will be working, and some output can usually be generated even when the program is not complete. These early results can be shown to the eventual user. In this way, the user not only sees that something is happening but also has a look at what the programmers felt was requested. Any change of mind or omissions can be rectified early before extensive coding has been done, and changes can be made then instead of once coding is completed.

Which Is Best?

Which approach is best depends on the project. On small programs it probably makes little difference. In some cases, the needed program stubs for top-down testing can be as complex as the actual modules, and so there is little advantage in using it. The top-down approach can also overlook the fact that a planned lower-level module may be impossible to write, and this factor may cause major problems if not discovered early. In actual practice, we often end up by using a mixture with some coding and testing proceeding from the top and some from the bottom.

TEST DATA

The selection of appropriate data for testing a routine can greatly ease the problem of detecting errors. The first test of the program or module should be the simplest possible. The purpose is to see if the program will execute at all. This is often called a *smoke test* (plug it in and see if smoke comes out). The first few tests are used to verify the basic organization of the program, for if the basic organization is incorrect, it is frivolous as well as difficult to check out the intricacies of the program.

Thus a test that follows the typical flow of the program will uncover gross errors. If gross errors are present, the program will easily spin off in any direction at the speed of several million operations a minute. If an elaborate test is used for the first test and the program does not work, we will not know if the program fails to work for all cases or merely for this specialized case. A complicated set of test data will produce either a very simple failure that could have been found with a much simpler set of test data or a failure as complicated as the test data producing output impossible to diagnose.

Keep your arithmetic simple. If a program will add 11.11, 22.22, and 33.33 correctly, it will add 12.56, 45.92, and 34.79 correctly. Simple test data is easier to hand check. The purpose of test cases is to see if the program works correctly, not to test the ability of the machine to perform arithmetic.

Even though it is desirable to use simple data, it is also desirable to obtain as much information as possible during each test run and to make as few runs as possible. We would like to obtain many units of information from each test run, but items being tested must not interfere with each other to the point of obscuring information in case of errors. Good tests should also help to indicate the error source if errors develop.

Some testing requires "miniaturization" of the program — that is, reducing the amount of data to a reasonable level below the regular amount of data. For example, a program may usually require a 50 × 50 matrix, but checking out test cases of this size is prohibitive by hand. So a test matrix of 5 × 5 may be used. But if program changes are then required; there is some danger either that existing errors may be obscured or temporarily eliminated by the changes or that new errors may be introduced in the program by the changes that are made to facilitate program testing.

Similarly, if a routine works for a loop of 5, it should work for a loop of 105 (as long as sufficient storage space is reserved). For loops, loops of size 0, 1, or a negative value (careful) often produce interesting results. If a loop is supposed to do N iterations, the most common error is to do $N - 1$ or $N + 1$ iterations.

Test data should increase in complexity stepwise. With each new test run one new section of the program is assumed to work correctly (at least under one case). Stepwise testing makes it much easier to pinpoint an error when results are incorrect. If test data simultaneously tests several untested sections of the program and the program blows up, it is difficult to know which of the several sections caused the blowup.

Eventually the tests should test all sections of the program. In this way, routines with errors in them will not be skipped because they do not affect the results in that particular case.

When testing a program, the goal is not merely to see if the program executes for each set of test data but to see that the program executes *correctly*. So test data should be chosen so that the programmer can calculate the correct answer *before* the program is run. If the answer is calculated after the test run, it is too easy to assume that it is correct.

Types Of Test Data

There are three general categories of test data:

1. constructed data,
2. actual data with modifications, and
3. actual data in volume.

Each type of data is usually needed to test a program.

Constructed data is the first test data used. *Constructed* test data refers to data that the programmer creates (constructs) to test the program. There are two types of constructed test data: controlled and random. The controlled test data are used to see if the program works at all. Controlled test data has the advantage that it can be created to test particular situations that might rarely occur. Such creation allows the maximum control over test data. Also, selection of the right data will minimize the necessary work needed to hand check results. The drawback with controlled test data is that only those problems that the user recognizes as problems are included in the test data.

So, the use of random test data should not be overlooked. Random test data are often created by a special program provided for this purpose. Controlled test data may consistently avoid the errors in the program. Random test data has the advantage of indicating errors that may not be apparent otherwise. The disadvantage of using random test data is it may be difficult to check the results to see if they are correct. But if the errors resulting are gross enough (abnormal termination), they will be quite apparent.

Modified actual data has some of the advantages of both other types of data. By careful, selective modification of real data, specific tests can be made with the program. The use of real data avoids the sometimes awesome task of preparing large masses of data.

Another advantage of using modified real data is that it adds an element of reality to the testing process. The introduction of real data can pinpoint many problem areas that could never be discovered by constructed data. One reason for modifying real data is to test error routines. Deliberate introduction of errors in data is the only way to ensure that the error-checking routines work.

The final set of test data is volume testing by using actual live data. If this step can be done with a parallel run of an older system, less hand checking will be needed on resulting calculations. Generally there are many surprises in store for the programmer when using real data. Often this is where a failure of communication between the user and programmer is discovered. Oversights by both programmer and user are frequently revealed here.

Occasionally parallel runs will demonstrate that the older system had, in fact, been incorrect in part. Checking of expected output without a parallel run is normally a time-consuming job, if at all possible. Parallel test runs of at least three cycles are commonly necessary for complete testing.

When doing parallel runs, the volume of output often prohibits eye comparisons. Instead a program can be written to compare outputs. Printed results can be directed to a tape or disk so that the comparison program can compare the entire file for differences. Moreover, all new output test files should be compared against the previous set of test files each time the production programs are modified.

Seemingly, all three types of test data are needed to do a complete job of testing. Each type has advantages and disadvantages if used alone; but when used together, they tend to balance each other, thereby providing the best possibility of thorough testing.

When hand calculating results to check out test calculations, sufficient care should be taken to get correct results. Otherwise you could compare your incorrect hand-calculated results and the computer printout and spend many hours looking for a bug in the program when the problem is in your calculations.

Classes of Test Data

Since we cannot hope to try all possible data, we want to select data that is representative. We wish to select our test data so that each test represents a class of data. This is an often-overlooked aspect of testing. Once the program has correctly processed a class of data, we have some assurance that the program will process other data in the same class correctly.

If we had a program that was to read weekly hours and calculate pay, then we could select the classes for hours. Obvious classes are

Hours
0
35
40
50
100

Since the program is to calculate overtime pay, we would like values under, at, and over 40 to ensure that it is working. Then zero is always interesting, as is one large value. You should also try some incorrect values, such as negative values, and a very large value.

In selecting the classes of the data, some knowledge of the code of the program is usually needed. In the preceding example, we need all the classes shown. A group of additional numbers over 40 would not tell us much more than the 50 does — that is, if the program work correctly for overtime pay. And if any of the classes were omitted, we would not have as much faith in the program. The point is to try to discover the classes and to try a case or two for each class. Amateurs tend to overtest one class and skip others.

Each test case should represent a different class of data.

The process of using classes of test data recognizes the economics of testing. As noted before, exhaustive testing is impossible, so we want to select classes of test data in such a way that, when we test it, we have some assurance that this class will be handled correctly.

Solutions for Test Data

If test data is to be used, we must be able to figure out if the program-generated answers are correct. There are several ways to obtain correct answers:

1. calculate the answer by hand calculations,
2. obtain results from a book, article, or set of tables, and
3. obtain the answer from another computer program.

It is important that the results produced by the program be compared with corresponding data obtained *independently* from a different source. Obviously the first method is the most undesirable, since it may require a great deal of work to calculate the answers by hand.

All the preceding techniques require us to know what the expected output values are. Sometimes this knowledge is not possible or practical for all test data. Then two additional methods are possible if the tester has detailed knowledge of the program algorithm.

The first method requires knowing the magnitude of the output values. The magnitude can usually be determined by rough analysis and knowledge of the algorithm. Any output values that exceed the expected ranges can be checked out more carefully.

The second method is by manipulating the test data in a controlled manner. By carefully modifying input values, we should be able to predict direction and magnitude of change in the resulting output values. These factors should partially indicate whether the program is operating correctly.

Generating Test Data

In order to improve the testing process, ways of generating test data are necessary. For card data, such methods can be as simple as providing standard test cards. Standard test cards usually include

1. A card with   0 in columns 1-9,
                                  1 in columns 10-19,
                                  2 in columns 20-29,
                                  etc.

2. Cards with   1 in column 1,
                           2 in column 2,
                           .
                           .
                           .
                           9 in column 9,
                           0 in column 10,
                           1 in column 11,
                           .
                           .
                           .
                           9 in column 19,
                           0 in column 20,
                           1 in column 21,
                           etc.

3. Cards with   80 columns of zeros
    Cards with   80 columns of ones
    .
    .
    .

    Cards with   80 columns of nines
4. Cards that alternate zeros and ones.
5. 80 column alphabetic cards:
                           A in column 1,
                           B in column 2,
                           C in column 3,
                           etc.

This type of test data can be used to check out fields. For example, if columns 27–32 are used for input, then records with data like cards 1 and 2 can be used. The output would look as follows.

      222333   (Read each column as a number.)
      789012

This example clearly indicates the columns that were read (i.e., 27, 28, . . . , 32). It proves one of the most basic things to be tested — that is, that the correct columns of records are being read. Then test cards of types 3–5 can be used to ensure that zeros and alphabetic data are handled correctly. Another method that is used to make fields stand out is to use the same letter or number throughout a field but use a different character for each field. Then field separations are more easily recognized.

No one should expect all the testing problems to be completed by using these test cards, but many simple tests can be accomplished with them. The cards should be readily available in a card rack where the programmer can reach them.

Both COBOL and PL/I make heavy use of files; so test data are needed to test files. Utility programs can usually be used to create files. IBM offers the utility program IEBDG (data generator) that provides a "pattern" of test data that can be used in testing. In addition, some installations provide special test generator programs that will generate test files. The general principle of these test generator programs is that they use the file description in the program to be tested to generate test files. A test generator program can be an in-house program or one that is purchased from a software house.

Test Cases

The actual testing of a program can be broken into three phases.

1. Testing the normal cases
2. Testing the extremes
3. Testing the exceptions.

These three phases should include all necessary testing.

The goal is to ensure that all valid data yields correct results and that all invalid data always yields error messages.

TESTING NORMAL CASES

The normal cases include the most general data for which the program was planned. Very few programs will work for all data. Instead the data is usually restricted to a data domain — that is, to the data that the program will process correctly. This phase of testing attempts to prove that the program will produce correct results for most general sets of expected data.

TESTING EXTREMES

This is the second phase of testing. After the normal cases have been tested, the extremes should be next. The extremes include fringes of the input range that are to be accepted as valid data. For nonnumerical data, use typical and similar cases that contain all expected characteristics. For numerical data, take values at the end of the allowable range, varying for minimum and maximum field length. Obvious examples are very large numbers, very small numbers, and zero amount transactions. Each program has its own extreme data that must be selected by the programmer.

The process of using extremes for test data is referred to as a *boundary test*. Boundary tests are often the most fruitful place to look for errors. If a program works correctly at the boundaries, there is a good chance that it will work everywhere. There is another type of extreme, the extreme of volume — that is, too few or too many records. What happens if there are no transactions or only one. Does the program still work?

The *null* cases are always of particular interest. The null case for numerical input usually consists of zero values. For character strings, the null case is the blank string or null string. For pointers, it is the null pointer. The null case is one of the best test cases, since it will certainly turn up as data sometime in the life of the program. And the null case, if untested, often causes a program to do strange things.

It isn't always obvious which values will test the extremes. For example, suppose that a program had to read in four positive integer one-digit numbers. A naive approach would be to use the following to test the extremes.

	A	B	C	D
Test group 1	0	0	0	0
Test group 2	9	9	9	9

At first glance, they would seem to be the extreme values.

The preceding sets of numbers are good test cases, but they probably are not the desired extremes. They are the extremes only if the calculation is

$$\text{ANSWER} = A + B + C + D$$

But if the calculation being performed is

$$\text{ANSWER} = \left(\frac{A + B}{C}\right) ** D$$

Then a value of $C = 1$ would give the largest possible answer.

$$\text{ANSWER} = \left(\frac{9 + 9}{9}\right) **9 = 2^9$$

$$\text{ANSWER} = \left(\frac{9 + 9}{1}\right) **9 = 18^9$$

Therefore it is possible to select the numeric values that will produce the extremes only if you are familiar with the actual calculations being done. This situation illustrates an often-overlooked fact. There are extremes for input and extremes for output. Generally the extremes for input do not generate the extremes for output. The major reason for wishing to use the extremes in test calculations is to ensure that intermediate result fields have sufficient space to handle the calculation that are required.

Test situations can be forced by loading in data as constants to create the test conditions desired. If the extreme conditions that you want to test are the result of long calculations, it may be difficult to manufacture data to create the condition that you wish to test. For instance, if you wish to test the condition of a calculation turning negative, a relatively rare situation, then you can easily do so by adding a statement in the program to reset the necessary variable to negative to complete the test. Care must be taken to remove this modification once testing is completed. An easy way to remember to remove it is to insert a comment stating that it is a test statement or to punch TEST in columns 73–80 of the source test line as a reminder.

TESTING EXCEPTIONS

The final phase is the testing of data that falls outside the acceptable range. All programs are designed to process a restricted set of data. So if the program is not designed to handle negative or zero data, what happens when it is actually given this type of erroneous input? Or if arrays are used, what happens if the number of data elements exceeds the size of the specified arrays? What happens if strings are too long or too short? What happens if numbers are too large or too small?

The worst situation that can happen is that the program accepts the erroneous data and returns an incorrect but believable answer. It is not sufficient to say that the program wasn't designed for that data or to say that no erroneous data should be inputted. Erroneous data can be inputted through typing errors or a misunderstanding of input instructions. The program should forcefully reject all data it cannot process correctly.

If you are to be the sole user of the program, you may decide to live dangerously and skip adding program statements to reject bad data. But if the program is for others as well, there must be statements to reject any unacceptable data. These statements should be tested and the tests should convince you that you haven't overlooked any editing statements.

When testing the exceptions or the extremes, there are several hints that may save time. If there are edit checks that include range tests, try values on both sides of the range. Those values just inside or outside the range are the ones most likely to give trouble.

Data with blanks, numerics, and alphabetic characters should all be tried in various combinations. That is, try a blank field and an alphabetic field in fields that require numeric data. If relations between data fields are being tested, try permutations of correct and incorrect data.

Sometimes data with multiple input errors can cause unusual problems.

Another error of special interest is the error on the first or last transaction. That is, if the last transaction is incorrect, does the program still conclude correctly? You might even try an input file of one transaction with the transaction incorrect. This step should test all kinds of things. If these problems are not discovered during testing, they will certainly appear during production runs.

Now is the time to be curious and let your imagination run wild. Put in out-of-sequence data. Try a handful of data cards from the recycling bin. Try some data cards upside down. Try a data tape from another job. The first rule of data is: data will be incorrect. If your program is not designed to prevent the use of incorrect data, you will spend a lot of time looking for bugs when the fault lies in the data. Although it may be careless for a clerk to prepare incorrect data, it is unforgivable for the programmer to allow the program to accept incorrect data as correct.

Test the normal, extreme, and exception cases.

PATH TESTING

Flowcharts are useful during testing because they show paths in the program. This information can be used to locate critical paths in the program and to establish classes of test data. Once the paths are found, it is necessary to develop test data to check out each path. On a two-way branch, we would want test data to test each branch. Structured coding techniques should help simplify path testing, since there are usually less branches.

Develop test data for each path.

Paths are more easily tested in individual modules. The paths should be checked in unit testing. If path testing is postponed until modules have been combined, testing becomes much more difficult. Consider a module that has *n* paths to test. Then there is a second module that calls the first module from *m* places. If each module can be tested independently, we need to test *m* + *n* paths. But if the modules are combined and tested, we need to test *m* × *n* paths. Also, the more code there is, the more difficult it is to locate the error.

It should be obvious that traversing all paths in a program is an insufficient test of a program. Suppose that a program is to determine if three numbers are equal and the following algorithm is used.

```
IF ((X+Y+Z)/3 = Y)

    THEN  PRINT 'X, Y, Z, EQUAL'

    ELSE  PRINT 'X, Y, Z, NOT EQUAL'
```

Obviously if the test data simply checks out the two paths, the program will erroneously be thought to be correct.

SAMPLE TESTS

A very simple problem to test would be a module that calculates the diagonal of a box. Figure 5.4 shows a box with a diagonal drawn. The diagonal is equal to $\sqrt{(\sqrt{A^2 + C^2})^2 + B^2}$.

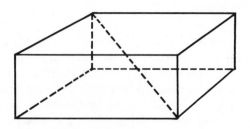

Figure 5.4

For test data, we wish to test the normal cases, the extremes, and the exceptions.

	Sides of a Box			Remarks
1.	1	1	1	A good first test.
2.	1	2	3	Another normal test.
3.	0	0	0	Should give you a zero answer.
4.	0	1	2	Not a box. What happens?
5.	1	0	3	Not a box. What happens?
6.	2	1	0	Not a box. What happens?
7.	1	-6	3	Incorrect data.

The first two tests are testing the normal cases. Tests 3–7 test the extremes or exceptions. If all these tests produce correct answers, we are fairly certain that the module works correctly. You might like to try some large or small numbers as an additional test. We can never be positive that a program will always work, but in this case we would have a high degree of expectation.

A second example of testing consists of finding quadratic roots of the equation $Ax^2 + Bx + C = 0$. In this program we read the coefficients A, B, C and use the quadratic formula

$$R = \frac{-b \pm \sqrt{b^2 - 4ac}}{2a}$$

to find the two roots. We have a few more items to test here.

	Coefficients			Remarks
1.	1	1	-2	A good first test.
2.	1	0	0.25	Another normal test.
3.	0	0	0	What happens here?
4.	0	2	1	Should get only one root.
5.	2	1	0	Should be OK.
6.	1	1	1	Complex roots.
7.	0	0	2	Not a valid equation.
8.	0	2	0	Should get one root.
9.	2	0	0	Should get two roots.

If all these test data produce correct results, we could be reasonably sure that the program would produce good results consistently.

These are two points to notice here. The first is that these routines were simple to test. If you use module programming, your routines can also be simple. The second point to notice is that the testing was done in a systematic fashion. We did not simply pick several random numbers as test data. Normally if random numbers are used for test data, it is too difficult to calculate the results by hand. Also, random numbers may not test all cases. It is better to carefully pick input that will test all the possible situations in the program. Good testing is thorough testing.

TESTING MATHEMATICAL SOFTWARE

In testing numeric software, there are three primary sources of errors in any numerical result. First, there is the result of error in the original data, which is called *intrinsic error*. Examples are errors in input (*transmitted error*) or limitations in measurement (*inherited error*) of input variables. This error is attributed to the uncertainty in the input value and is not correctable by any amount of computational sophistication in the evaluation procedure.

The second source of error is *analytic truncation error*. This type of error is caused by replacing an essentially infinite mathematical process by a finite process in the mathematical algorithm. An example is using only six terms of a series instead of the whole series, which is usually infinite.

The third source of error is *roundoff error*. It is caused by using finite-precision arithmetic in the computer. This last error is influenced by the number of places and the arithmetic base used to represent numbers in the computer. Roundoff errors are called *generated errors*, since they are generated by the computer program, assuming exact input data. The generated error on mathematical software is tested for by using data with known solutions and comparing the results with the known solutions. Known solutions are obtained either by theoretical knowledge or by calculating answers on another computer with greater precision and then comparing the two results. Precision is important in test cases because *nearly* correct programs are especially treacherous.

Comparing the results with known answers (in the forward) is called *forward error analysis*. Direct comparson of known results is often not possible or appropriate. Sometimes it is more appropriate to show that the computed solution to the problem is the exact solution to the original problem. This is called *backward error analysis*. Instead of measuring the difference between the computed solution and the mathematical solution, we measure the difference between the problem posed and the problem solved. An example is finding an inverse. Then the inverse can be multiplied by the original value to see how close the solution is. For those interested in mathematical software, a good first place to look is John R. Rice (Ed.), *Mathematical Software* (New York: Academic Press, 1971).

MODULES

Perhaps some of the programmers reading this chapter thought the testing examples were nice but nowhere near the complicated programs they do. Well, your programs can be simple if you use modules. Only very inexperienced programmers write single, long, untestable programs. It is virtually impossible to test a large monolithic program because of the large number of total logic paths. The more experienced the programmer, the shorter the modules used.

The major aim of modules is to produce readily testable units. Each module should do one task. Then in the testing of the unit, we must test only to see if this one task is completed correctly. Modules that have been individually tested have a much better chance of producing a correct program. All modules should be completely tested before they are combined.

Once the individual modules are tested, the paths and interactions between the modules should be tested. Even though the data areas might have been checked during debugging, it is a good idea to verify that all values being passed between modules are correct, since it is a very common area of trouble. Because the interaction between the modules is restricted by the parameter list, testing of a large program composed of modules is easier than a large program without modules. At this stage of testing there should be no logic errors in the individual modules. If an error is discovered, it would indicate that module testing was incomplete.

The chance of introducing errors when program changes are made is substantially reduced when small modules are used. Modules can also be easily included in a library. Then the use of the library programs automatically reduces the testing job, since the routines contained in the library are pretested.

Simulation of Modules

A common situation is the need to simulate a module. Possibly a needed module is not ready but is needed to complete testing of another module. In order to start testing the completed module, the missing module can be simulated. There are two possibilities: dummy modules or substitution modules.

Dummy Modules. A dummy module is one that has only an entry point and a return point. It is used to test a higher-level module when the needed module is not ready or not required. It is often useful to have a statement in the dummy module that will indicate it was called.

Substitution Modules. A substitution module is used for testing when a dummy module cannot be used. The substitution module actually does some calculation but usually only in a very simplified manner. It is needed because a higher module calls the substitution module to return some values so that testing of the upper module can be completed.

Another reason to use a substitution module is that the needed module may require too much computer time or special output to use the real module; therefore it is advantageous to use a substitution module to speed up testing.

Hints on Testing Modules

Testing of modules can be made easier by placing the data in the top module. This step results in easier testing because then all data is external to the lower modules being tested. For example, perhaps the I/O module requires a fairly complicated coding that will take a long time to program. Many of the other modules may be programmed earlier. To avoid delay in testing the other modules, a substitution I/O module could be set up to provide test input data. Since all the data is kept in the top module, it would be fairly simple to program a substitution module to provide test input data. Then the other modules can proceed in testing without having to wait for the I/O module.

Each module should be short in length and thus easily comprehended. Each module should have a limited number of paths and should process a small amount of data. If the module has all these conditions, it should be relatively simple to test the module, using all the extremes of the data, and to test each process path.

Another method to test modules is to use an "initial" statement in the module to start testing. The initial statement can provide the first values to test the module. This method avoids the problem of actually having to pass values to the module. It provides a good way to first test the module. But you will still need to test the module and pass values to it, since errors may exist in the passing of values that would be overlooked by the initializing test method.

PROGRAM LIBRARY

As the subroutines are coded, debugged and tested, they should be put in a library. If you are using programming teams, this step can be handled by the programming librarian. A program library reduces the size of test decks and, more importantly, ensures that all of the programs that require one particular routine are actually using the same version.

Sometimes it is desirable to have two program libraries: one a test library and the other a production library. The test library can contain subroutines with test aids (or debug aids) built in. By using the statement

IF TESTING THEN ...

described in the debugging chapter, we can usually obtain the same result with only one program library.

FILE TESTING

When processing records in which the record changes, the record should be printed out before and after each change. Similarly, when the response to a record depends on what is in the record, the record should be printed. This process will facilitate testing, since it allows the tester to avoid reading dumps of files.

A set of test records should be created early in the testing process to reduce duplication of effort. Utility programs are available normally for convenient generating of test records. A record generator program can greatly facilitate testing of programs. The program should be able to generate records for testing when data formats, including size, character, and normal contents of each field, are given it.

SYSTEM TESTING

So far this chapter has been devoted to program testing. Yet a larger test situation often exists — that is, system testing. The system may include several programs and in-between clerical tasks.

System testing proceeds from the simple to the complex. The testing of large systems is commonly divided into the following steps.

Unit Testing. The *unit test* is the lowest level of testing. The innermost routines are tested first. Testing should include all possible valid inputs and a sufficiently large collection of erroneous input to test all error routines.

Module Testing. The module can be a single program of a system or a system routine. Programmers should test their own modules before releasing them to the next step.

System Testing. The modules are put together and tested as a group. Major errors in coordinating the system are discovered here. The tests should be prepared by the person who prepared the program specifications.

Product Testing. Here the complete package is checked out, including documentation.

Field Testing. This is often called validation. The system is released to a restricted group of users. The system is closely watched for errors. Documentation shortcomings can be corrected here. This restricted group of users should be encouraged to run test cases of their own and to attempt to "crash" the system.

Release Testing. The product is released for general use. The user always completes the final testing. It is at this stage that we discover how thoroughly the previous testing has been done.

Several helpful observations can be made about organized testing patterns like the above.

1. Take only one step at a time, holding as many environmental factors constant as possible.
2. In the actual tests, proceed from the simple to the complex. The volume of test entries and the complexity of test entries should increase gradually.
3. If a program chronically fails at a given level of testing, it should be demoted to the previous level for additional testing.
4. An analogous rule is that the amount of difficulty encountered at any step of testing varies inversely with the thoroughness of the preceding steps of testing.
5. Loose control over the coding and debugging only delays the ultimate problems until testing.
6. Careless program testing reveals itself during "production" runs.

TESTING AIDS

Testing aids are programs that help automate the testing process. Such aids are also called *automated testing aids.* Testing tools allow a small programming team to examine a large volume of code, a situation that is otherwise impossible. Before discussing testing aids, let us review several other aids that are quite useful in testing. First, a good debugging compiler is needed. Discussed in Chapter 4, these are useful because they uncover a multitude of errors that would otherwise need to be discovered during testing. Eliminating syntactic errors is an essential step in achieving a correct final program. The greater the number of errors discovered by the compiler, the fewer errors remain to be uncovered by testing. The current trend is to include more and more error diagnostics. PL/I presently has about 1000 error diagnostics, including warnings.

The second testing aid in the compiler is the run-time package associated with the compiler that does automatic error correction. The language system can point out arithmetic overflow/underflow, division by zero, and illegal ranges for supplied subroutines. The better compilers, such as FORTRAN WATFIV and COBOL WATBOL, also indicate array subscripting errors, illegal branches, and mismatched subroutine parameters. Since they require run-time overhead, these options are less available, ranging from hardly being available at all to 136 execution-type errors in PL/I. Errors detected by the compiler are certain to be caught; consequently, they are not left to wait for some special combination of errors that cause later program failure.

Next, the compiler should have a trace available and should be able to monitor selected variables. Both options are useful, for then it is possible to trace both logic paths and the changing values of variables in a program.

The next testing aid needed is a means to store testing input so that it can be reused. It can be as simple as a deck of cards for a small program or a complete set of programs for a complicated system. What is needed is a method that allows us to store, add, and modify test data. The test data is saved in order that it can be run against the program whenever the program is modified.

Test Data Generator

Although the preceding tools are useful and necessary, they are not what is known as proper testing aids. The first actual testing aid is the *test data generator* (TDG). A test data generator generates data that will be executed by the program being tested. Such data is often useful as a first test of the program to see if the module or program is going to hold together. However, several problems are involved in using this. First, it is necessary to learn how to use the TDG. And learning how to do so may take more effort than creating the test data by hand, at least on small projects. Next, TDG's main ability is to generate large amounts of test data. But it is not simply volume that is needed. What we want is a small amount of carefully selected test data that will exercise the program being tested. Moreover, test data must usually be generated in a particular sequence, often with very complex relationships (i.e., master and detail files), in order to be useful. Different packages solve these problems better than others. The table shows some commonly available Test Data Generators.

Table 5.1 Test Data Generators

IEBDG	IBM OS Utilities
	IBM Corporation
PRO/TEST	Synergetics Corporation
	One Garfield Circle
	Burlington, Mass. 01803
MetaCOBOL	Applied Data Research
	11661 San Vicente Blvd.
	Los Angeles, Cal. 90049

Other test data generators are discussed in Stanley M. Naftaly, *COBOL Support Packages* (New York: John Wiley & Sons, 1972).

File Print Utility

This testing aid is used to print the tape or disk files that a new program has created. It allows sight checking of files, a process that is often necessary and desirable. A program of this type is usually available as a standard manufacturer-supplied utility. Desirable characteristics are as follows. Each new record starts on a new line. It has the ability to print several representations — for example, character, decimal, and hexadecimal. It is also able to print a desired number of records and to start and stop at any record card.

File Comparer

A *file comparer* is a program that reads two files and prints out any differences. A file comparison program can be used to compare old test output to new test output to see if any discrepancies appear.

Programs must be retested when any additions or changes are made to a production program. The best approach is to save all old test input in a file and pass it through the modified program as a test. However, someone must then sit down and manually check all the new test output to see if it is correct. Manual checking of the output is so time consuming and boring that it is usually not done.

A better approach is to direct all test output into a file and then use the file comparison program to compare the new test output to the latest checked file of test output. The file comparison program reads the two files and prints only differences. Then someone must sit down and check out the differences. Finally, this new test output file becomes the master test output file to be used next time.

Profilers

Profilers were first discussed in Chapter 3. A profile of a program is useful during testing because it shows which statements were executed as well as how many times. Frequently, during debugging and testing it is useful to know how many times a particular statement was executed. A module or set of code not executed will show up on the profile and indicate a need for further testing. A useful addition to profilers is the ability to keep cumulative statistics in a data file of the system being tested. These cumulative statistics allow the tester to locate sections of code that are undertested. See Projects at the end of the chapter for a list of profilers.

Test Harness

A *test harness* is a program that passes input to a module and collects output that is either printed or placed in a file. A test harness is also called a *driver*. This device is used to execute a module of a program so that it can be tested. Sometimes the test harness is simply a small program to test out a single subroutine. In other cases, the test harness can be quite complicated. A good test harness will print the input parameters and any returned values. Top-down testing eliminates some of the need for a test harness by using the main program as the driver.

USE YOUR PROGRAM TO CHECK RESULTS

A program can be used to help check out the answers. This process is often called *self-checking* software. For example, if a module was to find a square root, the best approach would be for the test

routine to call the square root module and then print out the returned square root, the square of this supposed root, and the difference between the input argument and the square of the returned root.
This procedure is called a *reversal check*. Other examples when a reversal check can be done include matrix inversion, Fourier transfor-
mations, encoding when the reversal is the decoding, and many
conversions. When testing a module, the driver or test harness can be
used to verify the reversal check so that humans have less work to
do. If a great deal of volume is involved, the driver can be set up so
that it reports only failures, thereby reducing the total output.

To illustrate, if the output is the solution of a set of mathematical
equations, its correctness can be verified by substituting the solution
to the equations and checking for consistency. In some cases, a simple relationship may exist among the output variables, and the correctness of the output can be verified by checking this relationship.
Examples include a sorted array or some group of totals that must
balance each other (cross totals).

In most cases, the correctness of the output can only be verified
by an algorithm that is just as complicated as the program being
tested. Even then it is still often possible to check the reasonableness
of the output. For instance, paychecks should not be below or above
a set figure and the program can easily check this fact.

Yet it is important to be careful not to let the program convince
you that an incorrect answer is correct. If you have the computer
print out the intermediate calculations and then verify each step, all
you have done is verify that the machine can multiply correctly. You
have not verified that it did the correct mathematical operations in
the correct order. In the square root example, calculations were done
in two different ways and the results compared. This procedure is
not foolproof, but it is still a good check.

VALIDATION

At some point, testing is considered completed. The program has
been tested thoroughly with test and real data. The data preparation
and operating instructions are reviewed and considered complete. If
possible, release the program to a restricted number of users. A restricted release provides an additional testing phase before the program is completely released.

All final testing is done by the user. Computer manufacturer's
software is always tested by the user. Very seldom can the programmer have foreseen and tested all possible areas of difficulties. Users

normally report any errors they find, which can then be fixed and the program retested. Then the test data previously developed can be used to retest after changes.

Once the program has passed this limited usage test, it is ready for final release. All input instructions and documentation should be completely updated.

ADEQUATE TIME FOR TESTING

One way to help guarantee adequate testing is to schedule sufficient time for it. It has been suggested that testing time will equal programming time. Since the tendency is to schedule only time for programming, this factor might indicate why all programming projects are late. Time should be scheduled for planning, coding, debugging, and testing. Then if the planning is two weeks behind schedule, it is obvious that everything else will also be two weeks behind schedule.

On systems in which thorough testing is required, extra time is needed. On the Apollo program, according to estimates by NASA, testing accounted for 80% of the cost of developing software. This figure is high because of the thoroughness required in Apollo testing, but similar estimates for the development of operational software have produced figures of 30 to 60% of the total development cost as the amount assigned to testing.

Testing Schedules

If program testing is divided into categories, it is much easier to control testing. Very often a set amount of time is scheduled for all testing, so trouble in one area steals test time from other areas.

Schedule adequate time for testing.

A set amount of time should be scheduled for each step of testing. Then if unit testing is two weeks behind schedule, management will be warned early that the job production schedule will be delayed two weeks if additional resources are not allocated. Frequently, in order to keep on schedule when delays have occurred, later steps of testing are simply just skipped.

Testing schedules allow tighter control over testing and early warning if testing is not going according to schedule.

A Program Test Schedule

Quite often it is desirable to keep track of how program testing is progressing. At least two factors are of interest.

Are we maintaining our schedule?
Is the program being properly tested?

Both questions are important as well as difficult to answer. But there are techniques that can help to indicate the status of program testing.

Large program systems are generally divided into subsystems or components. These components are then composed of the smallest identifiable program units. There may be many levels and many units at each level. The normal testing method checks the smallest unit first, then combines the units and continues testing those until the complete system is tested.

An approach to organized testing is to develop a library of test cases while the program is being coded. This should be a parallel development effort by a different group from the programming group. This situation assumes that the test group (test groups are covered later in this chapter) and program group both use the same program specifications. If the specifications are not clear, then the tests designed usually will not match the programs. Thus these tests help prove the clearness of the design specifications. Separate design of test cases verifies both program testing and specification testing. If a program will not run with the supplied tests, this fact may indicate a specification failure rather than a test failure or program failure.

Once the test cases are designed by the test group, a status report can be kept of the following rates of progress.

What percent of tests has been tried?
What percent of tests has been completed successfully?

By keeping daily records of test results, management should be able to obtain some indication of program testing progress.

If an effort is not made to develop systematic test cases, it is doubtful that any true indication of status or success of testing will be found. Too many programming systems have failed from the lack of any careful long-range test planning and from the lack of understanding the intensive and exhaustive effort necessary for comprehensive system testing.

HOW WELL HAS A PROGRAM BEEN TESTED?

Sometimes, on a program, it is desirable to know how well the code has been tested. If the program is large with many logical decisions, then a pessimistic evaluation would be that most programs have not been very well tested. But it still would be useful to have a yardstick to determine how well the program has been tested. Some of the items to use in an evaluation are:

1. the percent of code actually executed during tests. We should hope for 100% here.
2. the percent of the total number of branches that has been taken in both directions during testing. Again, we would try to obtain 100% here.
3. how well the program has been segmented. Segmented programs are usually easier to test and hence are better tested.
4. the extent to which various interlock situations have been explored.

The weakest part of the testing is generally the last one.

On a large program it would be impossible to test all logical paths and data dependencies, but all major paths should be covered. Then the programmers are required to use their intuition to decide which untested paths would be most productive to test (i.e., the paths most prone to error). At this stage, program testing is no longer a science but becomes an art. Since the combinations and permutations of logical paths may be astronomical, a large program can never be completely tested. But there are two paths of special interest: the path of minimum input and the path of maximum input. These paths are usually easily identifiable and should be tested. Some of the factors that the program tester should consider are the importance of the logical paths, the prior testing completed, the vulnerability to failure, the cost of testing, and possible payoff.

RETESTING

During testing it is common practice to make changes in the program because of errors found while testing. These changes are particularly vulnerable to producing new errors. This situation occurs because you are concerned with removing the present error, and it is easy to overlook other problems that may be introduced. Program modification is also quite vulnerable to introducing errors. If previous test data has been saved, the old test data can be used to ensure that new errors have not been introduced.

Every program unit should have a set of test cases permanently associated with it for original testing and retesting after every program change. If the set of test cases is available for reuse and if it can be rerun automatically on demand, the programmer is less likely to skip the testing.

All saved test cases should be used as soon as possible when retesting. It is not advisable to use a few test cases, correcting any errors found, and then try additional test cases later. Instead, all test cases should be tried as soon as possible. If the code being tested is poor, it is best to find out immediately. Moreover, it is more efficient to correct many errors all at once rather than one at a time; or, in the worst case, it is cheaper to rewrite a module all at once rather than a little at a time.

These libraries of test input and test output are called *scripts.* Test data should not be used and thrown away. It takes a great deal of effort to create good test data; so the test data should be saved for reuse. The script must be documented in order that a later user can use it and understand it. The script may be used years later in regression testing after program modifications are made; therefore adequate documentation is vital.

Retesting is sometimes called *redundancy* testing or *regression* testing. When programs are first tested, we start with small, simple test cases and proceed to the large, complex tests. In regression testing we can start testing with the large, complex test and proceed to the small, simple test cases only if the former are unsuccessful. As we proceed backward to the simpler tests, the errors should be localized.

> *Retest after every program change.*

A TEST GROUP

One approach that has been tried is to establish a group of senior programmers to test all programs and systems before they are actually used for production runs. This approach, however, does not free the original programmer from testing his program. The testing group provides a final test for programs after the original programmer has certified the program as correct.

The test group can then consider the program a "black box" where, if specified input is provided, the outcome will be the desired results. Test groups are sometimes called professional idiots (not meant as an insult).

They include people who are good at designing incorrect data. That is, they design data that an idiot (hence the name) would use as input. The professional testers' job is to be destructive. Their goal is to attempt to cause the system to fail. If they make the system fail, they are successful. The original programmer wants to make the program succeed. So the original programmer and the testers have different goals.

A test group can thus gain proficiency in testing. Also, a fresh mind can often see problems that the original programmer may have overlooked. Sometimes, therefore, it is advisable to have a friend test your program.

Testing or validation done by a test group is sometimes called *acceptance* testing. The original programmers test the programs deductively and analytically, using their superior knowledge of the inner logic of the program. But the acceptance-tester approach is basically empirical, since the tester knows little of the internal logic of the program. The acceptance tester is in the middle between the program developer and the eventual user.

The acceptance tester must rely on the program specifications. If the specifications are vague or inconsistent, this fact will be discovered when the program is tested. The acceptance tester must decide if the program accomplishes the purpose set out in the original program specifications. If the program test group cannot determine from the specifications what the program is supposed to do, no testing can be accomplished.

In addition, the acceptance tester may determine such factors as:

Are the results accurate enough?
Is the documentation complete enough to allow easy use of the program?
Are error situations taken care of sufficiently?

Some advantages of using a testing group may be stated as follows.

1. The testing group does not disband at the end of each project. Thus it can accumulate testing experience and develop special tools to make testing more thorough and efficient.
2. The testing group's loyalty is directed to the user and not

against the colleagues who developed the programs. The test group's job is not to prove that the developers did their work correctly. Instead it is to prove that the program is acceptable to the ultimate user.

3. Since the testing group is working for the user, the group can influence the program developer to do adequate testing.

CONCLUSION

A programmer is judged by the number of errors that occur after the program is released for general use. So, it is better to have a reputation for being slow but producing good and thoroughly checked-out programs than to have a reputation for being fast but producing error-prone programs. The production of error-free programs is a time-consuming task.

A common piece of programming graffiti goes like this: Why do we never have enough time to do it right the first time but always have plenty of time to fix it later? Quick and dirty programmers tend to tarnish the reputation of all programmers, since these programs are also expected to turn out correct results. All important programs are always assigned to the programmer who turns out good, thoroughly checked-out code. Since your programming reputation is involved, it is wise to insist that enough time be allowed for proper program testing. Inadequate time produces inadequate results. Adequate time, however, should produce adequate results.

PROGRAMMING MAXIMS

Use a minimum number of test cases.

Since exhaustive testing is impossible, test wisely.

Start testing early.

Hand test the design first.

Try out a simple first version to test the basic design.

Try top-down testing.

Each test case should represent a different class of data.

Test the normal, extreme, and exception cases.

Develop test data for each path.

Schedule adequate time for testing.

Retest after every program change.

EXERCISES

Chapter Review

1. Define.
   (a) Program robustness
   (b) Specifications testing
   (c) Leg test
   (d) Smoke test
   (e) Unit test
   (f) System test
   (g) Product testing
   (h) Field testing
   (i) Release testing
   (j) Validation
   (k) Redundancy testing
   (l) Professional idiot

2. How does program debugging differ from program testing? Do you believe program testing should be a separate step from program debugging? Why?

3. What excuses are used for a program when it fails?

4. What are some of the advantages of setting up a testing schedule?

5. When is the artisan program tester needed?

6. What are some of the advantages of using subroutines when testing?

7. Name three ways of obtaining results for test data.

8. Why is retesting important?

Problems

9. Is it sufficient for test cases to test each exception or is it necessary to test combinations of exceptions?

10. What are the advantages of processing large amounts of actual test data even though one cannot check the accuracy of all results?

11. Find an example of a programming project that was scrapped during testing. What was the cause: poor testing preparation, inadequate design, change of goals, or other?

12. Use a simple program and calculate the number of unique paths within the program. Is exhaustive testing possible for this program? What are some techniques for cutting down the number of paths?

13. Develop test data for
    (a) GCD (greatest common divisor). Accepts two integers and gives the greatest common divisor.
    (b) LCM (lowest common multiple). Accepts two integers and gives the lowest common multiple.

14. Develop test cases for one of the following problems. Determine the "classes" of test data needed for each problem. What is the minimum number of test cases needed in each problem? What are the boundary points?
    (a) A square root function.
    (b) The program reads three numbers that are supposed to be sides of a triangle. Then the program prints whether the numbers represent a scalene, isosceles, or equilateral triangle
    (c) The program reads two dates and returns the number of elapsed days.
    (d) Read *N*, and then read *N* numbers and print the maximum and minimum value in the group of numbers.
    (e) Read an item and check to see if it matches any item in stored array.

15. By checking your programming manuals, determine the acceptable range of the argument for the functions below.
    Logarithmic–10   Cosine
    Logarithmic–*e*   Hyperbolic sine
    Sine   Hyperbolic cosine
    Write a program and try exceeding the range and note what happens.

16. Any mathematical function is not completely accurate because of errors inherent in computation. See if you can find in a computer manual the error range in some commonly used supplied math functions, such as SQRT, SIN, TAN . . . .

17. Take a program and prepare the following test data.
    (a) Constructed data
    (b) Actual data with modifications
    (c) Actual data in volume

18. Given the formula

$$Y = \frac{ab}{cd} - \frac{c+d}{a-b}$$

prepare test cases for
(a) the normal cases.
(b) the extreme cases.
(c) the exceptional cases.

19. Think of a program that failed during a production run. Would a well-planned testing practice have uncovered the error?

20. What automatic testing routines are available for your programming language?

21. What utility programs are available for program testing?

22. Develop some test data for the following program. Write a seat-reservation system for an airplane company. There are five flights daily. The flight numbers are 142, 148, 153, 181, and 191. Your company takes reservations only one week in advance. Your program must accept reservations, cancellations and refuse reservations when a flight is full. In order to reduce test input, use a plane capacity of six passengers. There are three classes of seats: first, coach, and student. The program can be made more complicated by allowing first-class passengers to bump coach passengers, coach passengers to bump student passengers, and so on.

23. Using your own programming experience, figure out what percent of your time is used for coding, debugging, and testing.

24. Take a program that you are familiar with and design test cases for
(a) the normal cases
(b) the extreme cases
(c) the exceptional cases.

25. Write a program to find the cube root and use your program to check the accuracy.

26. Write a program to find roots of quadratic equations

$$ax^2 + bx + c = 0$$

Use the formula

$$\text{Roots} = \frac{-b \pm \sqrt{b^2 - 4ac}}{2a}$$

Use the program to check out the roots you find. That is, substitute the calculated roots into the input equation to see if the result is zero. Test the program by using your own test data.

Next, use the following test data.

a	*b*	*c*	*a*	*b*	*c*
1	2	1	6	5	-4
1	-1	-6	$6*10^{30}$	$5*10^{30}$	$-4*10^{30}$
1	-10	1	10^{-30}	-10^{30}	10^{30}
1	-1000	1	1.0	-4.0	3.9999999
1	-10000	1	1.0	-4.0	4.0
1	2	3	1.0	100.0001	0.01

Finally, reprogram the problem by using extended precision and see if the results improve.

27. Develop test data for this program. Your teacher, Ironsides Gradehard, believes in "survival of the fittest." Here is the grading algorithm. Calculate the mean (u) and standard deviation (s) of the class scores. Let t_i be the test scores. then

$$u = \sum_{i=1}^{n} \frac{t_i}{n}$$

$$s = \left(\sum_{i=1}^{n} \frac{(t_i - u)^2}{n} \right)^{1/2}$$

Grades are assigned according to the rules below.

A for scores greater than or equal to $u + 2s$.
B for scores greater than or equal to $u + s$ but less than $u + 2s$.
C for scores greater than or equal to $u - s$ but less than $u + s$.
D for scores greater than or equal to $u - 2s$ but less than $u - s$.
F for scores less than $u - 2s$.

28. Your computer handles a maximum of six significant digits. But you had to do addition with eight significant digits. You have decided to solve this problem by splitting the input values into the left and right four digits and doing the addition. For example, the number 00123456 would be input as 0012 and 3456.

```
00123456          0012  3456
65432100  becomes 6543  2100
                  6555  5556
```

Your program must accept both positive and negative numbers. Develop the test data for this problem first. Then program and test it, using your test data.

Projects

29. Some test data generators were listed in this chapter. Find out what other similar packages are available and evaluate their usefulness. Develop a checklist of what a good test data generator should have.

30. Several other test packages were described. Find out what is available and evaluate their usefulness. Hetzel's *Program Test Methods* has several references on different types of test packages.

31. *File comparison.* Locate or write a program that will accept two files and compare the two files, printing only the differences. Document the program and make it generally available at your installation. A program called FILCOM is usually available on PDP computers; it is written in BASIC-PLUS.

32. Gather some statistics on the features below.
    (a) Time spent at design, coding, debugging, and testing stage
    (b) Size of program
    (c) Programmer language
    (d) Programmer experience
    Then try to find some correlation between some of this data. For example, does programming language or the amount of time spent in the design phase affect the amount of time spend testing or debugging? If this interests you, consult Barry Boehm, "Software and Its Impact: A Quantitative Assessment," *Datamation*, May 1973. Also see G. Weinberg's *Psychology of Computer Programming.*

33. Here are several methods of evaluating software reliability.
    (a) *Mean time between errors (MTBE).* The average up-times between interruptions to service.
    (b) *Mean time to repair (MTTR).* After an error is found, how long does it require to get it properly corrected?
    (c) *Percent up-time.* What percent of the time is the software operational?
    (d) *Number of bugs versus calendar months.* Plot the number of

bugs versus calendar months and use the slope of the curve as a rough measure of progress.

Discuss or try some of these methods for evaluating reliability of your software.

34. Write a program to generate a covering set of test cases for your compiler for one of the following.
    (a) Arithmetic expressions
    (b) Subroutine call statements
    (c) DO loops.

    The above generated set should generate all and only sets of syntax correct tests.

35. Develop test data that will adequately test one of the supplied functions. Examples are absolute value, square root, sine, cosine, and so on. What will be the critical values for each function?

36. Many people have been trying to prove programs are correct much as mathematicians prove mathematical theories are correct. Investigate the present status of proving the correctness of computer programs. What impact do you think program proving will have on programming?

37. It would be convenient if we had a method to measure how well a software system has been tested. Several guidelines are given in this chapter. Try to develop some method to measure how well the code has been tested. Also, see the debugging section in Chapter 4.

38. *Program testing log.* Similar to a diary, it is a written account of the progress made during testing. It can be used at the end of the project to evaluate the success of the testing plan. Also, the log will tend to make the programmer more careful because no one likes to write down something like "Test number 2 had to be rerun because I set it up incorrectly." On some program, try keeping a program testing log.

39. *Profilers.* Several software packages that analyze the execution sequences that the program goes through are available. These programs count how many times each statement is executed (profilers) and sometimes also analyze code for errors and non-standard features. Some of the packages are
    (a) COTUNE (for COBOL Profiler) and FOTUNE (for FORTRAN Profiler). CAPEX Corp., 2613 North Third Street, Phoenix, Ariz. 85004.
    (b) PROFILE. CACI, Inc., 12011 San Vincente Blvd., Los Angeles, CA. 90049.

(c) MetaCOBOL available from Applied Data Research, Route 206 Center, Princeton, N.J. 08540.

(d) *RXVP* available from General Research Corp., 5383 Hollister Ave., Santa Barbara, Ca.

(e) PET (Program Evaluator and Tester) available from McDonnell Douglas Astronautics Company.

The last two are described in Gilb's *Record 1973 IEEE Symposium on Computer Software Reliability* and his *Software Metrics*. Look up the preceding packages and find descriptions of similar packages. Find out what the similarities and differences are. Then draw up a checklist of useful features for program testing.

40. *Dual code.* If it is difficult to work out solutions for test cases, one method is to have a separate group code the problem in a different programming language. Since testing is so costly and both programs can use the same design and analysis, the extra coding is often not a major cost. Try a problem in which dual code is used. See Gilb's *Software Metrics* (listed in Chapter IV) for more information on dual code.

41. Collect some data on types of errors made in programming. Two interesting articles are: Albert Endres, "An Analysis of Errors and Their Causes in System Programs," *IEEE Transactions of Software Engineering*, June 1975 and Barry Boehm, "Software and Its Impact: A Quantitative Assessment," *Datamation*, May 1973.

42. *Measures of complexity.* Here are some suggested measures of program complexity.

(a) Number of unique paths in the program

(b) Number of IF statements (and the percent of all statements)

(c) Average size of modules

These items can be measured by a computer program. Write a program to do so. You might decide that some programs are too complex and cannot be tested or maintained and should be rejected and rewritten. Suggest a guideline.

43. One suggested measure of software reliability is

$$1 - \frac{\text{number of inputs with execution failures}}{\text{total number of inputs}}$$

(from Gilb's *Software Metrics*, p. 146). Evaluate it as a software metric tool.

44. *Test inspection.* Test inspection is a team evaluation of the test

thoroughness. A checklist for test inspection, developed by Rodney Larson, is reproduced in Appendix B of Glib's *Software Metrics*. On some program, set up test inspection to evaluate the thoroughness of testing.

REFERENCES

Boehm, Barry W., "Some Information Processing Implications of Air Force Space Missions in the 1970's," *Astronautics and Aeronautics*, January 1971.

——, Robert K. McClean, and D. B. Urfrig, "Some Experience with Automated Aids to the Design of Large-Scale Software," *IEEE Transactions on Software Engineering*, March 1975.

Conway, Richard, and David Gries, "Program Testing," *Primer on Structured Programming using PL/I*. Cambridge, Mass.: Winthrop Publishers, 1976.

Elmendorf, William R., "Controlling the Functional Testing of an Operating System," *IEEE Transactions on Systems Science and Cybernetics*, October 1969.

Gruenberger, Fred, "Program Testing and Validating," *Datamation*, July 1968.

A Guide to Testing in a Complex System Environment. IBM Corporation, GH20–1628.

Hetzel, William C. (Ed.), *Program Test Methods*. Englewood Cliffs, N.J.: Prentice-Hall, 1973.

Hice, G. F., W. S. Turner, and L. F. Cashwell, *System Development Methodology*. New York: American Elsevier, 1974.

Hughes, Joan K., and Jay I. Michtom, *A Structured Approach to Programming*. Englewood Cliffs, N.J.: Prentice-Hall, 1977.

Management Planning Guide for a Manual of Data Processing Standards. IBM Corporation, C20–1670.

Maynard, Jeff, *Modular Programming*. Philadelphia, Pa.: Auerbach Publishers, 1972.

Rustin, Randall (Ed.), *Debugging Techniques in Large Systems*, Englewood Cliffs, N.J.: Prentice-Hall, 1971.

If a program is worth writing, it is worth writing correctly.
If you haven't made mistakes, you will get the right answer.

Program in haste, debug at your leisure.

6

101 Programming Problems

NUMBER PROBLEMS

1. An automorphic number is one that appears at the end of its square — that is,

$$5^2 = 25$$
$$25^2 = 625$$

Write a program to find some automorphic numbers.

2. Write all the prime numbers between 100 and 300. A prime number N is divisible only by 1 and N.

3. Every integer number can be factored in a unique way into powers of prime numbers. Write a program to do so.

4. The *Goldbach conjecture* states that every even number can be represented as the sum of two prime numbers. Check his conjecture for the first 500 even numbers.

5. Write a program to read two integer numbers and determine if they are relatively prime. Two numbers are relatively prime if they have no common divisors.

6. *Twin primes.* Twin primes are two numbers that are primes and have a difference of two — that is,

$$3 \qquad 5$$
$$11 \qquad 13$$

Find 15 twin primes.

7. *Mersenne primes.* A Mersenne prime is a prime number of the form

$$2^p - 1$$

where p itself is prime. Write a program to find some of these numbers.

8. Pythagorean numbers can be described as follows.

$$a^2 + b^2 = c^2$$

where a, b, c are integers. Write a program to find five values for c that are Pythagorean numbers. For example,

$$3^2 + 4^2 = 5^2$$

9. A perfect number is an integer that is equal to the sum of all its factors except itself. Write a program to find three perfect numbers. For example,

$$28 = 1 + 2 + 4 + 7 + 14$$

10. Write a program that reads a real number and prints the number in scientific notation. For example,

$$123.42 \rightarrow .12342E{+}03$$

11. *Fibonacci numbers.* Here are the rules for Fibonacci numbers.

$$F_1 = 1$$

$$F_2 = 1$$

$$F_{i+2} = F_{i+1} + F_i \qquad (i \geqslant 1)$$

Thus $F_3 = 2$, $F_4 = 3$.
(a) Print the first 15 Fibonacci numbers.

(b) Print the ratio of each successive pair of Fibonacci numbers.

(c) Someone noticed that if we multiply 1.618 times a Fibonacci number, we almost get the next Fibonacci number. Try this and calculate the difference for each pair of Fibonacci numbers.

12. Write a program to read in a decimal number and print its binary, octal, and hexadecimal equivalent.

13. Compute the correct arithmetic sum and difference of two integer numbers 100 digits long.

14. Write a program that will read two binary numbers and do binary addition. If you feel brave, try binary division.

15. Write a program to read N, M, and calculate N/M to 25-place accuracy.

16. Write a program to read two integer numbers and find the greatest common divisor (i.e., the largest integer that will divide both input integers). The least common multiple of two integers is the product of the two numbers divided by their greatest common divisor. Find the least common divisor, too.

17. Amicable numbers are two numbers, each of which is equal to the sum of all the exact divisors of the other except that number itself. For example, 220 and 284 are amicable numbers, since 220 has the exact divisors 1, 2, 4, 5, 10, 11, 20, 22, 44, 55, and 110, whose sum is 284, and 284 has the exact divisors 1, 2, 71, 142, whose sum is 220. Write a program to find some more amicable numbers.

18. Write a program to find all the proper divisors of an integer number N (i.e., all numbers less than N that divide N).

19. (a) Write a program to find the smallest integer that can be written as the sum of two cubes in two different ways. For instance, the cubes are 1^3, 2^3, 3^3, ... So $9 = 1^3 + 2^3$, but it is not the sum of any other pair of cubes.

   (b) Generalize the preceding problem. That is, finding the smallest integer M such that it is the sum of two nth powers in at least two different ways. For example,

$$\text{For } n = 1, \quad M = 2 = 0^1 + 2^1 = 1^1 + 1^1$$
$$\text{For } n = 2, \quad M = 25 = 0^2 + 5^2 = 3^2 + 4^2$$
$$\text{For } n = 3, \quad M = ? = I^3 + J^3 = K^3 + L^3$$
$$\text{For } n = 4, \quad \ldots$$

20. Write some programs that cause arithmetic overflows for
    (a) integer arithmetic.
    (b) real arithmetic.
    One approach is to calculate powers of 2. A faster way to get
    an overflow is to calculate factorials (i.e., 5 factorial is 5!
    = 5*4*3*2*1). Also, write a program to get real arithmetic
    underflow.

21. Using integer values for *I, J, K, L*, find some numbers such that

$$(I^3 - J^3) = (K^2 + L^2)^2$$

GAME PROBLEMS

22. Here are some games that are easily programmed.
    (a) Tic-Tac-Toe   (b) Blackjack
    (c) Tower of Hanoi   (d) Guess a word, by guessing
                                  one letter at a time until the
                                  word is guessed.

    (e) Nim   (f) Craps
    (g) Slot machines   (h) Roulette
    (i) Chinese Fan Tan   (j) Magic Squares
    (k) Hexapawn   (l) Kalah
    A game can be programmed so that an individual plays against
    the machine. Another interesting approach is to have the ma-
    chine play both sides. One strategy is to program one side to
    play a sophisticated game and then have the other side use a
    different playing strategy or have it make random moves. By
    printing the moves, you can often watch an interesting game.
    Donald Spencer's *Game Playing with Computers* (Rochelle Park,
    N.J.: Hayden Book Company, 1976) discusses computerized
    game playing.

23. A bucket contains ten black balls and five red balls. You draw a
    ball and then put it back. Then you add a ball of the same
    color to the bucket. Write a program to simulate 100 drawings
    of balls from the bucket.

24. *Missionaries and cannibals.* Three missionaries, three cannibals,
    and a boat are on one side of a river. The boat will hold a maxi-
    mum of two people. If the cannibals ever outnumber the mis-
    sionaries on either side of the river, the cannibals will eat those
    missionaries. Write a program that computes how to get all the
    missionaries and cannibals across the river without the mission-
    aries being eaten.

25. *Chess problems*
    (a) Five queens. Five queens can be placed on a chessboard so that every square is dominated by at least one of the queens. Write a program to figure out how to do this.
    (b) Twelve knights. Twelve knights can be placed on a chessboard so that every square is dominated by one of the knights. Write a program to figure out how to do this.
    (c) Eight bishops. Do the same for eight bishops.

26. *Crossword puzzles.* A good crossword puzzle has little unused space and uses a group of words involving one subject. Write a program that, when given a list of words, generates a crossword puzzle.

27. *Chess fans.* This is called the knight's tour. Write a program to have the knight visit each of the 64 squares without landing on any square more than once, or, write a program so that the knight goes the maximum distance without ever crossing his own path.

28. Read in a student name, address, class, and major. You are the school president and must send each student a "personalized" computer letter. You must use his name, class, and major in the content of the letter. Compose a letter welcoming the student back to school, and write a program to generate these letters.

29. *Random numbers.* A simple check for randomness is to total the number of times each digit appears in a string of random numbers. That is, you would expect zeros to appear 10% of the time, ones to appear 10% of the time, and so on. Write a program to read 100 random digits and print the percentage for each digit.

30. Write a simple mate-matching program.

31. Write a program that simulates rolling a pair of dice 1000 times. Keep count of the number of combinations of each possible outcome. Compare your results to the theoretical outcome by calculation.

32. Write a program to calculate the odds on possible poker hands.

33. Write a program to deal cards. Then deal 1000 poker hands and accumulate statistics on how many pairs, three of a kind, four of a kind, etc., appear. Compare your computer-generated results to a table of poker hands.

34. *Bridge fans.* Write a program that deals a hand of bridge and then makes an opening bid.

35. *The game of life.* In *Scientific American,* February 1971, the following simulation is described.

At time t a square is alive if either

(1) it was blank at time $t - 1$ and exactly three of its neighbors were alive or

(2) it was alive at time $t - 1$ and either two or three of its neighbors were alive.

Otherwise the square is blank.

A neighborhood is the eight squares touching any internal square.

X	X	X
X	Y	X
X	X	X

The 8 Xs are Y's neighbors.

This is an archetypal checkerboard simulation. It is important to calculate the configuration for each cycle as efficiently as possible. Your job will be to simulate a 15 × 15 configuration with the following squares initially alive.

$(3, 8), (4, 7), (5, 7), (5, 8), (5, 9), (10, 7), (10, 8),$
$(10, 9), (11, 7), (12, 8), (3, 2), (4, 3), (5, 1), (5, 2)$
$(5, 3), (9, 1), (9, 2), (9, 3), (10, 3), (11, 2).$

Write a program to simulate five cycles.

36. *Ringworm problem.* Simulate the infection of ringworm by using an 11 × 11 array of skin cells. Start with the center cell infected. Each time unit, an infected cell has 0.5 probability of infecting each of its healthy neighbors. After six time units an infected cell becomes immune for four time units and then becomes healthy again. Simulate this infection and print out the array for each time unit, showing which cells are infected, immune, or healthy.

GRAPHIC PROBLEMS

37. *Graphics.* Use the line printer to draw the following pictures.
   (a) Print a large box.
   (b) Print a triangle.
   (c) Print a checkerboard of 1-inch squares. Shade the squares.
   (d) Read a word and print it 2 inches high.

(e) Plot a simple curve.

(f) Read a radius and print a circle.

(g) Use overprinting to develop a shading chart. Then try to print a simple picture.

38. Use the figure given here.

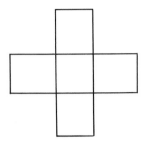

Write a program that prints all the arrangements of the digits 1-8 (five at a time) in the figure with the condition that no two consecutive digits can be in any adjacent squares.

39. *Chess players.* The queen can move vertically, horizontally, or diagonally as far as desired. Write a program to read the row and column of the queen as input and mark the square the queen is on with a Q. Mark the squares the queen could move to with *'s, and mark all other squares with +'s. For example, a chessboard with a queen in the second row and third column would look as follows.

```
+ * * * + + + +
* * Q * * * * *
+ * * * + + + +
* + * + * + + +
+ + * + + * + +
+ + * + + + * +
+ + * + + + + *
+ + * + + + + +
```

CRYPTOGRAPHY PROBLEMS

40. Being an amateur cryptographer, you want to read alphabetic data and count the number of times that each character appears. Write a program that prints frequency counts for each of the 26 letters of the alphabet and spaces. The most common letters of

the English language in order of importance are ETOANIRSH.
Compare this to your results.

41. Computers are an ideal tool for encoding and decoding secret
    messages. Write programs to do so by using the following
    method
    (a) *Caesar substitution.*
        Substitute C for A.
        Substitute D for B.
        Substitute E for C, etc.
    (b) *Rail fence transposition.* This is a rearrangement method.
        Select the 1st, 4th, 7th, . . . characters and place them to-
        gether, followed by the 2nd, 5th, 8th, . . . characters, fol-
        lowed by the 3rd, 6th, 9th, . . . characters.
    (c) *Gronsfeld method.* This method uses a numerical key and
        modifies the traditional Caesar system. Using a key 31206
        and the plain text record PROGRAMMING, the following
        encipherment is obtained.

Key	31206	31206	3
Plain	PROGR	AMMIN	G
Cipher	SSQGX	DNOIT	J

        To encipher P using the key digit 3, simply begin at P and
        count forward 3 in the normal alphabet; the substitute is
        S. To encipher R with key 1, begin at R and count forward
        1 in the normal alphabet; the substitute is S. For decipher-
        ment, count backward in the alphabet. Two factors are
        evident: there are 10 possible substitutions here (for the
        digits 0–9) and we lose some of the weakness of the pre-
        vious systems.
    (d) *Transliteration.* Another common method is to use rec-
        tangles to scramble the message. We can inscribe the alpha-
        bet into a rectangle by using a vertical path as follows.

1	A E I M Q U Y
2	B F J N R V Z
3	C G K O S W
4	D H L P T X

    The inscription consists of taking the elements off horizon-
    tally. We will do the rows in this order 2 4 3 1. The coded
    message would appear like this.

    BFJNR VZDHL PTXCG KOSWA EIMQU Y

The key is the size of the rectangle and the interchanging of rows. Write a program to encode and decode messages by using this method.

CHARACTER STRING PROBLEMS

42. Read an alphabetic character string and print out the characters in reversed order.

43. Read a five-character alphabetic character string and print all permutations of the characters.

44. Student names are punched on cards so that the last name is first, followed by a comma, then the first name and middle initial. Write a program that reads these cards and prints the names in sequence — first name, middle initial, and last name.

45. Write a subroutine that accepts character string, a single character, and then returns a number indicating how many times the single character occurs in the character string. Modify the subroutine so that it searches for a substring instead of a single character.

46. Write a program that reads in a sequence of numbers. Print the longest subsequence of monotonic increasing magnitude.

47. (a) *Roman numbers.* Write a program to add roman numbers. Write a program to multiply roman numbers. Here are some roman numbers and their decimal equivalents.

Roman	Decimal
I	1
II	2
III	3
IV	4
V	5
VI	6
•	
•	
•	
IX	9

Roman	Decimal
X	10
L	50
C	100
D	500
M	1000

Restrict the input Roman numbers to MMM (3000). Input and output should be in roman numbers.
(b) Morse Code.
Write a program that will read dots (.) and dashes (–), which are Morse code, and have the program translate it. Also, go in the other direction.

STATISTICS PROBLEMS

48. (a) Read in N and then read N numbers. Print the mean, standard deviation, maximum value, minimum value, and range.
   (b) Print the mode, first quartile, second quartile (median), and the third quartile.

49. Write a program to compute statistics of customers. Data cards will look as follows.

Field	Columns
Customer number	1–4
Age (in years)	6–7
Sex (0 female, 1 male)	9
Marital status (0 single, 1 married, 2 divorced or separated)	11

Print out this information.
(a) Percent under 21 years old
(b) Percent 21 or over
(c) Percent male, female
(d) Percent single

(e) Percent married

(f) Percent divorced or separated.

Label all output.

50. A group of students took an examination in which possible scores range from 0 to 100. Write a program to print a bar graph showing the number of students that fell in the intervals 0 to 10, 11 to 20, and so on.

51. Write a program to read in an array of student names and test scores. There are 15 students and five test scores for each student. Compute the average for each test. Then compute the average score for each student. Next, compute the student average, using the best four test scores. Finally, print the names of the students who received an average test score higher than the average, using the four-test average.

COMPILER PROBLEMS

52. Write a program for a compiler that will read cards with arithmetic expressions and check for unmatched parentheses.

53. Write a program for a compiler that will read arithmetic expressions and determine if each is a valid expression. Assume that all variable names are only one character long. Here are three invalid arithmetic expressions.

$$A = B/{*}C$$
$$D = E * (A - B$$
$$F = G + 5 +$$

54. Write a program that reads an arithmetic statement and then does the arithmetic in the correct order. Operations are restricted to

$$( ) = - + * /$$

For example.

$$A = 5 * 3 - 4 / 2$$

In the above, the * is done first, then the /, and, finally, the subtraction.

55. Read in three numbers in any order. Put the numbers in order and print the ordered numbers. Next, modify the program to read N, then read N numbers, sort the numbers, and print the numbers in ascending order.

56. Write programs to do sorts by using these techniques.
    (a) *Bubble sort.* Place the smallest element in A(1). Put the second smallest element in A(2). Put the third smallest element in A(3), and so on.
    (b) *Merge sort.* You will need four arrays: A, B, C, D. Start with all elements in array A. Start with a_1 and put a_i in C until $a_i > a_{i+1}$. As soon as $a_i > a_{i+1}$, put a_{i+1} into array D and continue to put elements in array D until $a_i > a_{i+1}$; then switch back to array C. When array A has been exhausted, you will have a series of sorted subsequences in arrays C and D. Next, take the first subsequence of arrays C and D and merge them together in sequence, placing them in array A. Take the second subsequence in array C and D and merge them together, placing them in array B. Then take the third subsequence in array C and D and merge them together, placing them in array A. Continue merging until arrays C and D are exhausted. Then arrays A and B are merged in a similar manner. This process is continued until one array contains all the numbers in sequence.
    (c) *Radix sort.* Starting with the least significant column, order the numbers so that the least significant column is in order. Proceed to the higher-order columns, ordering them one at a time, taking care not to scramble the order of the less significant columns. To make it easier, use only positive integer numbers. If you wish to make it more difficult, drop this last restriction. A card sorter uses a radix sort.
    (d) Develop another method of sorting and program it.
    (e) Compare the different methods of sorting to see which is faster. One method of comparing the time used is to generate 1000 random numbers, sort them, and see which sorting method is fastest.

MATHEMATICS PROBLEMS

57. Write a program to read in three numbers.
    (a) Determine if it cannot be a triangle.
    (b) Determine if it is an equilateral triangle.

    (c) Determine if it is an isosceles triangle.

    (d) Determine if it is a right triangle.

58. Write a program to read in four numbers. Can they form a quadrangle? Square? Rectangle? Parallelogram? Rhombus?

59. Write a program to read the coefficients of three linear equations and find the solutions for the three unknowns.

60. The famous computer scientist Professor Abort Easycode is engaged in testing his new computer by trying the $81*10^9$ possible solutions to the problem of reconstructing the following exact long division in which all of the digits, except one in the quotient, have been replaced by a star.

```
              **8**
     *** / *******
          ***
          ****
           ***
          ****
          ****
```

    (a) Each * denotes a digit between 0 and 9 and all leading digits are nonzero. Find a solution to the above.

    (b) How many actual solutions are there?

61. Write programs to compute 20 terms of the following.
    (a) $\pi = 4(1 - 1/3 + 1/5 - 1/7 + \cdots)$
    (b) $e = 1 + 1/1 + 1/2! + 1/3! + 1/4! + \cdots$
    (c) $\sinh x = x^1/1! + x^3/3! + x^5/5! + \cdots$
    (d) $e^x = 1 + x/1! + x^2/2! + x^3/3! + x^4/4! + \cdots$
    (e) $\sin^{-1} x = x + 1/2 \cdot x^3/3 + 1/2 \cdot 3/4 \cdot x^5/5 + 1/2 \cdot 3/4 \cdot 5/6 \cdot x^7/7 + \cdots$

62. Write four subroutines to perform complex arithmetic, one for each of addition, subtraction, multiplication, and division.

63. Write programs that will add, subtract, and multiply polynomials. Use vectors to store the coefficients of each polynomial.

64. *Newton–Raphson method.* The square root of A can be found by using the iterative formula

$$x_{i+1} = \frac{1}{2}\left(x_i + \frac{A}{X_i}\right)$$

where A = a positive number

       x_i = the current approximation of the square root of A

  x_{i+1} = the next approximation of the square root of A

Use this formula to find the square root of numbers and stop when

$$\frac{(x_{i+1})^2 - A}{A} < 0.001$$

Compare your answers to the results obtained by using the SQRT function.

65. Write programs to find the roots of

$$2X - 1 - 2 \sin X = 0$$

using these methods.
(a) Bisection method
(b) Iteration method
(c) Newton–Raphson method.

66. (a) Write a program to solve the following, using Simpson's rule.

$$\int_0^2 \ln \sqrt{1 + x}\, dx$$

(b) Write a program to solve the following, using the trapezoidal rule,

$$\int_0^{\pi/4} \frac{\sin^a x}{\sqrt{1 + \cos^2 x}}\, dx$$

for $a = 1.0, 1.1, 1.2, \ldots, 2.0$

ARRAY PROBLEMS

67. Write a program to read in an array of 100 elements. Then count how many groups of three adjacent positive numbers are in the array. Five positive adjacent numbers would mean a count of three.

68. Write a program that reads in a vector of length 30. Each element is to be modified as follows.
(a) If the value of the element is less than the subscript, square the element.
(b) If the value of the element is equal to the subscript, reverse the sign of the element.

(c) If the value of the element is greater than the subscript, subtract one from the element.

69. Write a program to find the determinant of arrays.

70. Write a program that will add arrays of any size. Write a program that will multiply arrays.

INTEREST PROBLEMS

71. Calculate the new balance if $1000 is deposited at 5% for 10 years with interest compounded quarterly. Next, calculate interest compounded monthly. Finally, calculate interest compounded daily. Compare the results.

72. If you wanted to accumulate $1000 by the end of 5 years, how much would you need to deposit each year? Assume that the interest rate is 5% compounded yearly and that you make identical deposits at the first of each year.

73. Manhattan Island was purchased by settlers in 1626 for $24. If the $24 had been deposited in a bank at 6% interest compounded annually, how much would their bank account be worth now?

74. Your bank has a billionaire depositer. Write a program that calculates compound interest (6% compounded monthly) for his account. If he doesn't receive all his interest, he will move his account to another bank, and you will lose your job.

75. If a person borrows $500 at 1½% per month, how much has she paid and how much does she still owe after one year if she makes payments of $7.50 per month? What if she makes payments of $10 per month?

76. Using the preceding problem, how many months must the person pay if she pays $10 per month?

BUSINESS PROBLEMS

77. Calculate taxable income by deducting $750 for each dependent and a standard 10% deduction. Read name, social security number, yearly pay, and number of dependents.

78. Write a program to calculate average mileage. Read in starting and stopping speedometer mileage and the number of gallons of gasoline purchased.

79. Since you are poor, you may wish to write a program to analyze your expenses. Write a program to keep track of expenses over three months. Obvious expense categories are food, housing, transportation, entertainment, and educational expenses. Add any other classifications you wish.
    (a) Find the total expense for each category for each month.
    (b) Find average expense and the maximum and minimum expense for each category over the three months.

80. Write a check-balancing program for a bank. The master input record consists of

Customer name	20 characters
Customer account number	5 digits
Present balance	6 digits

    Detail transactions consist of

Customer account number	5 digits
Transaction amount	6 digits

    If the transaction is positive, it is a deposit. If the transaction is negative, it is a check. Customers are charged 15¢ for each check they write with a maximum charge of $3. Customers with a minimum balance of $300 are not charged for checks. Write a program to balance the accounts, showing all transactions for the bank's customers. If any check would overdraw an account, print a warning message, charge a $5 bad check charge, and don't process the check.

81. Write a program to calculate weekly pay. Read the data.

Name	20 columns alphabetic
Employee number	9 columns numeric
Number of hours worked	4 column field 99.9
Hourly pay rate	5 column field 99.99
Dependents	2 column field 99

    Overtime is paid after 40 hours at 1½ time. Deduct 5% for social security but never deduct more than $20 in one week. Deduct 2% for state tax. Deduct for federal tax according to

Dependents	Tax Rate
0	16%
1	12
2	9
3	6
4+	5

    Print a report indicating all pertinent information.

82. The READY water company charges these rates:
    0.015 per gallon first 100 gallons.
    0.011 per gallon after first 100 gallons.

    Write a program to read
Customer name	20 characters
Customer number	4 digits
Last meter reading	4 digits
Last meter reading	4 digits

    Do calculations necessary to print out
    Customer name
    Customer number
    Last meter reading
    New meter reading
    Amount used
    Charges on Rate 1
    Charges on Rate 2
    Total charges

    Stop the program when finding a negative customer number and print totals for
    Total amount used
    Total Rate 1
    Total Rate 2
    Total charges

83. A company bills its customers the last day of each month. If the bill is paid by the 10th of the next month, the customer gets a 1% reduction or $2, whichever is larger. If the bill is paid after the 10th but by the 20th of next month, the customer pays the regular bill. If the bill is paid after the 20th, there is a $1 or 1% service charge, whichever is greater. Write a program to read
Customer number	5 digits
Date of billing	6 digits month day year
Date of payment	6 digits month day year
Bill amount	XXX.XX
Amount paid	XXX.XX

    Calculate the due amount and print any differences between amount paid and amount due.

84. The county property tax office needs assessment totals for the types of land classifications. County tax assessment rates are

Land Type	Assessment Rate (per acre)
1	1.01
2	1.21
3	1.49
4	1.87
5	2.31

Each input record contains the following:
    Parcel number
    Land type
    Length in feet
    Width in feet.

Calculate and print the total assessment for each land parcel (indicate the square feet and acreage). An acre is equal to 43,550 square feet. Next, print summary totals for each land type. Include
    Land type
    Number of parcels
    Total square feet
    Total acres
    Total assessment
    Percent of all land.

85. The National Losers Society gives out scholarships to campus losers. The minimum requirements are
(a) C (2.5) grade-point average or lower.
(b) at least a Junior standing (3) or higher.
(c) over 30 years old.
(d) married — 0 unmarried, 1 married.
Write a program to read student names (20 columns alphabetic) and the requirements; print all names eligible for awards.

86. A company pays its salespeople 5% commission on total sales less than $1000 and 6% if total sales are $1000 or greater. If the salesperson has been with the company for over 10 years, he or she receives an extra 1% commission. Salespeople who have been with the company more than 10 years have an even employee number. Input is a salesperson's name, number, and total sales. Calculate the commissions. Print all input and the commissions. Print totals for sales and commissions.

87. A pair of socks cost $1.05 each, or $10.25 a dozen, or $110 a gross. Write a program to calculate the price on sock purchases.

For example, 13 socks would cost $11.30 ($10.25 + $1.05). The storekeepers are kindhearted and wish to warn their customers whenever they make an unwise purchase. For instance, a purchase of 11 pairs of socks costs more than a dozen. Fix the program so that it prints a warning message whenever a customer selects an unwise purchase.

88. Write a program to process revolving charge accounts. The data is punched as follows.

Account number	5 digits
Name	20 characters
Street address	20 characters
City–State	20 characters
Zip code	5 digits
Old balance	5 digits
Payments	5 digits
Purchases	5 digits

A service charge of 1½% on any old unpaid balance is charged, with a minimum of 50¢, if there is an unpaid balance. The program should print out new bills to send to the customers.

89. A manufacturer buys a machine with a life of one year to produce consumer goods. Costs are incurred in the production of the goods, and revenue (cash inflow) is generated by the sale of the goods. To calculate the return that the manufacturer earns on his investment, costs are subtracted from revenue to produce a return figure. This return figure is then divided by the initial investment to compute a rate of return.

   Assume that the machine costs $8000, that revenue from sales was $12,000 and that the costs incurred, including operating the machine, totaled $10,800. Write a program that calculates return and rate of return and outputs machine costs, sales, total costs, return, and rate of return. Your output should appear as

```
Machine
  Cost    Revenue    Costs   Return    Rate
 8000.00 12000.00 10800.00 1200.00   0.15
```

90. Problem 89 must now be expanded to allow the machine (project) to have a life in excess of one year. This modification forces the analyst to deal with uncertainty that results from estimating future magnitudes of sales and costs.

   It is known from analysis of historical data that this machine has a useful life of 10 years, that sales, on the average, grow by 5% a year, and that, on the average, costs increase by 8% per year. Although these percentages are correct in the long run, actions of competitors, economic conditions, and the like tend to make the actual rate of change of costs and sales vary rather drastically from the average rates. The effect of these exogenous forces can be simulated by using a random number generator to modify the average annual changes in cost and sales. Although rather marked variations will occur, the net effect of inclusion of the random variation will be zero.

Since it is reasonable to assume that the changes in sales and costs are related, only one random number should be generated for each year. This number would be multiplied by the average change in sales and costs to produce the simulated change in the variables for a given year. The random numbers should have values between 0.5 and 1.5.

To the ouput of Problem 89, add the year numbers down the left-hand column of the page. Note that the output for year one is the same as the output of Problem 89.

91. The simple rate of return approach used in Problem 90 is not satisfactory to some managers. An approach that has gained institutional although not academic acceptance is payback period analysis. This technique computes the time necessary to recoup an initial investment.

The payback computation must take a cumulative form. That is, each year's return (cash inflows) is accumulated until the initial investment has been fully covered. For example, assume an initial investment of $31,000 and net cash inflows in the succeeding years of $10,000, $20,000, $10,000, and $10,000, respectively.

Year	Cash Outlay	Net Cash Flows Each Year	Accumulated
0	31,000	–	–
1	–	10,000	10,000
2	–	20,000	30,000
3	–	10,000	31,000
4	–	10,000	–

In this instance, assuming payments occur uniformly over each year, analysis of the third year reveals that the final $1000 needed to recoup the investment would occur after one-tenth of the year. Consequently, the payback period for this investment is 2.1 years.

Compute the payback period for the machine purchase analyzed in Problem 90. Your output should include the complete results of Problem 90 plus an additional line as output of the payback period.

92. Expand Problem 91 to include many investments. The basic data for each of the investments has been keypunched on data cards in the following layout.

Card Columns	Content
1–2	Machine number
3–4	Number of periods
5–14	Initial outlay = machine cost
15–24	Sales
25–34	Costs
35–44	Change in sales
45–54	Change in cost

It is possible that erroneously punched cards were not all removed from the data deck; hence your program must check for the validity of the data. Invalid data are defined as follows.
(a) A machine number less than or equal to zero or greater than 10
(b) A number of periods for the investment less than or equal to zero or greater than 15
(c) An initial outlay smaller than $1000
(d) An initial sales-estimate that is less than an initial cost estimate

If any of these invalid conditions exist, the whole data card should be ignored and your program should read another data card. The end of the data deck is signalled by an end-of-data card with an investment number of 99 and a number of periods of 99. Your output should appear like this:

Investment number	2
Number of periods	10
Initial outlay	8000.00
Initial sales	12000.00
Initial cost	10800.00
Rate of change for sales	0.050
Rate of change for costs	0.080

Period	Sales	Cost	Return	Rate
1	12000.00	10800.00	1200.00	0.15
2	12127.42	10983.49	1143.93	0.14
3	11995.32	10792.05	1203.26	0.15
4	11538.07	10133.84	1404.22	0.18
5	12457.86	11426.41	1031.45	0.13
6	12536.89	11542.39	994.50	0.12
7	12600.14	11635.56	964.57	0.12
8	13096.13	12368.40	727.73	0.09
9	13919.05	13611.91	307.14	0.04
10	13540.53	13019.64	520.88	0.07

Payback period   7.08

93. Refer to Problem 92. Instead of computing values for the return in a given year from sales and cost estimates, assume that future returns themselves have been estimated and keypunched. A data deck has been prepared that includes project data and the associated future returns.

The first type (of which there is only one) contains the project data in the following layout. Validity checking is not necessary.

Card Column	Content
1-2	Project number
3-4	Life of project
5-14	Initial outlay with the decimal point punched

The second type (of which there are an unknown number) contains the estimated returns.

Card Column	Content
1-2	Year number
3-12	Return with the decimal point punched

These cards (type two) must be checked for validity. Invalid conditions are defined as follows.

(a) A year number less than or equal to zero

(b) A year number greater than the life of the project
(c) A return value less than zero

The end of the data deck is indicated by an end-of-data-card with a year number of 99.

Note that since the year number is punched on the data card, there is no need to have cards in order. Your program should read a type-two data card, test it for validity and assign the return value to a one-dimensional array so that the position of the value in the array corresponds to the year in which that return will be earned. Although it is unlikely that any project will have a life of 99 years, it is suggested that the array for storing returns be dimensioned 99 so as to allow for all possibilities. If a data card does not exist for a given year, the return for that year should be assigned a value of zero.

After all the values have been assigned, print out only that part of the array that pertains to the life of the project and payback period for the project. The output should appear as follows.

1	8	16000.00
4		3600.00
3		1900.00
12		8000.00
1		1000.00
7		6300.00
6		6700.00
8		5200.00
5		-1400.00
5		5400.00
99		0.00

Period	Return	Rate
1	1000.00	0.06
2	0.00	0.00
3	1900.00	0.12
4	3600.00	0.22
5	5400.00	0.34
6	6700.00	0.42
7	6300.00	0.39
8	5200.00	0.32

Payback period   5.61

94. The Local Gas Company bills its customers according to these rates.

First	500 cubic feet	$1.10
Next	3,000 cubic feet	0.130 per hundred
Next	32,000 cubic feet	0.125 per hundred
Next	100,000 cubic feet	0.120 per hundred
Next	150,000 cubic feet	0.100 per hundred
Next	400,000 cubic feet	0.095 per hundred
Next	685,500 cubic feet	0.087 per hundred

The input record has these fields.

Name	16 characters
Street address	16 characters
City–State	16 characters
Meter begin	7 digits
Meter end	7 digits
Date from	6 digits
Date to	6 digits
Meter number	6 digits

Write a program to prepare bills for the gas company.

CHANGE PROBLEMS

95. Write a program that makes change with the rules that one is always given the fewest number of coins. For example, if you give the grocer $1.00 for a 21¢ item, he will give you back a 50¢ piece, a quarter, and four pennies.

96. Write a program to print the number of different ways that a dollar bill can be broken into change. Assume that there are pennies, nickels, dimes, quarters, and half-dollars.

97. The old English currency system used pounds, sillings (12 shillings = pound), and pence (20 pence = shilling). Write a program for a cash register that accepts a payment amount and purchase price and then calculates correct change.

CALENDER PROBLEMS

A year is a leap year (i.e., February has 29 days instead of 28 days) if it is a multiple of 4 except that a multiple of

100 is a leap year only if it is also a multiple of 400. January 1, 1800, was a Wednesday.

98. Write a program that reads any date (month, day, year) and prints the day of the week.

99. Write a program to find the next three-day weekend caused by the 4th of July.

100. (a) Write a program to generate a calendar for the present year.
   (b) Write a program to read two dates and calculate how many days have passed.
   (c) Write a program to read a year and then generate a calendar for that year.

101. Friday the 13th.
   (a) What is the probability of the 13th of the month being a Friday?
   (b) Write a program to count how many Friday the 13ths occur in this century.
   (c) Why is the 13th of the month more likely to be a Friday than any one of the other days of the week?

Appendix

Team Projects

Actual programming is usually done with others. It is only on small projects that one person can design, code, and debug a whole program. So one of the skills you need to learn is how to work and communicate with others on a programming project. Good communications skills are necessary if the programming project is going to be successful.

By doing projects in teams, we more closely simulate the conditions of actual software development. For too long program teaching has perpetuated the myth that programming is an individual activity. Even the most casual observation will reveal that most programming projects are cooperative ventures.

At the end of each of the first five chapters of this book a selection of projects that can be done by a team or class has been included. In addition, many of the other programs scattered throughout the chapters are suitable for team projects.

Each team should do the entire programming project, using many of the suggestions given here. This includes top-down design, algorithm selection, structured programming, debugging, and a testing group. Depending on the team's inclination, it may be feasible to try the chief programmer team organization. As an added suggestion I would like to remind the reader to be sure to set up a schedule and project goals. (See Chapter 2.) It is often interesting to assign programs or modules to different groups of individuals and then compare the results.

Hopefully, the team project will serve as a vehicle for trying out many of the techniques included in this book. These techniques are not the last word in the art of programming; so the team projects should not only help people learn those discussed but also offer a basis of scrutiny of the techniques themself from which even better suggestions may evolve. In addition, the team project also provides a means of involving students in a project larger than the ones usually attempted.

Before doing one of the projects, develop a cost figure; that is, what would you charge the user for doing the project? If your price is too high, you might not get the job. If your price is too low, your company will lose money. Either way you may lose your job. Also, you may subcontract parts of your job to other groups. Keep some records and see how your bid compares to the actual cost. Some guidelines on software prices can be found in Ray W. Wolverton, "The Cost of Developing Large-Scale Software," *IEEE Transactions on Computers*, June 1974.

Several references should be read by people working on team projects. They are listed next.

REFERENCES

Baker, F. Terry, and Harlan Mills, "Chief Programmer Teams," *Datamation*, December 1973.

Brooks, Frederick P., Jr., *The Mythical Man-Month.* Reading, Mass.: Addison-Wesley, 1975.

Weinberg, Gerald, *The Psychology of Computer Programming.* New York: Van Nostrand Reinhold Company, 1971.

Index

A

Abbreviation
  standard 16
  variable names 15
Abends 188
Abstruse programs 2
ACM 52
Active listening 205
Adaptability 101
Aho, Alfred 52, 174
Aids
  debugging 211-215
  testing 267-269
ALGOL W, tracing options 214
Algorithms
  collected 52
  efficient 47-52, 123
  incorrect 179-180
  selection 46-52, 119, 123
Alignment
  decimal 135
  storage 136

Allen, F. E. 174
Alphabetizing lists 19-20
Amicable numbers 287
Anagrams 39
Analysis
  forward error 262
  backward error 262
Antibugging 206
Apollo 271
Applied Data Research 283
Arguments
  order 20-21
  wrong mode 186
Arithmetic
  errors 210
  fixed point 133
  operations 131
Armstrong numbers 171
Aron, Joel D. 93, 109, 111
Array errors 210
Art of programming 35
Assembly lists 137-138
Assertions 209

Attitude 217
Attributes
  defaults 195
  indentation 28
Armstrong, Russell M. 111
Automatic checks 216
Automorphic numbers 285

B

Backup programmer 95
Bail, William G. 175
Baker, F. Terry 68, 111, 312
Barron, D. W. 236
Basic block 141
BASIC-PLUS 216
Bebugging 218, 223
Beckman, M. 101, 111
Bergerson, Howard W. 39
Black box, testing 244, 275
Blank lines 9-10
Blank spaces 10
Block
  basic 141
  structure 24-30
Blocking 158-160
Bloody instructions 176
Blowups 189
BMD 57
Boar, B. H. 237
Boehm, Barry W.
  errors 66, 283
  modifications 101
  references 111, 284
  software impact 281
Bohm, C. 110
Bottom-up testing 248
Boundary tests 257
Breakpoints 215
Bridge 289
Brooks, Fredrick P., Jr.
  efficiency 114
  IBM 360 OS 59, 94
  reference 312
Brown, A. R. 237
Buddy, programming 37, 44
Buffer 158-160
Buxton, J. N. 93, 111

Bugs (*see also* Errors)
  arresting 206
  catalog 210-211
  diary 222, 223
  first 179
  preventing 219
  psychology of 197
  system 234

C

CACI, Inc. 282
Caesar substitution 292
Calculation of constants 130
Calender problems 308-309
Cancellation 198
CAPEX, Corp. 282
Cards
  efficiency 157
  errors 182
CASE 76-85
Cashwell, L. F. 284
Change problems 308
Character strings 293
Characteristic errors 177, 234
Check digits 208
Checkerboard (*see* Chessboard)
Chess problems
  eight queens 173
  knights 168, 289
  queen 289, 291
Chessboard
  cutting 109
  example 72-74
Chief programmer teams 93-199
  additional members 95-96
  advantages 96
  member responsibilities 94-95
  problems 97
  reflections 97
  size of 97
Classes of test data 253
COBOL
  decimal alignment 135-136
  file names 14-16
  paragraph names 22
  spacing 9
  storage alignment 136
  support packages 116
Code bums 115

Coding
  actual 90
  assembly 137-138
  avoidance 65
  consistency 43
  forms 193
  obscure 42
  pseudo 88-90
  simple 42, 183
  skeleton 88
  structural 74-88
  top-down 88-93
  tricky 42, 219
Cohn, Laurence S. 174
Comments 3-9
  correct 9
  directory 5
  explanatory 5
  how many 7
  indenting 9
  placement 8
  prologue 4
Compiler
  debugging 116, 185
  error checking 214, 216, 267
  error messages 228
  limits 236
  optimizing 116
  production 117
Complex variables 13
Complexity
  dimensions 42, 61-62
  measures 109, 283
  types 69
COMPUTATIONAL 135-136
Computerization need 106
Conditional expressions 147
Connection complexity 69
Conrow, Kenneth 40
Constants, calculations 130
Conway, Richard 284
Cornell University 116, 185
Correctness 183
COTUNE 282
Cratered 189
Critical region 114
Cross totals 270
Cross word puzzles 289
Cross-reference list 193, 234
Cryptography 291-293

D

Dahl, O. J. 39, 109, 111
Data
  actual 252
  constructed 251
  dependency 220
  domain 70
  errors 210, 240
  filter 208
  representation 52
Day, A. Colin 52
Davis, P. J. 87
Debugging 176-237
  aids 202, 233
  expensive 217
  failure 205
  foreign 236
  on-line 215-216
  output 201-202
  partner 191, 205
  psychological 227
  quality 218
  systems 235
  time 176, 219
  training 176
  types 187
  versus testing 177
Decimal alignment 135
Deck marking 182
Defaults, dependence 195, 220
Defensive programming 206
Design
  hand test 246
  program 41-112
Desk checking 194, 201
Determinacy 192
Development Support Library 98-100
Diagonal matrix 170
Dijkstra, Edsger W. 38, 111, 238
Dimensions 61, 209
Directory comments 5
Disk files 161-162
Distributed complexity 69
Divide and conquer 67
Documentation
  bad 103
  need for 33
  when start 65, 102

DO UNTIL   76-85
DO WHILE   76-85
Dog tags   208
Dressing example   65
Driver   269
Dual code   283
Dummy module   90, 264
Dumps   211-212
Durability   239-240

E

Earthquake proof   61
Echo printing   182, 196
EDP Analyzer   101, 112
Efficiency   113-175
   algorithm   47-52
   concern for   114-115
   estimates   121
   possible improvement   121
   versus maintenance   115
   versus readability   115-116
   versus reliability   113
Ego-less programming   38, 96
Eight queens problem   173
Elmendorf, William R.   284
Emulation   101
END OF JOB   205
Endres, Albert   283
Enforcer   38, 111
Engineer, logic circuits   74
English currency   308
Equivalence   128, 154
Errors (*see also* Bugs)
   analysis   180
   analytic truncation   262
   breakpoint   215
   characteristic   234
   checking facility   214, 216
   data   181
   design   246
   documentation   181
   execution type   267
   general   181
   generated   262
   handling routines   235
   inherited   262
   input/output   196
   intrinsic   262
   isolation   207

Errors (*cont'd*)
   locating   199-206
   mathematical   87
   problem definition   179
   roundoff   262
   seeding   218
   semantic   181
   spurious   185
   transmitted   262
   type of   212-213
   typing   193
   undetectable   186
   underflow   195
Error messages
   standardization   234
Evanescent bug   212
Explanatory comments   5
Extensions   110

F

Factorials   24, 47-49, 109
Failure, debugging   205
FETE   174
Fibonacci numbers   286
Field testing   266
File comparisons   268
File name   14-15
File processing   158-162
Fingernails   144
Firewalls   207
Flowchart   180
Folding   130
Foreign debugging   236
FORTRAN
   alphabetic lists   20
   efficiency   113-175
   GO TO   87-88
   statement numbers   21, 37
   structured coding   83-85
   style   1-40
   virtual memory   127-128
FOTUNE   282
Four color problem   174
Fragile   102
Friday the 13th   309
Functional complexity   69
Functions   56-57, 140
   inverses   229
Future Shock   101

G

Gaines, R. Stockton 237
Game of Life 290
Game problems 288-290
Gardner, Martin 39, 174
Geller, Dennis 237
General Research Corp. 283
Generality 53-55
Generated errors 262
GIGO 208
Gilb, Tom 218, 237, 283
Glitch 182
Global variables 69, 71, 106, 127
GO TO
  controversy 109
  effect on optimization 118
  example 63
  guidelines 78
  locality 127
  myths 87
  too many 86
Goals
  modest 59
  set 60, 64
  simplicity 41-43
Goldbach conjecture 285
Gould, John D. 227
Granholm, Jackson W. 67
Graphic problems 290
Gries, David 284
Gronsfeld method 292
Grouping modes 136-137
Gruenberger, Fred 107, 221, 284

H

Halphern, Mark 237
Hand testing 64, 244
Hardware epoch 178
Harrison Malcolm C. 52
Hetzel, William C. 284
Hice, G. F. 284
History of programming 11
Hoare, C. A. R. 39, 111
Hopcroft, John 174
Horner's method 47
Horowitz, Ellis 52
Hughes, Joan K. 247, 284

I

IBG 159
IBM Fellow 98
IBM 360 OS
  cost 97, 101
  errors 94
  leap years 59
Identification 11
Idiots, professional 275
IEBDG 256
IF
  complex 28
  ELSE 81-82
  errors 82
Immediate detection 207
Indenting 24-29, 37
Indenting comments 9
Independence, module 68
Indiana University 57
Ingalls, Daniel H. H. 174
Inherited error 262
Input/output (*see also* Output)
  editing 222
  efficiency 156-162
  errors 160, 196, 210
  field width 43
  formats 58
Instant insanity 173
Integer
  truncation 35
  variables 13
Interblock gap 159
Intrinsic error 262
Invariant expressions 145
Iteration 75

J

Jackson, Michael 16, 40
Jacopini, G. 110

K

Kelly, John R. 112
Kernighan, Brian W. 40, 211, 237
Keyword search 172
KISS 41
Kludge 67

Knuth, Donald E.
  Art of Computer Programming
    51-52
  FORTRAN programs 38, 174
  GO TO 87, 109
  programming as an art 36
  sorting 170
Kreitzberg, Charles B. 175

L

Labyrinth 180
Large programs 41
Leap years 59, 308
Ledgard, Henry 40
Leg test 241
Lexicographic labeling 23
Librarian, programming 95
Library 56-57 (*see also* Development Support Library)
Load modules 163
Locality 127
Logic
  decisions 220
  errors 180, 211
  expressions 149
  traces 204
Loops
  avoidance 142
  combining 147
  efficiency 129, 143-147
  errors 210
  infinite 189, 204
  optimization 143-147
  organization 142
  unrolling 146
Lore, computer 165

M

Macbeth 176
Magic Marker 182
Magnetic tapes 158-160
Magnitude problem 97
Maintenance 45, 101-102
Manhatten Island 299
Maps 190, 192

Mathematical
  errors 87
  software 263
Matrix problems 170-171
Maynard, Jeff 112, 284
McClean, Robert K. 284
McGowan, Clement L. 112
McKeeman, W. H. 172, 173
Mean time
  between errors 281
  to repair 281
Mersenne primes 286
MetaCOBOL 283
Michtom, Jay I. 247, 284
Mills, Harlan 94, 98, 110, 111, 312
Minotaur 108
Missing filling 114
Missionaries and Cannibals 288
MIT 179
Mixed data types 134
Mnemonic names (*see* Variables names)
Mode
  correct 134
  grouping 136-137
  subscript 155
Modifications 2, 11, 55
Modules 67-72
  coupling 69
  disadvantages 163-164
  dummy 90, 264
  errors 210
  simulation 263
  substitution 90, 264
  testing 264, 268
  trouble prone 218
Monolithic programs 41
Morrison, J. E. 128, 175
Morse code 294
Moshman, Jack 67
Murphy's Law 220
Mutual suspicion 207

N

Naftaly, Stanley M. 116
NASA 271
National Opinion Research Center 57
Naur, Peter 112
NEATER 50

Nested loops
  indenting 26
  ordering 143-145
Nested polynomial 47
Nested procedures 22
Nesting of structures 76
New York Times 93-94
Newton-Raphson 297
Non-numerical applications 52
Null case 257
Number problems 285-288
Numerical pathology 197

O

Obscure coding 42
On-line debugging 215-216
Operator (arithmetic)
  precedence 10
  reducing strength 33
Operator (person)
  careless 11
  convenience 59
  independence 220
Optimization
  compiler 116, 140
  machine-dependent 118
  subscripts 156
Optimizing 119-123
Output (*see also* Input)
  debugging 201
  selective 203
Overlays 125-126
Overload bug 213
Overtesting 253

P

Pages 126-127
Palindromes 39
Pandora's box 179
Paragraph names, selection 29
Paragraphing (*see* Indenting)
Parallel runs 252
Parameters, change prone 55
Parentheses 23-24
Parnas, D. L. 110
Partitions 107
Patch 190
Pathology, numerical 197

PDP 11 216
Percent up time 281
Perfect numbers 286
Perfect program 44
PET 283
Phone number search 172
PL/C 116, 185
PL/1
  decimal alignment 135-136
  file names 14-15
  optimizer 116, 186
  procedure names 22
  SORMGIN 201
  vertical spacing 9
Physical errors 182
Plagiarism 56
Plauger, P. J. 40, 211, 237
Point of detection 201
Point of origin 201
Poker 32, 172
Polynomial factoring 47
Poole, P. C. 237
Portable 101, 110
Prime numbers 107
  example 47-49
  problems 285-286
Printed output 157 (*see also*
  Input/Output)
Printing (*see also* Input/Output)
  file 268
  nice 58
Problem definition 44-45
Problems
  array 298-299
  business 299-308
  calender 308-309
  change 308
  character strings 293-294
  compiler 295
  cryptography 291-293
  games 288-290
  graphics 290-291
  interest 299
  mathematics 296-298
  numbers 285-288
  sorting 296
  statistics 294-295
Procedures (*see* Modules)
Product testing 286
Professional idiot 275

Professional standards 31
Profiles 120
  efficiency 114, 120-121
  testing 269, 282
Program buddy system 37, 44
    (*see also* Reading programs)
Program debugging 176-237
Program design 41-112
Program efficiency 113-175
Program standards 44
Program structure 42
  indentation 27
Program style 1-40
Program testing 238-284
Programming
  art 35
  defensive 206
  languages, selection 53
  structured 62-93
  teams 93-98
  tricks 183
Project goals (*see* Goals)
Projects, team 311
Prologue comments 4
Proper program 75
Pseudo code 88-90
Psychological barrier to coding 65
Psychological bugs 197, 228
Puberty 45
Pythagorean numbers 286

Q

Quadratic equation
  efficiency 148
  testing 261
Quality assurance 61
Quantum Chemistry
  Program Exchange 57

R

Rail fence 292
Randell, Brian 93, 111, 112
Random numbers 289
Range checks 208
Readability 1-40
Reading programs 35, 37, 44
Reasonability checks 208

Records
  names 15-16
  processing 156-162
Recovery bug 213
Redesign 122
Reducing strength 133
Redundancy code 208
Redundancy testing 274
Redundant instructions 138
Regression testing 274
Release testing 266
Reliability, software 281
Repeated calculations 138-141,
    144-145
Repeated elements 171
Report headings 129
Report writing 176
Reserved words 13, 35
Resequencing 21, 37
Retesting 273-274
Retrofitting 60
Reversal check 270
Rewriting 2, 88, 103
Rice, John R. 263
Ringworm 290
Ripple effect 69
Robustness 55, 239-240, 242
Roman numbers 293
Roundoff error 262
Rules for abbreviation 16-87
Rules of style 7
Rustin, Randell 175, 237, 284
RXVP 283

S

Sahni, Sartaj 52
Samet, P. A. 175
Sammet, Jean E. 111
Sampson, W. A. 237
Satterthwaite, E. 237, 240
Schedule testing 271-272
Scientific American 39, 174, 240
Scowens, R. S. 40
Scripts 274
Search strategy 199-200
Selection 75
Selective printout 203
Self-checking software 269-270

Segmenting programs   119
Semantic error   212
Semaphore bug   212
Separator   14
Sequence   75
Sequence numbering   11
Sequential files   158-162
SHARE program library   40
Shneiderman, Ben   175
Shooman, M. L.   237
Side effects   70
Sieve of Eratosthenes   49, 107
Signature on programs   31
Simmons factorial conjecture   109
Simplicity goal   41-43
Simpson's rule   298
Simulation of modules   263
Simulator   104
Skeleton coding   88
Small programs   41
Smith, Ronald G.   40
Smoke test   250
Software
   costs   312
   epoch   178
   errors in design   66
   production   32
Software Metrics   218
Software Tools   211
Soma cube   173
SORMGIN   203
Sort problems   170, 296
Space dimension   61, 209
Space saving   124
Spaghetti   41
Sparse matrix   171
Specifications   2
   freeze   46
   testing   243-244
Spencer, Donald   288
Splitting words   17-18
SPSS   57
Standards of style   2-3
Stanford University   116, 186
Statements
   length   43
   numbers   21
   placement   18
Statistical programs   57
Status report   273

Stethoscopes   209
Stevenson, Harry P.   112
Storage   125
   alignment   136
   map   190, 192
Strength, module   69
Structured programming   62-93,
   74-88, 109
Structured walkthrough   85, 246-247
Stub   90
Style   1-40
Subroutines   (*see* Modules)
Substitution module   90, 264
Subscripts
   check   214
   efficiency   150-156
   form   156
   efficiency   150-156
   mode   155
   optimization   156
   range checks   216, 224
Super-programmer project   93
Suspicion, mutual   207
Switches   43, 204, 265
System testing   266
Symmetric matrix   170
SYNCRONIZED   136
Synopsis   180
Syntax
   errors   183-186
   messages   228, 234
   problems   295

T

Table searching   170
Tapes, magnetic   158-160
Team projects   311
Technological change   177
Terminator errors   211
Test
   cases   256-262
   group   274-276
   harness   269
   inspection   283
   leg   241
   number of   242
   samples   260-262

Test data   250-260
  classes   253
  extremes   256-258
  generating   254
  generator   267-268
  normal cases   256
  solutions   254
  standard   254
  types   251-254
Testing   238-284
  acceptance   275
  adequate time   271
  aids   267-269
  art vs science   238
  black box   244
  bottom-up   248
  boundarys   257
  design   245
  early   244
  economics   253
  exceptions   258-259
  exhaustive   61, 242
  field   266
  file   265
  how much   241
  how well   273
  log   282
  mathematical software   262
  methods   248
  miniaturization   250
  module   266
  path   259
  product   266
  redundancy   274
  regression   274
  release   266
  schedules   271
  smoke   250
  specification   243
  system   266
  top-down   248
  unit   265
Tetrahedral matrix   170
Time dimensions   61, 209
Timing bug   212
Toffler, Alvin   101
Tooth   114

Top-down
  coding   88-93
  design   63-66
  difficulties   93
  testing   248
Tower of Babel   1
Tower of Hanoi   172
Traces   204, 213-214
Transliteration   292
Transmitted error   262
Traveling salesman   108
Triangular matrix   170
Tricky coding   42, 183
Tridiagonal matrix   170
Truncation   35, 229-230
Turing machines   110
Turner, W. S.   284
Twelve Days of Christmas   107
Typing errors   193-194

U

Ullman, Jeffery   174
Unit testing   265
University of Waterloo   116, 185
Unreadable programs   31
Unrolling loops   146
Unswitching   147
Up-time   281
Urfrig, D. B.   284

V

Validation   270
Variables
  errors   210
  initializations   130
  names   12-14
  traces   214
  undefined   191
Virtual memory   126-128

W

Waite, W. M.   101
Walkthrough, structured   85

Warning messages 163
WATBOL 116, 185
WATFIV 116, 185
Weinberg, Gerald 38, 96, 237, 281
  312
Whirlwind I 179
Wichman, B. A. 40
Wirth, Niklaus 112
Wolf Island 171–172
Wolverton, Ray W. 312

Writing programs, in English 64

Y

Yourdon, Edward 112

Z

Zelkowitz, Marvin, V. 175